Sanford Weinstein, EdD, MSW

Family Beyond Family: The Surrogate Parent in Schools and Other Community Agencies

*Pre-publication
REVIEWS,
COMMENTARIES,
EVALUATIONS . . .*

"**D**rawing upon his extensive experience as a social work practitioner, college professor, and researcher into group process, Dr. Sanford Weinstein answers many questions by presenting a clear and cogent model for understanding the relationship between individual human development and group life. This highly readable book sheds new light on issues of child abuse, violence in children, and the role and capacity of surrogate families to positively influence the psychosocial functioning of children at risk.

The suggested interventions are soundly rooted in well-documented theory. The material is an excellent resource for clinicians, educators, and other human service providers involved in the process of constructing supportive, protective, and supervisory services for children."

Stephen Weiss, PhD
*Director of Programs
in Early Childhood
and Elementary Education,
New York University*

"*Family Beyond Family* provides a blueprint for accomplishing the goal of raising children in a stressful society and offers an alternative to the failing nuclear family–that is, the surrogate family. The surrogate family includes those in schools and other community organizations who can provide for children's needs when the nuclear family cannot. Dr. Sanford Weinstein is well-equipped to make this prescription given his background in social work and health education, and his many years of experience educating and counseling children and their families.

Of particular interest to this reader is the last section of *Family Beyond Family* that includes discussions about violent children, abusive families, dangerous communities, and the ethical implications for surrogate parents and families. These very practical concerns are often overlooked by less meticulous authors when they discuss the roles and responsibilities of schools and communities.

I highly recommend *Family Beyond Family* to anyone concerned about the welfare of our children and the breakdown of the American family. It will sometimes frustrate you, while at other times it will exhilarate you. It is must reading if we are to survive the present age and emerge into a new and improved one."

Jerrold S. Greenburg, EdD
Director of Community Service,
College of Health
and Human Performance,
University of Maryland

"One need not be a psychologist or social worker to fully understand this very readable book. I found *Family Beyond Family* written with a minimum of jargon and a maximum of meaning.

Family Beyond Family can serve as a guide for educators involved with the performing arts. People who lead and teach music, drama, and dance in school, community, and professional settings will find this book addresses a very real need. We know how to deal with developing skilled performers, but have been forced to operate intuitively in responding to the human needs of those performers, especially those coming from troubled families. Dr. Weinstein's book fills the void and provides theory and language that will lend logic and rationality to addressing those human needs without becoming embroiled in the turmoil of these troubled lives.

This book should be required reading in teacher preparation programs and an important part of the professional library for all who provide leadership in the performing arts."

Edward Lewis, PhD
Professor of Music,
University of Regina, Canada

"Widespread family disruption demands the attention of policy makers and practitioners in government, education, social services, and health care. *Family Beyond Family* provides extremely valuable understandings and practical suggestions for those in government and the human service professions who wish to face this challenge. Dr. Sanford Weinstein presents a logic that is elegant in its simplicity and is profoundly true to life. In fact, one may ask oneself, upon reading this very readable book, 'Hey, why didn't I think of this?'

Because of its richness and originality, this book is must reading for those willing to create family-like alternatives as part of professional practice in schools and social service agencies of all types. The economy, ease, and limitations of integrating the role of surrogate parent with traditional professional roles are convincingly demonstrated in Dr. Weinstein's narrative. This economy and ease makes *Family Beyond Family* compelling reading for policy makers and practitioners alike."

Robert D. Patton, MPH, EdD
Professor, Health Education,
East Tennessee State University;
Tennessee House of Representatives

"**N**ever in our history has society been so challenged to respond to the immense needs of so many impoverished and socially isolated community members. Serious misfortunes have led to devastating estrangement from family and community. Therefore, in the absence of meaningful family or other social connections, the opportunity for family-like experience may be truly a life saver.

This era of profound desperation lends an heroic and resolute quality to the words of Sanford Weinstein in his book *Family Beyond Family*. His writing is an immensely valuable and readable resource to social workers and others providing direct service to the socially isolated.

Dr. Weinstein presents understandings and practical suggestions for direct psychosocial assistance that are universally acceptable across the broad range of settings, age groups, cultural communities, and service modalities. They are useful in individual and group service, and prescribe a healthy balance between the needs of clients and the resources of service providers. In short, this book provides a sound and practice-oriented picture of 'what its like out there in the real world' for students and practitioners alike. It should be required reading for students and is a must for personal professional libraries."

Artie Reed, MSW, CSW
*Social Worker, Department
of Veterans Affairs,
Veterans Homeless Program,
New York City*

"**F**amily Beyond Family is an excellent summary of research on roles and functions of families and groups, showing both the successful and unsuccessful results of fulfilling and not fulfilling those roles and functions. It indicates the need for surrogate parents and families, and shows how those groups can provide nurturance for young people developing into adults. A strong point in this book is the practical approach to interpreting the research and to suggesting ways in which we as a society of surrogate families can 'help children survive disrupted child rearing in troubled families.'

The Haworth Press, Inc.

Family Beyond Family

*The Surrogate Parent
in Schools and Other
Community Agencies*

HAWORTH Social Work Practice
Carlton E. Munson, DSW, Senior Editor

New, Recent, and Forthcoming Titles:

Management and Information Systems in Human Services: Implications for the Distribution of Authority and Decision Making by Richard K. Caputo

The Creative Practitioner: Creative Theory and Method for the Helping Services by Bernard Gelfand

Social Work Theory and Practice with the Terminally Ill by Joan K. Parry

Social Work in Health Settings: Practice in Context by Toba Schwaber Kerson and Associates

Gerontological Social Work Supervision by Ann Burack-Weiss and Frances Coyle Brennan

Group Work: Skills and Strategies for Effective Interventions by Sondra Brandler and Camille P. Roman

If a Partner Has AIDS: Guide to Clinical Intervention for Relationships in Crisis by R. Dennis Shelby

Social Work Practice: A Systems Approach by Benyamin Chetkow-Yanoov

Elements of the Helping Process: A Guide for Clinicians by Raymond Fox

Clinical Social Work Supervision, Second Edition by Carlton E. Munson

Intervention Research: Design and Development for the Human Services edited by Jack Rothman and Edwin J. Thomas

Building on Women's Strengths: A Social Work Agenda for the 21st Century by Liane V. Davis

Family Beyond Family: The Surrogate Parent in Schools and Other Community Agencies by Sanford Weinstein

Family Beyond Family
The Surrogate Parent in Schools and Other Community Agencies

Sanford Weinstein, EdD, MSW

The Haworth Press
New York • London

The Haworth Press, Inc., 10 Alice Street, Binghamton, NY 13904-1580

Library of Congress Cataloging-in-Publication Data

Weinstein, Sanford.
    Family beyond family : the surrogate parent in schools and other community agencies / Sanford Weinstein.
        p.   cm.
    Includes bibliographical references and index.
    ISBN 1-56024-442-9
    1. Child development. 2. Parenthood. 3. Family. 4. Education. I. Title
HQ767.9.W45   1995
306.874–dc20
                                                                    94-45866
                                                                    CIP

CONTENTS

ABOUT THE AUTHOR

Sanford Weinstein, EdD, MSW, is Professor of Health Education at New York University and a practicing social worker. During his 24 years at NYU, he has served in numerous funded projects in public schools, nursing homes, community agencies, and clinics, seeking to address the needs of youth and adults struggling with family disruption. In this book Professor Weinstein has integrated his diverse experience as an educator and family therapist.

PART I.
INDIVIDUAL DEVELOPMENT, THE FAMILY, AND GROUP LIFE: FOUNDATIONS OF EDUCATIONAL PROCESS

Introduction

This book is a guide for teachers, recreation leaders, counselors, social workers, nurses, clergy, and other human service providers who work in an educative capacity with people. The material that follows is not about curriculum, administration, activities, programs, evaluation, or research. Instead, it addresses those important times after the planning and organizing have been done.

The focus is on times when educators or other human service practitioners and the people they help are together, facing each other, in real live contact. The purpose of this focus is to explore insights and understandings that may be of value in creating a positive social and physical environment in which to implement programs and activities, and to pursue a variety of restorative and growth-oriented goals.

These insights and understandings take into account individual development and some relevant aspects of human beings as social creatures. The family is examined as an educational prototype, as are some of the problems that may interfere with this important family function. Group experience is offered as a context for emotional and intellectual growth beyond the family.

The narrative crosses disciplinary boundaries in linking understandings about child and adult development, family systems theory, and group development. That researchers and writers in these fields rarely cross each others' boundaries is worthy of note, and understandable in this era of specialization. Still, practitioners in applied fields such as education, recreation and leisure, social work, and mental health treatment can ill afford to be so self-limiting. This is so because these practitioners are the primary agents of the community, outside of the family, to become prominent figures to children, adolescents, and young adults.

Suggestions that follow acknowledge that there is much variability in families' capacity to nurture their offspring. Thus, these suggestions seek to capitalize on parallels between family and non-family groups so that the latter may be of value when the former are deficient (Weinstein and Thayer, 1986; Northen, 1976; Unger and Powell, 1980).

A major premise of this writing is the repeated observation that surrogate experiences help children survive disrupted child rearing in troubled families (Ackerman, 1983; Zuravin, 1994). This is so because many children display an incredible ability to benefit from even the "smallest affective nourishment" to be found in their surroundings (Miller, 1981, p. 33). Thus, family circumstances in which parents have little, if anything, to give need not damage children if parents do not prevent children from seeking emotional sustenance elsewhere.

No doubt, parental alcoholism, drug addiction, and mental illness are terribly destructive, but many children seek and find alternate sources for support and protection. Such children in need often turn to teachers, athletic coaches, arts instructors, clergy, and others for this purpose. To some degree, to be valued by a few special people in the community beyond the family is important to all children (Kagan, 1976).

Many children who were too damaged or whose parents made it too difficult to find alternative sources, have already found their way into institutional care. When this too fails, they find their way as "street kids" and runaways who sustain themselves emotionally through addiction, and materially as prostitutes and thieves (Lundy, 1992). Current estimates of homelessness among street kids suggest that as many as a million may be living this way throughout the U.S. (Lundy, 1992, p. 2).

A second premise is that positive and constructive interpersonal relationships are the most important growth-promoting experiences for those seeking support and protection beyond their family (Rogers, 1962; Yalom, 1975). Such relationships may be formed with those occupying positions of authority and with peers (Yalom, 1975). They are of value to those in need of healing and those merely seeking self-enhancement. Since most educational activity occurs with groups of people, educational settings offer many possibilities for such relationships. The key is the creation of an environment to promote and support healthy interaction.

REFERENCES

Ackerman, R. *(1983)*. *Children of Alcoholics: A Guide to Parents, Educators, and Therapists*. New York: Simon and Schuster.

Kagan, J. (1976). "The Psychological Requirements for Human Development." In N. Talbot (ed.), *Raising Children in Modern America: Problems and Prospective Solutions*. Boston: Little, Brown and Co., pp. 86-97.

Lundy, K. (1992). *A Qualitative Study of Street Kids: Living on the Edge*. Unpublished doctoral dissertation, New York University.

Miller, A. (1981). *The Drama of the Gifted Child*. New York: Basic Books.

Northen, H. (1976). "Psychosocial Practice in Small Groups." In R. Roberts and H. Northen (eds.), *Theories of Social Work with Groups*. New York: Columbia University Press, pp. 116-152.

Rogers, C. (1962). "The Interpersonal Relationship: The Core of Guidance." *Harvard Educational Review*, Vol. 32, No. 4, pp. 416-429.

Unger, D. and Powell, D. (1980). "Supporting Families Under Stress: The Role of Social Networks." *Family Relations*. Vol. 29, pp. 566-574.

Weinstein, S. and Thayer, S. "Family Stress." In R. Patton (ed.), *The American Family: Life and Health*. (1986). Oakland, California: Third Party Publishing Co., pp. 420-439, pp. 566-574.

Yalom, I. (1975). *The Theory and Practice of Group Psychotherapy*. 2nd ed. New York: Basic Books.

Zuravin, S. J. (1994). "Does Abuse as a Child Result in Irreparable Harm in Adulthood? No." In E. Gambrill and T. Stein (eds.), *Controversial Issues in Child Welfare*. Boston: Allyn and Bacon, pp. 36-41.

Chapter 1

Individual Development and Group Life

An extensive literature argues convincingly that evolution made social existence a requirement for human survival (Yalom, 1975). In primitive cultures, social groups formed around kinship and territory (Gough, 1971). Such groupings not only provided for procreation, cooperation, and mutual protection, but served as a medium through which the human organism's profound need for propinquity was met. Thus, the survival value of group existence goes well beyond the mere pooling of physical assets for life-sustaining tasks. The processes of group existence were and remain the mechanism through which psychological development occurs, and the emotional life of the individual is maintained (Sullivan, 1953).

The needs that undergird group life have prehuman origins in our evolutionary ascendence, and require more than mere territorial proximity for their satisfaction (Hayes, 1951; Harlow and Zimmerman, 1959; Morris, 1967). For most of us, these needs are the stuff of life and are about intimate social exchange. The group is the medium for such exchange because norms, expectations, and cohesiveness are the fabric of group life. This fabric creates the necessary constancy, predictability, and trustworthiness to permit contact with others to be meaningful and sustaining.

FIRST DEVELOPMENTAL CRISIS: BIRTH TO AGE THREE

The issue of trust becomes important at birth (Fraiberg, 1959) and remains so throughout life (Larzelere and Huston, 1980). Interactions may include physical, verbal, and nonverbal forms, but regardless of form, contact must occur in contexts where meanings have at least some emotional depth, permanence, and reliability. These qualities are the foundation of trust.

At birth and for a time after, we need direct and unequivocal physical closeness (Bowlby, 1969; Thayer, 1988). Because the very young are incapable of abstraction, and symbols mean little to them, the predominant external stimuli to which an infant's physiology responds are touch and taste. Variation in sights, sounds, and smells has important value in promoting growth (Kagan, 1976), but it may not replace the concrete in establishing the necessary bonding and trust for an infant's well-being.

We have known about the essential core of such needs since medieval times (Ross and McLaughlin, 1949, p. 366). We apparently forgot these early lessons until reminded by observations of infants deprived of contact in institutional settings. These children withdrew into themselves and eventually died, despite having other needs for food and protection met. Such terms as "hospitalism" and "marasmus" became labels for this deadly condition (Spitz, 1945, 1946).

Thus, a painful process produced rediscovery that very young childrens' affiliation needs must be met through direct physical contact. We also know that the quality and tone of contact can communicate love, indifference, and displeasure, but tender loving care is most sustaining when it is not overly threatening, and is reasonably consistent and predictable. In this way, trust becomes a major interpersonal issue with serious implications for survival at the very beginning of life.

Fortunately, the touching associated with infant feeding, cleaning, play, dressing, and moving about is natural to daily existence in most human families. Parents confirm and reconfirm trust and survival as babies are carried, held, rocked, caressed, bathed, hugged, and kissed. Older siblings, aunts and uncles, grandparents, and family friends are often enthusiastic contributors, too.

This beginning period of life is regarded by many as most important in the development of healthy, well-functioning maturity. Ideally, our experience is one of unbounded intimacy with seemingly omnipotent adults who, in response to a whimper or cry, gratify our fundamental needs. The singular demand for return is only that we thrive because we can do absolutely nothing but breathe, suckle, swallow, defecate, and cry out.

With adequate response, we are euphoric as we feed at mother's breast, and she and others put in place the building blocks of our adult happiness and success. For, we learn to love ourselves as we are loved, to soothe ourselves as we are soothed, and to cope with noxious and overwhelming stimuli as we are sheltered from them. Thus, instruments of parental care eventually become instruments of self-care, and we grow to trust ourselves as we were able to trust our families (Kohut, 1971, 1977).

It is a time of danger, too. In the absence of adequate and trust-worthy response to their inarticulate protestations, the very young recede into despair and may withdraw from life itself. In situations where parental response is disturbed, inconstant, or minimal, life may be sustained, but not without irreparable damage. Neglect, abuse, and erratic care become acts of betrayal from which there may be no recovery.

Still, the organic and fragile core of neonatal life begins to change as developmental processes give strength and push us toward maturity. Helplessness and dependence recede because physical development increasingly supports personal independence and social interdependence. In healthy child rearing, each new capacity is met with new demands for self-sufficiency as we are toilet trained and taught to feed and clean ourselves. Though many modes of physical contact become archaic and regressive as time passes, new avenues open. Adult utterance of the word "no!" becomes prominent as we acquire speech, and our need for propinquity remains.

Fortunately, the transition to self-sufficiency and reduced physical contact is matched by our own needs for autonomy, and the increasing gratification provided by symbolic exchanges of words and objects (Thayer, 1988). Physical growth and development provide tools for psychological growth and development. They also create powerful striving for emotional separation and personal individuality (Mahler, 1968). This striving is reawakened and intensified with the onrush of puberty and the teen years.

SECOND DEVELOPMENTAL CRISIS: ADOLESCENCE

Sadly for some of us, separation is confused with moving away, and individuality confused with selfishness. Adolescents struggle with the nagging dilemma of family closeness in the face of needs for greater privacy and change in interpersonal boundaries and limits. The emergent attraction of the peer group is a significant and possibly confounding part of life at this time.

The manner in which we resolve these separation issues is an important test of our capacity to trust and a building block for growth toward healthy adulthood (Boss, 1980). Since the press for separation is inevitable, the real question asks how much violence and destructiveness will be associated with its occurrence. If individuality becomes synonymous with ostracism, we become isolated. If separateness is associated with power struggle, we become powerless. If conflict is associated with futility, we become cynical and poor at conflict resolution. And finally, if puberty and the push to sexual expression are associated with loss of status, self-esteem is threatened.

Thus, our needs for closeness place us in a double bind. Early in life, nearness to others is necessary for survival and development. Later, healthy development requires the imposition of boundaries and limits on nearness, and these limits are often sources of confusion and conflict (Solomon, 1973; Boss, 1980). In this way, maturation tests the substance of family relations as adults fear for the future of rebellious children, and adolescents feel constrained in their quest for the real and imagined freedoms of adulthood.

For some adults, their own unresolved separation issues are rekindled. Their need to control the unbridled sexuality, egocentrism, and impulsiveness of youth may be more reflective of narcissistic fears about self than truth about young people. The mixture becomes increasingly volatile when one adds feelings of resentment, abandonment, and betrayal (Stierlin, Sevi, and Savard, 1971). The terrible fantasy is that the children will leave without a backward glance, destroy themselves with their hedonism and nihilism, and never return.

Simultaneously, personal growth and disappointments by parents erode a young person's illusions of parents' perfection. These processes and events elicit increasing ambivalence, and painful acceptance of the fact that one's parents and other adult relatives are merely human beings. They are no longer idols as they were in the eye of the child, because they have flaws and strengths as do all people (Kernberg, 1975).

Therefore, the young person's need is for life to be reflective of who one is, rather than a facsimile of the life from which one has come. In pursuing this, the adolescent's or young adult's self-perception is of creating a life in which one has established appropriate and necessary propinquity with peers. In this view, separation is not abandonment, but, rather, it is creating, as an adult, a domain from which to reestablish propinquity with one's family. In these ways, growing up not only presents enhanced capabilities, rights, and freedoms, but also new relational responsibilities. Family members and others must scramble to adjust to the emergence of a new adult.

INDIVIDUAL DEVELOPMENT: A TEST OF FAMILY HEALTH

It is difficult for many young people to imagine that the family may have a hard time with their maturity. But, the truth is that developmental change in individual members forces changes in family relationships (Weinstein and Thayer, 1986). Another truth is that change is invariably stressful and generally greeted with ambivalence regardless of how positive.

Therefore, resistance to change is not unusual and may be expressed in many hurtful ways. The ease and effectiveness with which resistance is overcome are usually good indicators of the emotional well-being of the people involved, and a sign of the health and flexibility of family structure (Minuchin, 1974). Prolonged resistance eventually takes its toll and exacerbates existing problems.

The evolving separation process is both intriguing and frightening for young people. The rights and privileges they seek are powerful incentives, but responsibilities associated with being alone and unprotected can be terrifying. The need to test oneself in the real world is sincere. However, young people also harbor a wish for freedom to return, without recrimination, to the safety of one's roots if the world proves too dangerous. Thus, in adolescence, status is sought as half-child and half-adult. This is a difficult rapprochement between mutually exclusive states of being and conflicting needs.

Unfortunately for some, rapprochement is not achieved because the world seems too terrifying or family members create difficult problems. Some young people move away and others never leave, but the separation process remains incomplete. Neither tactic faces the task of establishing a definition of self that is realistic, reasonably self-contained, and stable (Kernberg, 1975). In the absence of such development, there is danger of isolating pseudo-autonomy or growth inhibiting over dependence (Kohut, 1977). The challenge is about establishing relations, with the peer group and family, in which dangers of engulfment and loss of self-determination at one extreme and isolation at the other are adequately addressed (Epstein, Bishop, and Levin, 1978).

Thus, human beings are born into primary groups as small, helpless, and partially formed creatures. These groups usually include several generations of blood relatives, and preceding generations provide support and protection to the young. Still, the status of the children in these groups is not static. Caregivers face constant demand for change in the way children's needs are to be met (Weinstein and Thayer, 1986). Maturation increases self-sufficiency, and the young person moves from being his parents' child toward being his own person. Thus, the real goal of this activity is to prepare the new generation that leaves to begin its own intergenerational groupings.

In the absence of insight about the separation process, ambivalence and conflict may pass from generation to generation (Schulman, 1973). The process may be subverted to the point where serious damage is possible to individuals and the family as a whole.

One may ask if the risks and problems described above are so difficult that the end of childhood marks the end of propinquity. The answer to this question is probably dependent on the quality of early childhood experience. In the extreme, experience may be so destructive as to preclude healthy separation and substantial relationships later in life.

Fortunately, such cases are infrequent because most families, despite imperfection, are not that destructive. Also, human beings are resilient and do not require perfect rearing for reasonably healthy maturity. Competent parents who meet primary requirements for support and protection during early childhood, and demonstrate a timely willingness to let go later on are usually good enough.

Thus, we spend our lives emerging from our primary group of origin so that we may join and create new groups. We enter our world as the new leaves at the periphery of the family tree, but development and aging push us toward the center of things. Eventually, we become the trunk from which our own new branches and leaves may sprout, and then we are the roots as successive generations take their place.

THE FAMILY AS THE PROTOTYPE FOR GROUP LIFE

The impact of the family on participation in other groups is profound. Family experiences train children for group living, and create lenses that bring relationships in other groups into focus (Napier and Gershenfeld, 1981). Such experiences teach meanings and responses to issues that are common to all groups. Further, the self upon which these issues impinge is shaped first by family influence, and later by other groups to the degree that one's experience of them is family-like.

Family membership status and behavior are dictated by role and age, and provide the formative experience for analogous roles in other groups. The authority of parents, peer status of spouses, and subordinate status of sibling children are childrens' first exposures to these roles. Thus, representations of many aspects of family life are often present in our perceptions of life in other settings, and our responses in these other settings may or may not be entirely functional.

Unresolved family issues often become areas of struggle for individuals upon entry to other groups. Power and intimacy are recurrent themes in maintaining the health of the family unit and these same themes are at the core of group life elsewhere. Response to these issues elicited by authority and peers may at times resemble responses elicited by parents and siblings.

As all individuals and families encounter their own developmental processes, so too must other groups as the passage of time brings change and crisis. Individual response to the interpersonal issues which are raised by change is indelibly formed in the family. Unsatisfactory family experience with transition and separation may create problems in coping with change in other groups.

Fortunately, the family training function usually has many strengths as well as some flaws. Most of us emerge with reasonably healthy capacities for observation of, participation in, and contribution to life in other groups. We also have our blind spots, irrational fears, and limits to what we can give comfortably. These areas of difficulty probably have origins in struggles and conflict in our family, and are about issues around which parents or other family members have shaken our trust.

SURROGATE FAMILY EXPERIENCE: FAMILY BEYOND FAMILY

Still, each group we join has the potential to become family-like in its meaning to us, and to acquire the power to be family-like as a resource. In so doing, such groups may supplement deficits in some real families' abilities to promote the growth and well-being of their individual members. This compensatory potential is important because most families are, at times, deficient in performing their functions and fulfilling members' needs. Some of these functions and needs are described above, but in the most ideal sense, a family is supposed to be a nest and sanctuary for adults as well as children. It is to provide love, acceptance, validation, encouragement, and a place where we are cared for when all else fails. When a family fails in these functions, it jeopardizes its members.

When it fails badly enough to begin producing damaged members, it is considered dysfunctional. At these times, experience with other family-like relationships may have preventative or reparative value for the individual (Unger and Powell, 1980). Such experience may also benefit the family as a member returns to the fold with renewed strength and new insights.

Though we would like to think of the family as a Rock of Gibraltar, it is not. In some ways it is surprisingly strong and resilient, but in others, the family may be very fragile. It is vulnerable to disruption by forces from within and without, and coping with these forces often drains resources which might be better spent meeting members' needs. Disruptive circumstances not only test a family's capacities to nurture and love, but its ability to resist becoming negative and hurtful.

Families become hurtful when they develop coping strategies that sacrifice one or more of their members as the price for preserving an illusion of well-being for the others. Such strategies are clearly evident in families troubled by alcoholism or drug addiction. Codependency is a term that describes non-addicted family members' efforts to cope without overt acknowledgement of the family drug problem (George, 1990). The result of this destructive balancing act is that the addict sinks further into the morass of his addiction, and the quality of life deteriorates for the others in the family. Eventually, attention is drawn away from the addicted member as a vulnerable member falls victim to the incredible tension and becomes the family problem.

This happens because a family operates as an interlocking system in which events affecting one member also affect the others to some degree (Minuchin, 1974). Thus, tensions between spouses can interfere with parental role and create difficulties for children. Conversely, illness or disability in a child can exhaust parents to the point where they have little to give each other as spouses.

The laws, customs, traditions, and love that are the glue of the system are also the windows of vulnerability for individual members. When circumstances are good, members have access to each others' strengths and assets, and the price of sharing is appropriate. When things are bad, members are trapped by their ties to each other and assaulted in perpetuity as destructive ways of relating become regular family fare. The assault intensifies to the degree that the boundaries between parts of the family system and individual members fail to work. At one extreme of dysfunction, these boundaries may block necessary communication, and at the other, they may be inadequate to maintain needed separation. This weakness in the family structure usually makes itself known at times when strength is needed most; at times of transition, change, and stress. The family problem may then explode and precipitate the breakdown of a member.

Those members in greatest need of family protection and support are at greatest risk during such times. The youngest, weakest, or most fragile is usually the first casualty to bubble to the surface when family tensions reach the boiling point. A child may begin to have repeated trouble at school, a mother may become addicted to the tranquilizers her physician prescribed to treat her anxiety, a father may develop an ulcer or high blood pressure, or an elderly aunt or grandparent may suddenly and inexplicably need placement in a nursing home.

Thus, the family is a somewhat precarious organization of interdependent parts whose purpose is to support and protect its members. The functioning of each part influences the other parts in a balance between overinvolvement and inaccessibility. The exchanges of love, energy, and other resources are fragile and finite, and require reasonable and appropriate management.

In view of the complexity of family life and the enormity of the potentially disruptive forces to which it is subject, it is no wonder that problems can develop. Unfortunately, these problems threaten and cause suffering for individual members. Still, the nature of the family as a group, primary though it may be, permits other sources of support to play a role in protecting and strengthening the individual. Thus, the family provides the skills and abilities for life in nonfamilial groups. These capabilities become the tools for growth and healing beyond the family at times when the family is unable to address its members' needs.

THE GROUP AS A MEDIUM FOR GROWTH
AND DEVELOPMENT

Just as families exist to meet the needs of individual members, so do other groups serve the purposes of the people who form them. In order to satisfy these purposes, norms or rules of behavior dictate individual member behavior and organized behavior of the group as a whole. Because many norms are invisible, and some groups are highly regulated and coordinated, we think of them as though they are real living organisms. At times we may think of the people in them in a manner that is parallel to the bodily organs of a person. This gives rise to a very serious question of whether such groups exist to serve their members, or members exist to serve their groups.

There is no doubt that the benefits of group life require subordination of individual needs to some degree. In some cases, personal needs are subordinated or neglected to the point that the individual becomes a victim. Examples abound of families, communities, and nations in which this has happened. In such instances, people appear to have been treated as though existence was meant to serve the group. The truth is that even in the worst of circumstances, these people were the victims of other individuals within the group.

Thus, families and groups exist as useful concepts for understanding various collectivities of people we encounter in everyday life. These collectivities are not living, breathing organisms with needs and desires, but rather creations which serve the needs and desires of the living, breathing human beings joined within them.

People join or create such groups outside of the family to affiliate with others they like, to participate in activities they enjoy, or to gain rewards and gratifications that are external to the group (Napier and Gershenfeld, 1981). These motivations hold true for the workplace, social gatherings, community involvement, educational programs, and recreational activities. Some people seek groups whose defined purpose is therapeutic treatment, or to provide self-help opportunity, but these are less-frequent choices.

This does not preclude the possibility for therapeutic value and/or personal growth to be derived from other kinds of groups. Positive and constructive shared experience, regardless of content or nature of activity, provides opportunities for new learning, and healthy changes in outlook about self and one's world. To experience success and love in concert with others has long been known to be a powerful stimulant to emotional growth and development (Rogers, 1962). This is especially true for those whose family life is deficient in these qualities.

ELEMENTS OF FAMILY SURROGATE EXPERIENCE

The ingredients for positive and constructive experience in groups are not unlike those necessary for a healthy family. The basic element is the creation of an atmosphere of trust. There must be enough stability, consistency, and predictability that group members become a reliable part of each other's life within limits appropriate to the salience of the group. Honesty is required to the point that members feel confident that others generally "mean what they say, and say what they mean."

Also, benevolence is a major foundation to trust. Awareness that members are alert to protect and support each other's best interests will minimize antitheses to trust, such as fears of abuse, exploitation, neglect, betrayal, and abandonment. Reciprocity plays an important role in the creation of such an awareness.

Flexibility, a sense of humor, and calm rationality during crisis are other important foundations of trust. Feelings and perceptions that the group is adaptable and effective in the face of demands for change, that the group has a healthy perspective and can laugh at itself, and that things do not fall apart when the group faces tension and pressure are powerful sources of comfort and confidence.

A further ingredient for positive and constructive group experience is good leadership. The question is not about who is leader; it is about whether leadership is adequate to bring order out of chaos, and how that leadership is shared. Satisfactory leadership usually emerges when members create a structure of rules and norms that reflect what they want the group to be like; e.g., its goals, methods, and values. Then, some individuals accept executive responsibility as needed, there is some provision for collective decision making, necessary tasks and labor are shared equitably, and there is adequate flexibility to incorporate individual needs and perspectives.

Effective and appropriate communication is another important ingredient. Communication is important to meeting goals and objectives, and also to the quality of experience for members. Communication is not an end in and of itself, but rather a means. When effective, it reduces conflict, permits information sharing, assures shared perceptions of issues and events, and provides reinforcing and corrective feedback.

Still, an often neglected aspect of constructive communication is about individual freedom to participate in it. Just as in the family, it is important to establish a satisfactory balance between engulfment and isolation. Access to others, others' access to self, and personal privacy require careful balance for communication to be experienced as beneficial rather than burdensome. An important adjunct to this is communication that accurately transmits information and respects individual sensitivities, vulnerabilities, and emotional defenses when possible.

Thus, groups do not automatically become a positive force in peoples' lives, nor do they inherently provide family-like experience for their members. But members can establish conditions that promote these values. Recognition that the group serves its members is an important place to start. Creating an atmosphere of stability and safety, leadership by consent, and healthy effective communication are the basics. Interaction that promotes shared vision of group destiny, a sense of inclusion, and a positive culture is the process (Patton and Cissel, 1990).

In these ways an environment may be created that is not only comfortable and pleasant, but can enhance members' receptiveness to growth-promoting experience. Needs to defend or resist are minimized, and a readiness to examine and internalize constructive messages is optimized.

Within such an environment, there are a number of things that group members can give and receive. One is optimism and hope, and a repudiation of despair and pessimism. A second is recognition that differences between people are a matter of degree rather than kind, and that people hold much in common regarding the human condition. Another is education, including information, role models, and opportunities to acquire new skills. Still another is the experience of reciprocity and giving. Meaningful interpersonal relationships beyond one's primary family is yet another contribution (Yalom, 1975).

INDIVIDUAL BENEFITS: STRENGTH, RESILIENCE, AND INSIGHT

Personal growth and development is the benefit to recipients of such exchange when groups become family-like to their members. This growth can occur in many areas of existence, but is particularly important to a number of critical feelings about self.

One such critical feeling is that of control of one's life. Recognition of the connection between one's behavior and life's outcomes is the essence of this feeling. It does not bestow immunity to tyranny, but instead emphasizes acquisition of knowledge, skill, and attitudes that support self-sufficiency and social interdependence. Healthy families strive to promote this in their members and so do consistent and responsive groups.

Another important self-evaluative dimension is that of perceiving oneself to be socially integrated. Not to feel alone is a rather simple yet powerful human need, but integration requires more than superficial proximity to others. Social integration refers to acceptance, respect, and a real place among others with whom one has joined. Recognition that others share the benefits and consequences of one's actions, celebrate one's triumphs, and mourn one's losses is a central notion. The availability of others' resources when one's own are inadequate affirms such recognition. These expressions of trustworthiness and benevolence in a healthy group promote socially integrative experience.

Positive self-esteem is yet another important dimension to which group participation can contribute. Such self-esteem goes beyond egotism. Its essence is a comfortable self-acceptance and includes a stable core that protects the individual from depressive dips and manic highs. Affection and acceptance (independent of talents, abilities, wealth, or appearance) acknowledges members' intrinsic worth and sends strong messages regarding self-esteem. Groups that realistically emphasize members' strengths rather than weaknesses make similar positive contributions.

A sense of personal freedom to be creative, to experiment, to try new perspectives and behavior, and to make mistakes is another important feeling about self. Feelings along this dimension do not support capricious, impulsive, careless, or potentially destructive behavior. These feelings confirm flexibility and openness. That one can take time and opportunity to explore different options, that there is no one correct way of doing anything, and that tasks are challenges rather than threats are central notions to such personal freedom.

Just as families pick up a fallen child and apply first-aid to skinned knees, groups too can provide support to members whose well-intentioned efforts have gone astray. Encouragement to try again and acceptance of differences are important statements against personal and emotional confinement.

A final self-evaluative dimension is that of clarity of personal values and feelings. The essence of this dimension is one's awareness of one's own attitudes, morals, ethics, and emotional reactions concerning the events of one's life. It includes trust of self as a gauge of the qualitative aspects of living. To know one is angry, disappointed, elated, or has merely eaten enough of a good dessert is necessary to healthful living.

Thus, clarity along this dimension refers to awareness at the rational-intellectual and the visceral-emotional levels of experience and action. In some cases, conflict between these levels can produce emotional numbing that isolates consciousness from self. Feedback, self-disclosure of others, and acceptance can be important wedges into neurotic loss of contact with one's feelings and attitudes. Constructive group interaction can reduce isolation from self and enhance immediate experience.

The five self-evaluative dimensions described above form a general sense of well-being. They describe important strength and resilience to cope with the inevitable trials and tribulations of everyday living. Groups can contribute to well-being by enhancing growth along these dimensions. Creation of a safe and healthy social environment, and exchange of insight, wisdom, assistance, and support are keys to growth-promoting experience beyond the family.

REFERENCES

Boss, P. (1980). "Normative Family Stress: Family Boundary Changes Across the Life Span." *Family Relations*, 29, pp. 445-450.

Bowlby, J. (1969, 1973, 1980). *Attachment and Loss, Vol. I-III*. New York: Basic Books.

Epstein, N., Bishop, D., and Levin, S. (1978). "The McMaster Model of Family Functioning." *Journal of Marriage and Family Counseling*, 4, pp. 19-31.

Fraiberg, S. (1959). *The Magic Years: Understanding and Handling the Problems of Early Childhood*. New York: Charles Scribner's Sons, pp. 35-39.

George, R. (1990). *Counseling the Chemically Dependent*. Englewood Cliffs, New Jersey: Prentice Hall.

Gough, K. (1971). "The Origin of the Family." *Journal of Marriage and the Family*, November, pp. 760-770.

Harlow, H. and Zimmerman, R. R. (1959). "Affectional Responses in the Infant Monkey." *Science*, Vol. 130, pp. 421-432.

Hayes, C. (1951). *The Ape in Our House*. New York: Harper.

Kagan, J. (1976). "The Psychological Requirements for Human Development." In N. Talbot (ed.), *Raising Children in Modern America: Problems and Prospective Solutions*. Boston: Little, Brown and Co., pp. 86-97.

Kernberg, O. (1975). *Borderline Conditions and Pathological Narcissism*. New York: Aronson.

Kohut, H. (1971). *Analysis of the Self*. New York: International Universities Press.

Kohut, H. (1977). *Restoration of the Self.* New York: International Universities Press.

Larzelere, R. E. and Huston, T. L. (1980). "The Diadic Trust Scale: Toward Understanding Interpersonal Trust in Close Relationships." *Journal of Marriage and the Family,* Vol. 42, No. 3, pp. 595-604.

Mahler, M. (1968). *On Human Symbiosis and the Vicissitudes of Individuation.* New York: International Universities Press.

Minuchin, S. (1974). *Families and Family Therapy.* Cambridge, Massachusetts: Harvard University Press.

Morris, D. (1967). *The Naked Ape.* Jonathan Cape.

Napier, R. and Gershenfeld, M. (1981). *Groups: Theory and Experience.* 2nd ed. Boston: Houghton Mifflin.

Patton, R. and Cissel, S., eds. (1990). *Community Organization: Traditional Principles and Modern Applications.* Johnson City, Tennessee: Latchpins Press.

Rogers, C. (1962). "The Interpersonal Relationship: The Core of Guidance." *Harvard Educational Review,* Vol. 32, No. 4, pp. 416-429.

Ross, J. B. and McLaughlin, M. M. eds. (1949). *A Portable Medieval Reader.* New York: Viking Press, p. 366.

Schulman, G. "Treatment of Intergenerational Pathology." *Social Casework,* October 1973, pp. 462-472.

Solomon, M. "A Developmental Conceptual Premiss for Family Therapy." *Family Process,* June 1973, pp. 179-188.

Spitz, R. A. "Hospitalism: An Inquiry into the Genesis of Psychiatric Conditions in Early Childhood." *Psychoanalytic Study of the Child,* Vol. 1, 1945, pp. 53-74.

Spitz, R. A. (1946). "Hospitalism: A Follow-Up Report." *Psychoanalytic Study of the Child,* Vol. 2, pp. 113-117.

Stierlin, H., Sevi, L., and Savard, R. "Parental Perceptions of Separating Children." *Family Process,* December 1971, pp. 411-427.

Sullivan, H. (1953). *The Interpersonal Theory of Psychiatry.* New York: W.W. Norton.

Thayer, S. "Close Encounters." *Psychology Today,* March 1988, pp. 30-36.

Unger, D. and Powell, D. (1980). "Supporting Families Under Stress: The Role of Social Networks." *Family Relations,* Vol. 29, pp. 566-574.

Weinstein, S. and Thayer, S. "Family Stress." (1986). In R. Patton (ed.), *The American Family: Life and Health.* Oakland, California: Third Party Publishing Co., pp. 420-439, pp. 566-574.

Yalom, I. (1975). *The Theory and Practice of Group Psychotherapy.* 2nd ed. New York: Basic Books.

Chapter 2

Family Stress:
Adjustment to Crisis and Transition

This chapter describes the kinds of stresses that impair a family's ability to meet its members' needs. In so doing, the narrative will provide additional understanding about family circumstances that create the need for surrogate family opportunity in the first place.

Hopefully, this understanding will, in turn, provide insight into the private world of family from whence those needing surrogate family experience have come. As will be described, some individuals come from families that are in chronic and long-standing disarray. Others may be suffering through a transient but nevertheless painful period of crisis and transition.

Fortunately, in either case, the nature of the surrogate family experience remains the same, and the needs of participants differ in degree rather than kind. However, insight about such circumstances will permit the educator and other human service providers to be more sensitive and responsive to participants with differing degrees of need for alternative family opportunities.

Therefore, this chapter proposes a perspective that cuts to the heart of what family life is so the reader may better understand the nature of the "labor of love" in a family. By understanding how critical family functions are threatened by stress, the reader may become sensitive to the specific needs of families. Hopefully, this sensitivity will promote a respectful appreciation of the different ways family members organize to meet or defeat those needs, and a clearer understanding of the role of the surrogate family during times when needs might otherwise go unmet.

In order to more fully comprehend the role of the surrogate family at such times, one must understand the forces that impede a true family's ability to sustain its members' well-being. These forces, in combination with weaknesses and vulnerability in the way a particular family is organized, create the needs to which the surrogate family may respond in the large majority of troubled family circumstances.

Though flagrant abuse, neglect, and deprivation are obvious sources of pain for members of some troubled families, much family difficulty results from more subtle and insidious problems of relating between members. In some families, subtly destructive ways of relating are so ingrained and toxic that the family produces mental health problems, psychosomatic illness, and dangerous acting out among its members. This may happen even though family members live amid material abundance and nobody ever lays an angry hand on anyone else. Thus, the notion that "the pen is mightier than the sword" translates readily into the idea that the power for good and evil in family members' actions most often resides within words and meanings rather than physical confrontation.

Fortunately, families that produce and live within a consistently poisonous atmosphere are relatively uncommon. Most often, families that subject one or more of their members to undo bother do so only occasionally, and at times when the family as a whole is under stress. On such occasions, new needs and demands throw the family social system off balance. Family members seeking to restore their own individual equilibrium lose sight of each other's needs, rights, and obligations. Thus, stress occurs during times when family members must change or adjust some aspect of family organization.

Weakness in family relations increases the difficulty, costs, and destructiveness of making these changes. During more usual times, the everyday functioning of many vulnerable families is adequate even though it may not be optimal. Though the surrogate family is a source of emotional rescue for abused and neglected children, or for children of dysfunctional families, it is more often of value to those in need of temporary assistance during periods of family stress at home.

The concept of family stress is closely connected to our understandings about the nature of the family. Families, like other groups, exist to serve important functions and needs. At an intuitive and emotional level, our wish is for the family to be a nest, a sanctuary, a place where, when all else fails, we are taken care of. We need our family to be a place where we are loved, accepted, validated, and encouraged (Ackerman, 1958). We want our family to be a safe haven from the outside world, and at times we need family members to protect us from ourselves, too.

When a family does not provide these forms of support, protection, and guidance in adequately stable and consistent ways, we have good reason to suspect that it is dysfunctional. Unfortunately, the cold objectivity of the clinical term "dysfunctional" understates the disappointment, trauma, and deprivation that troubled families can create for their members. Flagrant or subtle and insidious neglect, abuse, betrayal, exploitation, and abandonment are experiences that distort and damage family members' consciousness of self, others, and their world.

THE SUBJECTIVE EXPERIENCE OF THOSE IN NEED OF SURROGATE FAMILY

Friends and neighbors are important, certainly. If they really sustain and love us we may say of them: "They are like family." What this means is that our peace of mind, strength, and well-being are critically dependent on the constant transaction of caring (Hafen, Frandsen, Karen, and Hooker, 1992). We give to and receive from those who are or represent family. Without what such people can give, we feel weakened and alone, our sense of self becomes fragile, and we are physically and emotionally vulnerable.

Truly, we are dependent in many ways on those with whom we live and love. If those with whom we share joy, tragedy, and conflict do not support and protect us during good times and bad, and help us grow stronger for happiness and difficulty yet to come, we turn to sad ways to dull our pain. For children, the consequences of such deprivations and the sad ways to which they may turn place them among those considered to be "at risk."

As described in Chapter 1, the life and health-sustaining reassurances offered by families do not come automatically, easily, or forever. Healthy families are not born, they are worked at. They are monitored and adjusted constantly as every important relationship demands.

To be with or live with others, whether we love them or hate them, is hard work. For the family to succeed, each member must strive to continually adjust and modify one's own performance as "mother," "father," "brother," or "sister." When adults and children in the family can bring these roles together in an integrated and coordinated fashion, they have become good at "familying" and "growing up."

Thus, the family, despite its liabilities and no matter what the divorce rate, can be and often is a stable, enduring group equipped to support and protect its members. In its absence or failure some sort of substitute or surrogate must be created to aid the individual to cope with the inevitable crises of life.

FAMILY TRANSITION, STRESS, AND DYSFUNCTION

To fully comprehend the vulnerability of the family, one must understand the stressful nature of family transition. The problem of family transition confronts all members with frightening questions; such as: "Can the family continue to serve its members when it faces change or when hard times come?" and "Will an individual member get lost as all others in the family clutch and scramble to keep their balance?"

The focus, here, is on the family rather than the individual member. The family is important because it is the larger integrated whole of which members are a part. For better or worse, family members are linked together by law, custom, and love to take care of each other, and therefore may be thought to be part of a social system (Lewis, Dana, and Blevins, 1994). Because of its integration, when an action, event, or person pushes or pokes one part, another part of the family social system shows some effect.

Not only is the family an intricate linkage of people, it is very much a living organism that goes through a developmental process or life cycle (Ackerman, 1966; Melson, 1980). It begins in a sort of infancy, passes through observable stages as it matures to peak size and strength, and then declines and wanes as do all living creatures. The family's passage through its stages of growth and development, while inevitable, is not without pain, struggle, and reward.

When these various forces to which the family is subject cause stress, the tensions they produce strain the family's capacity to healthfully serve its members. Sometimes stress comes from outside the family: from work, neighbors, or other sources. Sometimes, stress comes from within, as people grow and change and disagree. Whatever its source, stress tests the family's ability to provide resources and assistance, rather than to create obstacles and cause pain.

FAMILY STRUCTURE AND ECONOMY

The family is a system because it is a complex organization with smaller interdependent parts. The functioning of each part influences every other part. Minuchin and other family-oriented clinicians refer to the smaller parts as subsystems (Minuchin, 1974).

The subsystems are composed of people who occupy family roles, based primarily on age. These subsystems are siblings (brothers and sisters), spouses (husband and wife), and parents (mother and father). While extended families can include aunts, uncles, grandparents, and cousins, the discussion here considers what has been called "the nuclear family."

We may think of family subsystems as operating within an economy in which there are exchanges of attention, love, energy, support, and other resources. These fragile and finite resources require intelligent and responsible management or the family will lose its viability as a provider to its members.

Not only must families avoid squandering such precious resources, but exchanges between and within subsystems must exhibit a reasonable balance between giving and taking. Unfortunately, expected and unexpected events, or transitional crises in family life, threaten to deplete or unbalance this economy. When this happens families are subject to dangerous and potentially destructive stress.

THE NATURE OF FAMILY STRESS

The family plays many important roles that both relieve stress and cause it. The family may be the mediator or buffer of stress coming from outside, as for example, in a family member's loss of a personal friend. Here, the family may rally to support its vulnerable member.

On the other hand, the family itself may be the cause of stress. Something may be wrong with the way family members relate to one another. Even when only one member exhibits troubling symptoms of distress, the family as a whole may need mending in order to reduce its stress-creating style of living and relating.

Typically, family-induced stress occurs at times when new demands force alterations in a family's usual mode of operating. When this happens, one or another member's personal changes challenge the entire family's ability to adjust its way of operating.

There are several sources of stress for families. One source is the normal, natural developmental life tasks encountered by almost all families within a particular culture (Solomon, 1973). Examples are marrying, birthing, beginning and ending school, embarking on a new career, and retiring. A second, less predictable stress results from events that could happen to anyone, but happen only to a few in an unexpected and seemingly random way. Some examples are loss of a job, changing jobs, the death of a family member, having to relocate to a new community, or an automobile accident.

Because encounters with too much stress in too short a period of time can be devastating, Holmes and Rahe developed the *Social Readjustment Rating Scale* to identify people who are likely to become a physical and/or psychiatric casualty (Holmes and Rahe, 1967). Their rating scale examines a variety of common, stressful life experiences related to work, love, family, and everyday life.

Holmes and Rahe's work is relevant to this writing because it identifies "change" as the source of all stress. These writers emphasize that all change is stressful.

Their theory is that change, whether positive or negative, is stressful because change demands that we replace old ways with new ones. We are loathe to give up our old habits and patterns because they are familiar and comfortable. For this reason, the demand for new ways of relating, managing, and seeing oneself is stressful. If we fail to develop new skills, strategies, and tactics in response to this stress, we become dysfunctional and are at great risk of collapsing physically and emotionally.

Unfortunately, we all have limits to our adaptability. If changes or transitions are too frequent, too intense, or last too long, we will be pressed to the limits of our motivation. Such demands can overwhelm our problem-solving skills, and our spirit and courage. To hang on and cope in the face of relentless adversity is a difficult challenge.

Upon examination, the content of Holmes and Rahe's rating scale reveals that more than half of the most stressful life events are directly connected to important metamorphoses in family relationships. Whatever the actual cause of these changed relationships, and whether for better (e.g., marriage) or worse (e.g., marital separation), family members must develop new ways of relating in response to new roles and pressures. These pressures are inherently stressful. The more often such changes in the family occur, the more lasting the process of change, and the more powerful the impetus behind them, the more dangerous they are to individual members and the family as a whole.

Thus, much of the stress of our individual lives happens simply because we belong to a family. Though we have always known that the family is a powerful force in our lives, we now realize that the family's adjustments to transitional stress are a major factor associated with physical and emotional health and illness for individual members.

TRANSITION AND ADJUSTMENT IN THE FAMILY

As described above, transition times are difficult for all relationships, especially family relationships (Boss, 1980). During these times, family members must wrestle with changing interpersonal forces and newly emergent issues. Part of the stress comes about because new identities and roles threaten the comfortable balance of ritual and predictability that the family has come to know. Something inside the family shifts, what has been automatic in the past no longer works, and everyone has to make an adaptive or compensatory adjustment.

This is the notion of the family as a system, with elaborate connections tying everyone together. Even boarders in a rooming house have to adjust when one of their tablemates is very needy and is really packing away the food. Similarly in a family, when one of the members is psychologically very hungry and needs much supportive feeding, the family must cope with a new situation, a change, and the stress of adjustment.

Such times can include both positive and negative change. As described in Chapter 1, younger members of the family may acquire adult status and responsibility which other members may grant reluctantly and with resistance. Another instance may involve an aged family member going through emotional or physical decline, disrupting the routines of the family, and, in extreme situations, even intruding upon vital activities of other family members. Or, a spouse and parent may get an important promotion and have to devote longer hours, endure more erratic meal times, and have lots more money to spend on the family as a result of growing career success. Finally, consider the kinds of pressures for change created by the natural evolution of a child as he or she matures and expects increased privileges and autonomy.

Changes do not occur as instantaneous events. Family members directly and indirectly involved in any change must take time and pass through a process of accommodating to new arrangements. It is not merely that this or that family member alters a small piece of the family schedule. It is rather that many aspects of one or another family member may change. One's dress, working hours, income, self-image, and friends are a few among many such possibilities.

Unfortunately, the burdens and rewards of changes do not begin and end with the family member who has wrought them. The entire family, including some who do not even live in town, will weather the transition. Everyone will adjust in some way or other to new demands and requirements of life in the family.

Thank goodness, survival is not usually the issue. The issues are the psychological and physical costs to the family, what the legacy for future relationships will be, what patterns of conflict-resolution are left in the wake of the transitional crisis, whose ego has been eroded a little in the process, and so on. Thus, the consequences of family transitions have the potential to permeate every aspect of family life from the most casual to the most significant.

During stable times, when problems come from outside, individuals in the family are usually strong enough to help each other cope with stress. However, when the problems are a consequence of internal changes in the family, that is a different matter. Each member becomes a source of transition and stress for the others. They are all locked together in the struggle to adjust, and there may be such simultaneous demand for assistance with transition that no one family member can truly support any other. Everyone is too busy taking care of himself. The family as a needs-meeting system is taxed beyond its capacity to satisfy so many needs at the same time.

During these periods of crisis, when many old expectations are unmet, family members struggle with feelings of abandonment, betrayal, neglect, exploitation, and abuse. Whether or not members are behaving in these destructive ways, the family has become unpredictable and is therefore untrustworthy to its members. Adjustment and adaptation demand the re-establishment of predictability in some new workable form, and a renewal of trust.

FAMILY ATMOSPHERE:
INTERPERSONAL SHIFTS DURING CRISIS

Every family has an atmosphere that is very much a part of family response to transitional stress. In some homes, there is a coffee cup in the bedroom, a jacket hanging from a doorknob, and meals taken with few exchanges. In others, the house is neat as a pin and mealtimes are occasions for chatter and gossip. In some, children may be witness to affectionate kisses and hugs between their parents. In others, spouses come only as close as a light peck on the cheek. In many families, children come and go with minimal supervision, and in others the opposite is true.

Behind these everyday events and arrangements are unwritten rules about how family members should behave toward each other and the way family tasks and responsibilities should be handled. Of importance to the relationship between family atmosphere and family adjustment to stress are such questions as: "What kinds of issues underlie the way everyday events and arrangements are structured?" and "What organizing principles seem to connect these apparently random ways of being and doing?"

In answer to these questions, three major relationship forces or issues that relate to power, closeness, and belonging are prominent. Chapter 3 addresses these forces or issues in great detail. They are important because they govern the quality of experience in all groups and organizations (Bennis and Shepard, 1956; Shutz, 1958; Garland, Jones, and Kolodny, 1976). They are: (1) authority, (2) intimacy, and (3) membership.

Periods of crisis test how much control or authority family members can exercise in relation to one another. For example, the adolescent who asserts his independence in a manner that gets him into trouble with the law is raising many issues related to parental authority. And it may be that his parents were not too lax; rather their control was so restrictive, it precipitated a crisis.

Periods of crisis also test how honest and intimate family members will be with each other. For example, a teenager who discovers she is pregnant and wants assistance from her family never may have shared anything at all with them about her sexuality, or the extent of her involvement with her boyfriend. She just may be too shy, but one should not dismiss the possibility that her family gives clear messages that those things are not talked about.

Finally, periods of crisis test the limits tolerated by the family before a member runs the risk of being excluded or disowned. An example is the wife of an alcoholic who somehow manages to put up with her husband's irresponsible and embarrassing behavior. But, when he physically abuses her and the children, she offers him the ultimatum that he either get professional help with his problem or get out.

The examples above show how negative crisis tests family issues of authority, intimacy, and membership. However, family stress may be precipitated by positive as well as negative events. On the positive side, the teenager who has just passed her driver's license test is justly proud of an accomplishment that is a milestone marking her transition toward adulthood. The parents must now deal with issues of authority, control, intimacy, and belonging as they struggle with their daughter's new freedom and responsibility. The license to drive is only part of the problem. The real issue is "letting go."

As can be seen in the examples above, transitions force families to change the boundaries that separate children from parents, and force adults to adjust the balance between their roles as parents and spouses. At issue are new resolutions to problems of dependency versus autonomy, intimacy versus privacy, and individuality versus conformity in the family. As a result, periods of transition subject family members to pressures to change their relationships with one another and the outside world.

Family atmosphere is the medium in which such change occurs. If the atmosphere is rigid, closed, and adversarial, then change will likely occur amid bitter fighting and terrible emotional or even physical violence. If, on the other hand, the family's atmosphere is open, flexible, and cooperative, change is more apt to occur through negotiation, compromise, and consensus.

These negative and positive extremes of family atmosphere link with adjustment because crisis says very directly: "Things cannot be the same." Family atmosphere is the major determinant to whether the family will do it the "hard (painful and expensive) way" as is the case in the negative extreme, or the "easy (constructive and efficient) way" as in the positive.

If this experience or that change was only slightly stressful, most families' usual coping style would probably see them through periods of transition. When a family is confronted by a crisis, the old ways are no longer adequate. A shift will take place in critical family relationship dimensions.

CONSEQUENCES OF INADEQUATE ADJUSTMENT TO FAMILY TRANSITION

When a family repeatedly deals with crises ineffectively, the consequences may include creation of a secretive, nondisclosing, closed atmosphere (intimacy); ceaseless and vicious power struggles (authority); and the sense of being an outsider in one's own family (membership). In this way everyday family styles become independent, chronic sources of pain and suffering that family members come to take as the way life is.

Family members no longer question, and in fact may never have questioned, the way the family operates or what relational pathology is swallowed with breakfast or eaten at dinner. The children in the family start out vulnerable and dependent, and may never be encouraged to question the way things are. Similarly, the parents may be caught in a conspiracy designed to conceal their own fragile parenting skills.

In these ways, some family styles, adaptive and maladaptive, are passed from generation to generation (Schulman, 1973). Many family therapists have noted that even when people live alone, the ghosts of their families are always there. When we live with others, these ghosts find their way into the marriage bedroom, the dining room, and playtime with the kids.

Unfortunately, poor adjustment to transition does more than make the family an unpleasant place to be. The prolonged stress disrupts the individual's sense of self. One does not just feel bad! Prolonged family stress actually throws the individual off balance so that the usual and regular ways of going about things become impossible. The old ways just will not work.

This is the subjective experience of family members under stress. It is as if a fabric is starting to unravel. Coping skills and strategies cannot cover the gaps, yet life must go on. Bills must be paid, children tended to, spouses considered, and meals prepared. This is the demand side of the family equation.

On the supply side, each person's sense of self must be replenished as it is being exhausted by stress. We need validation of ourselves at all times, but especially during extreme transition. This emotional resupply and revalidation for members is one of the most important functions of the family.

Thus, periods of stress jeopardize critical feelings about the self. These self-evaluative dimensions can be threatened and stressed from within the family itself, by outside change stressors, or by some combination of internal and external family pressures.

As described in Chapter 1, there are five such critical feelings: (1) a sense of personal control (Rotter, 1966); (2) social integration (Dean, 1961); (3) positive self-esteem (Diggory, 1966); (4) flexibility and openness (Rokeach, 1960); and (5) clarity of personal goals and values (Raths, Harmin, and Simon, 1966). A brief description of each of these self-evaluative dimensions, and how the family influences them follows.

1. *Sense of personal control.* People need to feel that they are in charge of their lives, what they do matters, and that they can affect their world. One's belief in one's own control of life outcomes is an important source of reassurance and comfort.

2. *Social integration.* People also need to feel that they are an accepted, welcomed, respected, and important member of their family and other groups. Loneliness is a simple but powerful human experience that is the source of much pain. To avoid this pain, everyone wants to be part of the social world in which he or she is embedded.

In this instance, we are talking about blood ties, and the feeling that the family can be counted on to be there, whether they really want to or not. It is almost as if family members had no choice but to stand by each other. Feeling that one's own family is indifferent, and neither shares one's joys nor one's tragedies is a sad state of affairs, indeed.

3. *Positive self-esteem.* People also need to feel that within them are the assets and talents required to achieve the goals they value. Similarly, they need to recognize that they have special and prized personality characteristics and traits, that they are equipped to succeed, and that they are realistic in their positive self-confidence. Excessive stress gradually erodes self-esteem.

4. *Flexibility and openness.* People need to feel they can make mistakes, that there is room for error, and that consequences are reversible. Also, people need to know that there is time and opportunity to explore different options, there is not one correct way of doing anything, and that tasks can be viewed as challenges rather than threats. From this perspective, crisis is an opportunity for growth. Stress undermines this perspective.

5. *Clear personal goals and values.* People need to feel that they have direction in their lives, that they know what is good, bad, right, and wrong, and have a sense of what they want. Stress can throw long-held and cherished values into question. Even worse, people under stress may forget what is important to them and lose sight of their own values as they seek to adjust.

These self-evaluative dimensions provide one basis for identifying the healthy family and the unhealthy family. The adequacy with which a family adjusts to its own transitions has powerful impact on family members' positions of strength and weakness along the five self-evaluative dimensions. Repeatedly inadequate adjustments gradually accrue a terribly unhealthy legacy. Members' morale and mental health are eroded by feelings of powerlessness, isolation, and contempt for self. Their minds close as they seek comfort in that which feels familiar and safe, and their emotional lives become deadened as self is experienced with growing distrust.

SURROGATE FAMILY SUPPORT OF TRUE FAMILY

Because all families have the potential to move their members in any direction, those working with families seek to build on the strengths that exist in even the most disrupted families. Most important, members of families who are alert to the trials and tribulations of change can act on behalf of the entire family by helping all members cooperate and share in the work and benefits of successful transition.

For individuals besieged by forces of change and their family's inability to respond constructively to these forces, the surrogate family can provide some shelter from the storm of adversity. The surrogate family not only offers emergency support and protection, but also skills, insights, and renewed energy that one can bring back to one's own struggling family.

Thus, educators and other human service providers can safely assume that their efforts may resonate in positive ways far beyond the boundaries of the immediate work setting. The surrogate family opportunities they create may provide relief not only for participants but also for the troubled families from which participants come.

REFERENCES

Ackerman, N. (1958). "Behavior Trends and Disturbances of the Contemporary Family." In I. Goldston (ed.), *The Family in Contemporary Society*. New York: International University Press, p. 57.

Ackerman, N. (1966). *Treating the Troubled Family*. New York: Basic Books.

Bennis, W. and Shepard, H. (1956). "A Theory of Group Development." *Human Relations*, Vol. 9, No. 4, pp. 415-547.

Boss, P. (1980). "Normative Family Stress: Family Boundary Changes Across the Life Span." *Family Relations*, Vol. 29, pp. 445-450.

Dean, D. (1961). "Alienation: Its Meaning and Measurement." *American Sociological Review*, October, pp. 753-758.

Diggory, J. (1966) *Self-Evaluation: Concepts and Studies*. New York: Wiley.

Garland, J., Jones, H., and Kolodny, R. (1976). "A Model for Stages of Development in Social Work Groups." In S. Bernstein (ed.), *Explorations in Group Work.* Boston: Charles River Books, pp. 17-71.

Hafen, B., Frandsen, K., Karen, K., and Hooker, K. (1992). *The Health Effects of Attitudes, Emotions, and Relationships.* Provo, Utah: EMS Associates.

Holmes, T. and Rahe, R. (1967). "The Social Readjustment Scale." *Journal of Psychosomatic Research,* Vol. 11, pp. 213-218.

Lewis, J., Dana, R., and Blevins, G. (1994). *Substance Abuse Counseling: An Individualized Approach.* Pacific Grove, California: Brooks/Cole Publishing Company, pp. 143-146.

Melson, G. F. (1980). *Family and Environment: An Ecosystem Perspective.* Minneapolis, Minnesota: Burgess Publishing Company, p. 22.

Minuchin, S. (1974). *Families and Family Therapy.* Cambridge, Massachusetts: Harvard University Press.

Raths, L., Harmin, M., and Simon, S. (1966). *Values and Teaching.* Columbus, Ohio: Charles E. Merril Publishing Company, pp. 13-48.

Rokeach, M. (1960). *The Open and Closed Mind.* New York: Basic Books.

Rotter, J. (1966). "Generalized Expectancies of Internal versus External Control of Reinforcement." *Psychological Monographs,* Vol. 80, Whole No. 609.

Schulman, G. (1973). "Treatment of Intergenerational Pathology." *Social Casework,* October, pp. 462-472.

Shutz, W. (1958). *Firo: A Three Dimensional Theory of Interpersonal Behavior.* New York: Holt.

Solomon, M. (1973). "A Developmental, Conceptual Premise for Family Therapy." *Family Process,* June, pp. 179-188.

Chapter 3

Psychosocial Issues:
Important Understandings and Necessary
Resolutions for Healthy Group Experience

The preceding two chapters presented observations and notions about the challenges of being born into and growing up in a family. That family life affects the social and psychological well-being of the individual is clear. But as was described, families are vulnerable to disruption, and this disruption can cause members to suffer dire consequences. This is especially so when norms and rules that govern interpersonal relationships cause members to respond to one another in hurtful ways.

Also, these earlier chapters described how groups outside of the family can be a positive force in the life of the individual. Here too, positive health-promoting group experiences are not automatic. Therefore, the question arises as to what people must do to make nonfamily groups they join an enhancing experience in their lives. The material that follows attempts to answer this question.

In answering, the present chapter offers descriptions and explanations of some recurrent psychological and social issues that individuals confront when they join with others. The issues are psychological in that they address individual needs for safety, affection, status, and meaning, and are social because they pertain to how one can meet such needs through interaction with other people. The narrative that follows proposes that the manner in which participants resolve these issues and the content of their resolutions are keys to the success of one's experience in a group.

The concerns represented by these issues are relevant within the intimate confines of the family and the broader public domain of the community. They are points of intersection at which individual human needs collide with demands imposed by social existence. In the absence of satisfactory resolution, these issues may jeopardize the quality of shared experience, the productivity of collaboration, and the well-being of participants. Constructive resolution establishes safety that is foundational to trust, and salience that is the basis for deriving personal meaning from participation.

These recurrent issues were identified initially by observers who noted that the formation of a group is a process rather than an event (Bennis and Shephard, 1956; Yalom, 1975; Garland, Jones, and Kolodny, 1976; Schutz, 1958). These observers describe the process as one in which participants engage each other around issues of relationship. Together, members pass through a number of stages and milestones each of which addresses ambiguity about a specific aspect of interaction.

Though various investigators propose differing labels and some variations in concept when describing the issues, the following discussion is an interpretive synthesis of their disparate ideas. The synthesis attempts to pull together the various points of view in a way that draws on their value without violating the tenets basic to each.

As a model of group development, the concepts discussed here most closely resemble those of Garland, Jones, and Kolodny (1976). However, the intention here is not to describe group development per se, but to illuminate important psychosocial problems and issues that are now understood as a byproduct of discoveries about group development. A further intention is to integrate parallel notions about family so that opportunity for family surrogate experience can be built into group life.

Literature in the field of education contains reports that indicate understandings regarding these problems and issues are useful in designing educational programs and curriculum (Weinstein, 1980), and training educators and other human service providers for work with groups (Boucher and Weinstein, 1985). The material that follows describes how these understandings may apply to the creation of alternative social experiences for children and others whose family circumstances are less than ideal.

PSYCHOSOCIAL ISSUES AND GROUP LIFE

When a group first forms, or when one first joins an existing group, each new participant usually experiences some anxiety because of uncertainty about goals and purposes, ambiguity about how one should behave, and a lack of understanding about what to expect from others. Thus, in a new group, the unknown can be a source of considerable discomfort. This anxiety is a normal reaction to initial engagement in a new experience, and is a self-protective response to an important but, as yet unanswered question. This question asks about the trustworthiness and safety of participation.

The tensions and stresses associated with new experience, transition, and "social readjustment" have been made palpable by Holmes and Rahe (1967). These writers, whose research was described in Chapter 2, have not only identified life events and changes that are sources of distress, but have also documented their potential for negative impact on health.

Under many circumstances, joining a new group can be an extremely tense and stressful challenge. The quiet beginnings of social gatherings, reliance on disinhibiting effects of drugs and alcohol, and social purposes of formality and etiquette may be readily observed when people first come together.

To relieve these tensions and stresses, new participants observe, test, and explore in efforts to make clear that which is ambiguous and to discover what is unknown about participation. They seek relief through development and/or acceptance of a set of rules and social definitions that all can understand and follow. New participants discover and establish boundaries and limits of behavior. They then seek from others and grant to others permission to interact within those limits.

In so doing, group members confront and attempt to resolve important psychosocial issues of group living. Later in the life of a group, other ambiguities emerge as crisis, growth, and change repudiate aspects of earlier resolutions to these issues. Because the passage of time makes change inevitable, participants must confront psychosocial issues of group participation again and again.

In the absence of satisfactory resolution and later re-resolution, the social environment is unclear and participants struggle with undefined expectations, limits, and boundaries for acceptable be-havior. Under such conditions, interaction with others is experi-enced as unpredictable, potentially dangerous, and frightening.

STABILITY AND CHANGE IN FAMILIES, GROUPS, AND COMMUNITIES

Many writers describe the resolution of each issue as a one-time process. Implicit within such descriptions is the notion that stability is an important and positive aspect of rewarding group experience. This is true especially because stability is an important contributor to safety and trust.

Unfortunately, reality has an inconvenient way of intruding upon mice, people, and groups. Forces external to the group and within the members, themselves, inevitably precipitate crisis and change. Nowhere is the truth of the saying that "Life is something that happens while we are making other plans!" more evident than when a family, group, or community discovers that its old ways of doing things no longer work.

The problem of change is acknowledged by some writers who view the need for resolution of social and psychological issues to be recurrent (Homans, 1950; Schutz, 1958). This latter point of view is held in the present writing. That is, psychosocial issues are thought to require new resolutions as transition and change occur through-out the life of a group. The readdressing of interpersonal issues is the means by which groups adjust social interaction to new de-mands imposed by change.

This is very important for families. Family therapists consider an inability to adjust interpersonal relations to be an important aspect of family dysfunction. This is particularly so for changes demanded by members' growth, development, and aging. These practitioners also see this dysfunction as an important source of emotional distur-bance (Weinstein and Thayer, 1986).

Transition confronts the community with similar problems. How-ever, in the community, changes emerge from many sources. Some are imposed by persons in positions of authority, and others may involve reinterpretation of time-honored customs and tradition. Still others may emerge through organized but passive agreement, or evolve as social trends through acceptance by individuals as an unorganized aggregate (Roberts and Kloss, 1974; Weinstein, 1984).

Once initiated, new community rules and norms become genuine forces in the life of the individual in a variety of ways. One form of initiation is simple and passive adoption of disseminated ideas. Another more active and complex process is negotiated acceptance through dialogue and consensual decision making. And finally, people may resist or impose rules and norms by coercive confrontation and disruption (Cissel, King, and Patton, 1990).

These same mechanisms are at play in a small group in that groups evolve as microcosms of the larger community. The community will not lend support, or may actively seek to suppress, groups that violate basic values or threaten its safety. Thus, small groups must not only seek satisfaction of their own needs, but must achieve satisfaction in a manner that adequately addresses the demands of the surrounding community.

Therefore, resolution of psychosocial issues of group living requires participants to develop a structure of rules or norms that satisfies themselves and, to some degree, the community at large. The structure must provide adequate means of making sense out of group experience, and must be flexible enough to be altered when it ceases to function adequately.

AMBIVALENCE: A PSYCHOSOCIAL ISSUE ABOUT BEGINNINGS AND CHANGES

Ambivalence is the first issue people confront as they join together or collectively face change. Each such event initiates transition, and each transition demands an evaluation of and adjustments to impending alterations in life circumstance (Bridges, 1980). The evaluation invariably reveals that adjustments require forfeiture of positive elements and provide relief from negative elements of the old. Similarly, the new may offer its own attractions and burdens. These realizations often elicit powerfully conflicting feelings that are the essence of ambivalence.

Since our parents, ourselves, groups we join, changes we may face, and most aspects of life are neither perfect nor ideal, ambivalence haunts us continually. Therefore, our struggle is not to achieve perfection, but to find comfort in the face of the mix of positive and negative feelings that bombard us in perpetuity. The "coming to terms" with these ever-present mixed feelings is at the heart of constructive resolution to the psychosocial issue of ambivalence in a group.

According to Kernberg (1975), preparation for coping with ambivalence is a product of a major developmental challenge of early childhood. This challenge confronts the individual with the reality that the mother who loves, supports, and protects is the same person who punishes, withholds, and disappoints. Failure to incorporate this troubling reality, and merge one's view of the good mother with one's experience of the bad mother, may produce later difficulties in forming meaningful interpersonal relationships. Similarly, the beginnings of group life confront an individual with potential for good and bad in newly forming interpersonal relationships, and later adjustments to these relationships.

Extreme discomfort (such as anxiety or depression) during times when ambivalence is heightened may lead to overreliance on ego-defensive maneuvers. These maneuvers not only place barriers between the individual and his discomfort, but also between the individual and other people.

Coping with polarized feelings is not easy, and many of the most emotionally robust people would prefer to avoid such inner conflict rather than come to terms with it. In so doing, initial perceptions in a new group may be shaped by remote prior experience and individual personal needs rather than the objective facts of immediate circumstance.

This is especially true when participants attempt to "fill in the blanks" formed by the many ambiguities and unknowns of a new experience. Participants not only struggle to make sense of their experience, but are predisposed to make sense that minimizes ambivalence and inner conflict (Katz, 1960). Thus, the creation of self-protective illusion is an important aspect of initial encounters with new people in new circumstances.

Psychoanalytic thinking has generated terms such as "transference" and "countertransference" to identify the construction of illusion in the therapeutic relationship. Similarly, Sullivan (1970) refers to it as "parataxic distortion."

In the larger community, words such as "stereotyping," and "prejudice" refer to illusions promulgated by suspect social indicators. People often defend such illusions with the rationalization that there is a "kernel of truth," or "well-earned reputation" behind even the most outrageous illusory claims (Harding, 1964).

An extensive literature about "person perception" documents human tendencies to assign attributes to others based on superficial initial observations of appearance, symbols of social status, gender, and other immediately visible characteristics (Schneider, Hastorf, and Ellsworth, 1979). More recent reports document misplaced faith by many individuals in their abilities to accurately detect hidden purposes and ulterior motives through nonverbal cues (Goleman, 1991). Thus, immediate direct experience with a stranger can precipitate or perpetuate the generation of illusion.

For some, the illusory nature of initial group experience is seductive in its ability to evoke idealized expectations and a honeymoon of elation. For others, the illusion is so negative that they must resist powerful impulses to flee. Thus, "splitting," a tactic in which events, people, or a group are seen in the black-and-white terms of "all good" or "all bad," and denial, another tactic, are defenses against the competing negatives and positives of initial encounters with people or change. Not only are participants vulnerable to such psychological self-trickery, but leaders are too.

For a reasonably healthy person, these efforts to avoid ambivalence succeed only in delaying inevitable confrontation with one's own mixed feelings. Implicit in Sumerlin's (1979) theory about the formation of romantic relationships is the notion that movement toward disillusionment and true ambivalence begins with initial contact between people. According to Sumerlin, "illusion" in which one's perception of another is shaped by one's needs rather than by another's personal qualities and attributes is the first stage in the process. Then, there is disillusionment and disappointment as reality forces its way into consciousness, and seductive and coercive efforts fail to reshape interpersonal relationships into the illusory mold.

This is followed by a period of guilt about aggression and hostility expressed in the effort to maintain the illusion, and depression about the death of such a wonderfully gratifying dream. After a time of avoidance, effort is made to come to realistic terms with the mix of positive and negative feelings that the individual must face.

Thus, finding comfort in an ambivalent emotional state requires more than the mere drafting and acceptance of a psychological balance sheet. It also involves development of a readiness to give up comforting illusions and to face the disquieting facts of a situation.

The threat of loss of the familiar and comfortable, and prospects of having to cope with the new and unknown, are central to those disquieting facts. The problem of codependency in a family with an alcoholic member is an illustrative example of this. People in such families often cling to a problematic status quo because change is too threatening. In so doing, family members establish elaborate and destructive patterns to avoid confrontation about disruption caused by the alcoholic member (George, 1990; Lewis, Dana, and Blevins, 1988). In this environment, unexpressed tension and conflict associated with increasingly palpable ambivalence may turn the family into a veritable pressure cooker for mental illness.

Thus, the individual must eventually confront the fundamental questions about group life. "What do I stand to gain and what must I sacrifice if I join a group or embrace change?" In so doing, one must see past the illusions and distortions of ambiguous initial experience, and face tensions associated with change.

People may act to join and/or accept change, or withdraw and/or reject change, but psychologically, the issue is the inner conflict and tension associated with the decision. Fear about loss of safety, love, status, and meaning underlie this conflict and tension. Socially, individual concerns about choices, decisions, and changes raise issues for others (individually and collectively) when one expresses feelings, intentions, and beliefs about a change. Such outward expression of these inner feelings leads each member to contemplate the impact of any proposed change on self and group.

Thus, a problem for all groups is acknowledgement of ambivalent tension and conflict, and the availability of mutual support and assistance for individuals coping with prospective change. Health-promoting groups enhance potential to provide surrogate family experience by encouraging individual expression and responding in a reasonably helpful manner. In return, such groups also demand that the individual member consider the impact his decisions and actions have on others.

The expression of ambivalent feelings, and subsequent support and assistance, promotes individual growth in several important ways. Members are helped to face and make decisions, accept responsibility for the consequences of their choices, and live more comfortably with the inevitable combination of positives and negatives of every outcome.

Thus, for the individual, recognition of the connection between behavior and outcome is strengthened, and personal feelings, values, and attitudes may be clarified. Each member confronts his own decisions directly and vicariously as he observes and assists others facing similar struggles.

Dialogue and interaction about ambivalence are invariably important when groups first form, and as they face crisis and change. Therefore, the seeds of trust and benevolence may be planted early in group experience and become resources for coping with future transitional stress. This seems to be a remarkable parallel to the experience of birth into a family and early infancy as described in Chapter 1.

AUTHORITY: A PSYCHOSOCIAL ISSUE
ABOUT CONTROL AND DEPENDENCY

Very early in the process of joining together, members face the issue of control of behavior. In the primal and basic terms of psychoanalytic thinking, the concern is about the means through which the group will control its members' aggressive and sexual impulses. In operational terms, the concern is about how decisions will be made, the distribution of labor and responsibility, coordination of efforts, sharing of resources and benefits, and personal safety.

There are many possible resolutions that may successfully impose control, but resolutions that also promote growth and support surrogate family experience are more difficult to achieve. The issue is not about whether controls will be created, but how they will be developed, and what they will be.

Will controls be defined and imposed by an authority figure? Will they be developed by members as peers, or will participants and authority cooperatively produce them? These three alternatives illustrate the classic concepts of authoritarian, laissez-faire, and democratic styles of leadership. They also fit descriptions of authoritarian, permissive, and authoritative styles of parental control in the family (Baumrind, 1971). Authoritative parental control and democratic leadership appear to be equivalent, as do permissive parents and laissez-faire leaders.

There is ample evidence that democratic leadership and authoritative parenting are the healthiest when they are possible to achieve (Maccoby and Martin, 1983; Camp, Swift, and Swift, 1982; Kim and Stevens, 1987; Elings, 1988; Siegle, 1990). However, they require more skill, patience, and personal investment on the part of leaders than do authoritarian or permissive-laissez-faire methods.

Thus, a useful approach to understanding the problem of authority is a bipolar continuum with control centered in an authority figure at one pole and in the group members as peers at the other. The point on this continuum at which resolutions to authority issues fall is the product of many factors.

For example, a military unit, a prison rehabilitation program, a college debating team, a high school chess club, or a special education class for emotionally disturbed children face very different situational demands. The same holds true for differences in members' level of function and abilities to be self-managing. As the examples imply, in some cases resolutions toward the authority-centered end of the continuum are more functional, and in some, resolutions toward the peer-centered end are more functional.

In many situations, organizational mandates resolve the issue of authority before participants meet for the first time. This is so because the community provides a preexisting organization and social structure through which group experiences are offered and sanctioned. The community's laws, customs, and traditions demand compliance.

For example, in families, parents have power to control children. In school settings, so do teachers. Doctors, nurses, and social workers hold similar authority over patients in health care settings. The same observations apply to such diverse situations as recreation directors in community centers, clergy in religious organizations, and musical directors in bands and orchestras. Thus, as children venture forth from the shelter of the family, other adults in the community assume parental roles. This pattern persists into and throughout adulthood.

One consequence of our repeated experience with these aspects of family and community life is a commonly held expectation that special people will be present to direct and control behavior whenever one joins a group. We learn that leadership, responsibility, and control are inextricably linked to parents, educators, and other agents of the community when they are identified as authorities. Their authority may be derived from position in a social hierarchy, from charisma and other personal qualities, or from special skills and knowledge. Please note that each of these authoritative sources has analogues in early childhood illusions of parental omnipotence.

Unfortunately, we also learn that one reward for dependency on such people is escape from responsibility, and from tension produced by ambiguity and ambivalence. The idea of having our needs met through the ministering of benevolent parental figures is very seductive, indeed. The narcissistic gratifications associated with power and control, and the appreciative acknowledgements of dependent group members, are seductive to people in positions of authority, too.

Group leaders' and members' vulnerability to such gratifications may be compounded by performance anxiety (Weinstein, 1991). Members of groups such as athletic teams and performing arts ensembles may seek shelter in the shadow of coaches and directors as pressures of competition and exposure intensify dependency. This also may occur for teachers and others in positions of authority who face accountability demands (Weinstein, 1987). Such demands are sometimes imposed by employers and sanctioning organizations, and often intensify the need to be in control.

Thus, there is a mix of social experience and reciprocal need that evokes powerful expectations to have control invested in the authority of special people. One unfortunate result is that unconscious collusion between participants and leaders may produce an equally unconscious conspiracy of authoritative control and member dependency.

To be sure, there is need and a place for special people to assist in bringing order to the chaos that can, at times, mark life in some groups. This chaos is common to new groups and is frequently associated with change. Skilled leaders often can create and impose a reasonably functional structure of rules and norms during such trying times.

In some instances, dominant leaders may continue to regulate interaction and define individual experience throughout the life of a group. Continuous authoritative control beyond that needed during beginnings and transitions is possible, and often necessary, because some children and disabled adults need unrelenting direction.

This is especially true if health and safety are at risk. To provide less direction is to abandon these individuals to needs they cannot satisfy themselves. On a broader social scale, homelessness is one of the more visible consequences among the many that befall the very young, disabled, and mentally ill when agents of the community withdraw needed supervision, support, and protection.

In contrast, unneeded direction in a group hampers growth of interdependence and self-determination for more mature and functional people. For more capable individuals, the potential for sharing or distributing leadership on the basis of the demands of the moment and the diverse abilities of the members are great. A failure to develop and use this potential is damaging for several reasons.

First, interaction tends to occur primarily between leader and participant rather than between participants. Interaction that does occur between participants is likely to be shaped by needs for leader approval. This, in effect, deprives individual participants of access to the resources of the peer group.

Second, passivity and helplessness are taught and reinforced. This is especially so in situations demanding judgments, decisions, and containing opportunity for individual initiative. Clearly, effective functioning in such situations is a requirement of adulthood. Thus, repeated leader-centered resolutions to the issues of authority are regressive for more capable individuals because leaders remain parents and members remain children in perpetuity.

At times, teachers, parents, and others struggling with problems associated with leader-centered resolutions may react in the opposite direction toward the peer-centered end of the continuum. In so doing, they adopt a laissez-faire or permissive style that abandons group members to exercise self-control whether or not members are ready.

For some educators and parents, the tactic may be a reaction to narcissistic fears about being tyrannical and controlling. For others, an uncritical or orthodox dependence on a guiding ideology or philosophy may be the problem. In some situations, depression, burnout, incompetence, and hopelessness are so profound that people in positions of authority have little to give.

In all these cases, the needs of participants are subordinated to the needs of the leader. Members are subject to abandonment and neglect, and passive forms of abuse, betrayal, and exploitation to the degree that genuine needs for direction are unmet.

The discussion above describes powerful forces that shape the manner in which resolutions to the psychosocial issue of authority are achieved. The material below discusses concerns about the content of such resolutions. Just as authority-centered resolutions can produce repressive tyrants or benevolent despots, peer-centered resolutions can produce rampaging mobs or democratic groups.

Thus, a constructive "coming to terms" with the need for appropriate power and control involves assessments about the creation and preservation of adequate personal choice and initiative, and support and protection. In broad terms, the challenge is the exercise of power and the achievement of control that do not tyrannize, foster unnecessary dependence, or neglect needs.

Constructive resolutions prevent tyranny by demanding that participants separate the source of messages from the ideas and proposals these messages may contain. In so doing, the incidence of blind obedience, and blind reactivity and resistance to leadership, may be reduced. Terms such as overdependence, counterdependence, pseudoautonomy (Kohut, 1971), and dogmatism (Rokeach, 1960) are descriptive attempts to label and understand internal conflicts that lead to exaggerated deference and/or resistance to authority.

Basic to healthy resolutions to issues of authority are careful assessments of situational demands, and participants' needs and capabilities. Such assessments provide a basis to support and encourage participants to develop and exercise their own capacities for control. Similarly, participants should not be forced to do what they cannot. Thus, resolutions should avoid having leaders or others do for participants what they can do for themselves, and avoid being unresponsive when there is need for authoritative intervention.

Further, authoritative interventions should go beyond the needs of the moment. Needs should be satisfied in ways that promote an eventual shift of responsibility from authoritative figures to participants. Methods which teachers and others may use to promote such a shift include standard pedagogical practices such as didactic instruction and explanation, demonstration and role modeling, simulations and guided trials, coaching, and rehearsals. The principle here is illustrated by the adage that "If one gives a man a fish, he will eat today, but if one teaches him to fish, he will eat every day." Thus, the objective is to reduce groups' dependence on parental figures for direction and control, and to increase members' capacities to control and direct themselves.

Therefore, resolutions should assist leaders to "work themselves out of a job" by reducing group needs for authority-centered direction and control. The leader's old job is replaced to the degree that a cooperatively developed structure of norms and rules emerges to govern behavior in the group. When this is effective, a leader acquires new jobs as consultant and resource person.

Further, when ongoing groups establish a history, these rules and norms become a resource of time-honored customs and traditions. Behavior thus acquires a stable and trustworthy guide as history and precedent become part of the normative structure of the group.

INTIMACY: A PSYCHOSOCIAL ISSUE OF COMMUNICATION AND DISCLOSURE

The third issue that people confront when they join together is that of intimacy. The issue of intimacy arises early in group life and reemerges as change forces interpersonal realignments and adjustments. Again in primal terms of psychoanalytic thought, authority issues address means for controlling aggressive and sexual expression. In contrast, intimacy issues address anxiety about the degree to which such impulses may be expressed before members may impose control.

Thus, intimacy as a psychosocial issue is about limits and boundaries of interpersonal relationships. As described in Chapter 1, experience with these limits and boundaries originates in the family. Therefore, family is the primary frame of reference as participants test the appropriateness and possibilities for more deeply personal and family-like relationships with each other (Garland, Jones, and Kolodny, 1976). At this time, participants explore and cultivate the latent possibilities for family surrogate experience.

In operational terms, the form and content of communication, freedom of access to information, and privacy are at issue. The challenge is to establish patterns of communication that are optimal to the social needs of members and to the goals and purposes of the group.

In facing this challenge, groups address issues about disclosure and exchange at the rational-intellectual and visceral-emotional levels of experience and action. Also, they must decide about the degree to which communication may focus on reactions to interpersonal events as they occur. In this way, "head versus gut" and "there and then versus here and now" emerge in a struggle to define a second bipolar continuum.

This continuum lies between the overly personal and the overly impersonal. Members face decisions about the degree to which communication is to be limited to impersonal abstract concepts and ideas, or may include more personal feelings about immediate concrete events and experience with each other.

The impersonal end of the continuum emphasizes tasks and themes. It minimizes feelings, emotions, and "self and other as part of here and now social process" as focus of discussion. The less personal topical-theoretical flavor of the rational and intellectual is common to groups organized around themes, tasks, and activities, e.g., sports teams, performing arts ensembles, community action groups, recreational activity clubs, committees, academic courses, seminars and workshops, and discussion groups.

The personal end emphasizes feelings and explorations of members' role and behavior in the process and functioning of the group. "Growth-oriented" experiences offered by sensitivity training groups, consciousness-raising groups, support groups, and others develop and maintain an emotional-visceral flavor. In some settings, such as therapy groups, personal history may be a particularly important aspect of this focus.

In any situation, a reasonable expectation is that communication is primarily about content that is relevant to the purposes the group serves for its members. If people come together because of a shared interest in bicycling, they will want to talk about topics relevant to that interest. If they join together because of concerns about personal functioning, then that is what they will talk about. However, it is important to note that differences between groups with regard to intimacy are more a matter of degree than kind.

For example, even the most task-focused groups must pay some attention to creating and maintaining good working relationships between members. Intimacy must be established at levels that permit adequate information sharing, feedback about performance, and resolution of interpersonal conflict.

On the other hand, groups focused on social-emotional issues must handle some management tasks if they are to remain viable. Arrangements for meeting places, refreshments, costs, schedules, and other planning are among the less personal concerns that members of such groups must address.

The establishment of intimacy that is appropriate to the goals of the group and simultaneously provides members with access to each other is important. One may consider this to be an optimal resolution of the psychosocial issue of intimacy. Such a resolution creates a network of interpersonal resources members can rely upon to cope with individual and collective problems as they arise within the group. They may also turn to each other for support and assistance in coping with problems that are external to the group, if there is time and energy, and members so desire.

However, care must be exercised to establish a balance between engulfment and isolation, just as in the family. Despite the potential benefits, resolutions to the issue of intimacy present a double-edged sword to participants and leaders alike. The "freedom" to disclose is quite different from a "demand" to reveal, and access to communication is different from intrusiveness. Similarly, participants can become so overly involved in "sitting around and talking" that performance of tasks deteriorates.

MEMBERSHIP: A PSYCHOSOCIAL ISSUE
OF CONFORMITY VS. INDIVIDUALITY

The fourth issue groups face as they develop is that of conditions for membership. A fundamental aspect of this issue is the degree to which deviance from group norms and rules will be tolerated before the group suspends or revokes an individual's membership.

Rejection, diminished status, and withholding of privileges and rewards are the mechanisms through which many groups enforce rules and norms (Weinstein, 1987). In some settings, such as military units, penal institutions, criminal organizations, and street gangs, more aggressive and direct forms of physical threat are used for such purposes. However, when all recourse to persuasion and coercion are exhausted, the final alternative is rejection and ostracism.

As implied in Chapter 1, the individual pays for benefits derived from group membership by accepting reductions in personal freedom. Resolution of the psychosocial issues described above (ambivalence, authority, and intimacy) is the means through which demands and limits on individual behavior are established. Thus, group life is a balancing act in which the needs of the individual are weighed against the costs of group goals, purposes, and survival. Eventually, every participant is evaluated for conformity to expectations thought to be necessary to the functioning of the group.

A bipolar continuum may serve to describe this state of tension, similar to those used to describe tension around the issues of intimacy and authority, above. At what may be called the "conformist" end of the continuum, a group may require rigid and narrow adherence to all rules and norms regardless of situational demands or mitigating circumstances. This is probably best exemplified in the larger community by the military, athletic teams, orthodox religious activity, and some recreational organizations such as the Boy Scouts.

Tolerance for deviance in these groups is low. Punctilious responses of some conformist groups have filled the media with tales of conflict and legal confrontation. Recent events include the struggle on the New York Yankees baseball team about Don Mattingly's hair length, and rejection by the Cub Scouts of two atheistic

California boys who refused to acknowledge that part of the Scout Oath containing reference to God. The court martial and dishonorable discharge of a physician in the military reserve for refusing to serve in the Persian Gulf War is another more drastic example.

Groups operating toward the conformist end of the continuum are likely to adopt norms and rules that most closely resemble "rule ethics." Though such a system tends to respond to member behavior in terms of "black and white," and presents difficulty in the face of change and transition, it does provide a stable and consistent set of values upon which members can rely (Weinstein and Lagudis, 1980).

At the other, "libertarian," end of the continuum, a group may make few demands. Those may be flexible, broad ranging in interpretation, and responsive to situational problems and mitigating circumstances. This end of the continuum is exemplified by arts groups, liberal community organizing efforts, consciousness-raising and other growth-oriented groups. The varieties of dress, hair length, religious persuasion, political beliefs, and sexual orientation observable in such groups are indicators of libertarian acceptance.

Response to violation of rules and norms in groups at this end of the continuum are likely to resemble "situation ethics." That is, member behavior is evaluated in terms of circumstances and mitigating variables that are thought to be relevant. Deviant behavior may be tolerated or forgiven in some circumstances and not in others.

Though such an approach offers flexibility and aids response to change, the values and beliefs that underlie group reaction to individual behavior may become obscure and vulnerable to subversion (Weinstein and Lagudis, 1980). Some participants may disregard time-honored behavioral proscriptions and rationalize the selfish pursuit of personal rewards and gratifications. Under such circumstances, unconscious motives, expediency, and banal pretenses may abrogate high ideals and principles.

Some observers have detected a very real potential for hostile and authoritarian motives to corrupt people's seemingly benevolent intentions, and to contribute to divergence between rhetoric and behavior. For example, teachers espousing progressive educational beliefs, whose authoritarian practices identified them as "pseudo-progressive" (Pedhazur, 1969; Matioli, 1972), were found to behave differently toward children than teachers who were identified as truly progressive. Further, some supporters of the women's movement were identified as "pseudo-women's liberationists" because of their hostility toward men and their dogmatic views (Taleporos, 1974).

Thus, there are dangers associated with situational judgments that may cause ideals, values, and standards to lose clarity and definition. Such dangers may mitigate against consistency, stability, and benevolence necessary for trust in a group.

Because of this, resolution to the psychosocial issue of membership has an important part in a group's potential to offer family surrogate experience. There appears to be need for a core of stable and consistent values, standards, rules, and norms that participants may apply uniformly in considering each other's membership status. The experience of participation in a group that is stable and consistent fosters trust and a sense of social integration for an individual.

Simultaneously, there is need for enough flexibility and latitude within that group to permit useful and constructive adjustments to individual differences and change. Flexibility and openness to situational contingencies must be such that members can support each other's freedom to be creative, to experiment, to test new behaviors, and to make mistakes without jeopardizing one's membership.

Further, evenhandedness, equity, and fair mindedness in making assessments about individual behavior and membership is equally important. This is particularly important because people have a general tendency to respond more positively and tolerantly toward more attractive and highly esteemed individuals relative to those who are less attractive or have less status (Schneider, Hastorf, and Ellsworth, 1979). Such inequity not only is an assault on the self-esteem of lesser members, but also presents the problem of making "spoiled brats" or "monsters" of those who are indulged.

An obvious parallel exists between these concepts and the behavior of children in families with inadequate limits and boundaries. Less obvious is the narcissistic damage to both the favored and the less-favored individuals. Favored status produces guilt, anxiety, and an exaggerated sense of indebtedness. Less-favored status may at first produce frustration and anger, but despair, depression, and withdrawal will follow.

Thus, a group's readiness to say "no!" to problem members, and "yes!" to constructive diversity is important to the welfare of the group and the well-being of the individual. The response of others to individual action makes clear the connection between behavior and outcome, and thus makes personal control a tangible aspect of group life. These are among the many reasons that the psychosocial issue of membership is important to the quality of group experience and the creation of surrogate family opportunity.

TERMINATION AND SEPARATION:
A PSYCHOSOCIAL ISSUE ABOUT ENDINGS

Throughout the life of most groups, change and transition must be faced from time to time. The final such event occurs when the group itself ends. However, all changes may be viewed as an ending to an old way of doing or being, and movement into something new (Bridges, 1980).

As was discussed above, change is invariably stressful, and all cultures contain rituals and rites of passage to help ease the way. Wedding celebrations, baby showers, bar mitzvahs, confirmations, graduations, and funerals mark transitional events. Convention requires that family and friends gather to help. These events acknowledge predictable milestones in human development, and most cultures have established customs associated with them (Grollman, 1974).

The events just listed are among the multitude of anticipated changes people encounter as they progress from birth to adulthood and through the life span. However, there are many unanticipated changes and comings and goings for which there are no established patterns of ritual and social support. Examples of such very important transitions are divorce, a family move to a new location, the loss of a pet, a job change, illness and disability, and nursing home placement (Bridges, 1980).

Unfortunately, children are most likely to get lost in the turmoil and chaos precipitated by these sometimes sudden, unexpected events (York and Weinstein, 1980-81; Jewett, 1982). Children suffer partly because until recently their capability to comprehend loss and to mourn was poorly understood (Jewett, 1982, p. xi). Also, children do not have a backlog of experience to help them cope independently with momentous change. Because the adults upon whom children rely may be struggling with their own disequilibrium, children's needs go unnoticed at times when they need assistance most. Though some family members and friends may rally to help, not all adults in proximity are sufficiently responsive (Weinstein, 1991).

Analogues to the events discussed above constantly impinge on the life of on-going groups. New members join; old members leave; meeting places and schedules change; rules, norms, and leadership may change, and, of course, the group may end. The willingness and ability of members to provide support and assistance during such times is a strong indicator of a group's capacity for surrogate family experience.

In groups, just as in the family, there are events that may be anticipated and others that may not. In terms of coping, the difference between the two types of events is that preparation in advance may made for the former. Regardless of the nature of the event, the challenge is each member's adjustment to its impact.

Adjustment to change, transition, and endings is described as a process (Kubler-Ross, 1969; Cassem, 1974; Bridges, 1980; Brodsky, 1991). Though theories about the process vary, they seem to agree that adjustments involve, first, a period of avoidance-denial, then resistance-opposition, and finally, resolution-accommodation.

From a practical perspective, four tasks seem important for successful completion of the process. All are amenable to group assistance. The first is acceptance of the inevitability and finality of a change. The second is tying up loose ends and completing the unfinished business of the old, when possible. The third involves realistic evaluation of what is ending so its positives may be carried into the future and its negatives addressed in accommodating the new. And finally, preparation is needed for movement toward the new beginning. Thus, group members complete the cycle of issues, and a new status quo presents renewed ambivalence.

In cases where the group continues or survives the crisis, the psychosocial issues described above are encountered anew. However, in situations where one or more members leave, or the group disbands and ceases to exist, change takes on more powerful meaning. For some members, it represents the death of a part of the self (one's membership), and the loss of something of which one is a part (the group). For others, trust is shaken as feelings associated with earlier experiences of betrayal and abandonment are reawakened. For children, inclinations toward guilt and self-blame may be fanned. Also, the more salient the group is to its members, the more vivid and striking these representations and reactions are. Therefore, the death of the group becomes a powerful symbol of the transience of relationships and of life itself, and tests one's ability to trust.

For these reasons, impending termination of relationships or a group makes separation an important psychosocial issue. Still, good endings are important to completion of surrogate family experience. Endings would be most important for individuals whose real family experiences with separation were probably marked by conflict and struggle, as described in Chapter 1. Such individuals often carry with them a residue of anger and resentment, or guilt and self-recrimination.

Because endings are closely related to the quality of life in the group throughout its existence, groups generally end as they lived. If there is a great deal of discord and interpersonal struggle during the life of the group, it is likely that the ending will be marked by discord and struggle. The task of completing the unfinished will be overwhelming because of the sheer number of loose ends and the same unresolved problems that prevented completion earlier. The negativity that colored the quality of experience in the group will be reflected in evaluative dialogue, and members may have difficulty finding future applications of the experience. The finality and inevitability of the ending will be anticipated with relief and possibly, some sadness about lost opportunity and unrealized potential. Thus, groups in which surrogate family opportunities are limited are not likely to provide much opportunity upon closure.

Though a good ending may add little to marginal group experience, such an ending can preserve and enhance positive experience.

Memories of growth-promoting and other gratifying events add permanence through discussion and reflection. Positive values derived from the experience achieve added potential for use in the future as thought and planning about the future is shared. The ability to trust can be strengthened as one recognizes and confirms the reality of endings as part of the human condition and prepares for the inevitable endings of the future.

REFERENCES

Baumrind, D. (1971). "Current Patterns of Parental Authority." *Developmental Psychology Monograph*, Vol. 4, pp. 1-102.

Bennis, W. G. and Shepard, H. A. (1956). "A Theory of Group Development." *Human Relations*, Vol. 9, No. 4, November, pp. 415-437.

Boucher, C. R. and Weinstein, S. A. (1985). "Training Professionals to be Powerful and Collaborative." *Contemporary Education*, Vol. 56, No. 3, Spring, pp. 130-136.

Bridges, W. (1980). *Transitions: Strategies for Coping with Difficult, Painful, and Confusing Times in Your Life*. Reading, Massachusetts: Addison-Wesley Publishing Company.

Brodsky, M. S. (1991). *Testicular Cancer Survivor's Impressions of the Impact of the Disease on Their Lives*. Doctoral dissertation, New York University, 1991. Ann Arbor, Michigan: University Microfilms, No. AAC9134723.

Camp, B. W., Swift, W. J., and Swift, E. W. (1982). "Authoritarian Parental Attitudes and Cognitive Functioning in Preschool Children." *Psychological Reports*, Vol. 50, pp. 1023-1026.

Cassem, N. H. (1974). "Care of the Dying Person." In Grollman, E. (ed.), *Concerning Death: A Practical Guide for Living*. Boston: Beacon Press, pp. 13-48.

Cissel, W. B., King, R. A., and Patton, R. D. (1990). "Community Health Reform." In Patton, R. D. and Cissel, W. B. (eds.), *Community Organization: Traditional Principles and Modern Applications*. Johnson City, Tennessee: Latchpins Press, pp. 65-75.

Elings, J. R. (1988). *The Effects of Parenting Styles on Children's Self-Esteem: A Developmental Perspective*. ERIC Document Reproduction, service no. ED 298-396.

Garland, J. A., Jones, H. E., and Kolodny, R. L. (1976). "A Model for Stages of Development in Social Work Groups." In Bernstein, S. (ed.), *Explorations in Group Work*. Boston: Charles River Books, pp. 17-71.

George, R. L. (1990). *Counseling the Chemically Dependent: Theory and Practice*. Needham Heights, Massachusetts: Allyn and Bacon, pp. 50-54.

Goleman, D. (1991). "Non-Verbal Cues Are Easy to Misinterpret." *The New York Times*, September 17, pp. c1 & c9.

Grollman, E. A. ed. (1974). *Concerning Death: A Practical Guide for the Living*. Boston: Beacon Press, pp. 81-140.

Harding, J. et al. (1964). "Prejudice and Ethnic Relations." In Lindsay, G. (ed.), *Handbook of Social Psychology*, Vol. 2, Reading, Massachusetts: Addison-Wesley.

Holmes, T. H. and Rahe, R. H. (1967). "The Social Readjustment Scale." *Journal of Psychosomatic Research*, Vol. 11, pp. 213-218.

Homans, G. C. (1950). *The Human Group*. New York: Harcourt, Brace and Company.

Jewett, C. L. (1982). *Helping Children Cope with Separation and Loss*. Harvard, Massachusetts: Harvard Common Press.

Katz, D. (1960). "The Functional Approach to the Study of Attitudes." *Public Opinion Quarterly*, Vol. 24, pp. 163-204.

Kernberg, O. (1975). *Borderline Conditions and Pathological Narcissism*. New York: Aronson.

Kim, Y. and Stevens, J. H. (1987). "The Socialization of Prosocial Behavior in Children." *Childhood Education*, Vol. 63, pp. 200-205.

Kohut, H. (1971). *Analysis of the Self*. New York: International Universities Press.

Kubler-Ross, M. (1969). *On Death and Dying*. New York: Macmillan.

Lewis, J. A., Dana, R. Q., and Blevins, G. A. (1988). *Substance Abuse Counseling*. Pacific Grove, California: Brooks/Cole Publishing Company, pp. 145-146.

Maccoby, E. E. and Martin, J. A. "Socialization in the Context of the Family." In Musen, P. H. and Hetherington, E. M. (eds.), *Handbook of Child Psychology*. New York: John Wiley and Sons, 1983.

Matioli, M. J. *The Effect of Genuine Progressive and Pseudo-Progressive Educational Attitudes and Susceptibility to an Authoritative Source on the Marking Behavior of 4th, 5th, and 6th Grade Teachers and Students of Education Preparing to Teach*. New York University, Doctoral dissertation, 1972. Ann Arbor Michigan: University Microfilms, 1972, No. 26-608.

Pedhazur, E. J. (1969). "Pseudoprogressivism and Assessment of Teacher Behavior." *Educational and Psychological Measurement*, Vol. 29, No. 2, pp. 377-386.

Roberts, R. E. and Kloss, R. M. (1974). *Social Movements: Between the Balcony and the Barricade*. St. Louis: C. V. Mosby Company.

Rokeach, M. (1990). *The Open and Closed Mind*. New York: Basic Books, 1960.

Seigle, W. F. *Fostering Prosocial Behavior in Preschool Through Teacher, Student, and Parent Involvement*. ERIC Document Reproduction service no. ED 318-568.

Schneider, D. J., Hastorf, A. H., and Ellsworth, P. C. (1979). *Person Perception*. Reading, Massachusetts: Addison-Wesley Publishing Company.

Schutz, W. C. "The Interpersonal Underworld." *Harvard Business Review*, Vol. 36, No. 4, July-August 1958, pp. 123-135.

Sullivan, H. S. (1970). *The Psychiatric Interview*. New York: W. W. Norton and Company.

Sumerlin, J. R. *Development of Exclusive Romantic Primary Pair Bonds: Construct Validation of a Five Stage Theory*. New York University, doctoral dissertation, 1979. Ann Arbor Michigan: University Microfilms, 1980, No. AAC8010307.

Taleporos, E. (1975). *Women's Liberationists and Pseudo-Women's Liberationists: Their Beliefs about Sex-Role Socialization, Opinions About Social Issues, and Perceptions of Male-Female Relations.* New York University, doctoral dissertation. Ann Arbor, Michigan: University Microfilms, 1975, No. 08-567.

Weinstein, S. "Linking Health Education Content with Classroom Group Development." *Journal of School Health,* Vol. 50, November 1980, pp. 543-544.

Weinstein, S. "Social Realities and Measurement in the Scientific Study of Sex." *Journal of Sex Research,* Vol. 20, No. 3, August 1984, pp. 217-229.

Weinstein, S. (1987). "Disciplinary Action: Dealing with Problem Behaviors in Nonprofit Organizations." In Anthes, E. and Cronin, J. (eds.), *Personnel Matters in the Nonprofit Organization.* West Memphis, Arkansas: Independent Community Consultants, pp. 259-277.

Weinstein, S. "A Qualitative Study of Performance Distress: Useful Understandings and Helpful Suggestions for Coping." *Annual Journal of the New York Brass Conference,* March 1991, pp. 32, 34,36,38.

Weinstein, S. and Lagudis, M. "Health Ethics." (1980). In Dintiman, G. B. and Greenberg, J. S. (eds.), *Health Through Discovery.* Reading, Massachusetts: Addison-Wesley Publishing Company, pp. 505-518.

Weinstein, S. and Thayer, S. (1986). "Family Stress." In Patton, R. (ed.), *The American Family: Life and Health.* Oakland, California: Third Party Associates, pp. 420-439.

Yalom, I. (1975). *The Theory and Practice of Group Psychotherapy,* 2nd ed. New York: Basic Books.

York, J. and Weinstein, S. (1980-1981). "The Effect of a Videotape About Death and Dying on Bereaved Children in Family Therapy." *Omega Journal of Death and Dying,* Vol. 2, No. 4, pp. 355-361.

PART II.
SOCIAL CONSTITUENCIES
AND THE SURROGATE FAMILY

Introduction

The preceding three chapters describe hazards and challenges of growing up encountered because we live in families and participate in community social activities. As the narrative argues, life in the family can be as troubling as it is sustaining, and the same can be said for primary groups we join outside of the family. For this reason, the concept of the surrogate family is of great importance to educators and other human service providers.

The psychosocial issues described in Chapters 2 and 3 are the immediate and practical concerns around which people manage the hazards and challenges of life in families and other groups. Sustenance, conflict, and pain are all potential outcomes of a member's success or failure to satisfactorily resolve these issues. The professional practitioner's attempt to create surrogate family opportunities represents a purposeful and systematic attempt to promote success in resolving the issues and providing sustenance to those whose true families cannot.

The issues present families, group members, and leaders with a difficult set of dilemmas. Individual concerns about safety, affection, status, and meaning are one side of each dilemma. And the subordination of such needs to the best interests of the group as whole is the other side. As described throughout the first three chapters, these dilemmas are:

1. Certainty vs. ambivalence
2. Control vs. freedom
3. Intimacy vs. privacy
4. Individuality vs. conformity
5. Transition vs. continuation.

The poles of the dilemmas each have attractions and rewards. Unfortunately, each pole has its dangers, too. Certainty can produce rigid ideology, but it also offers stable principles and values. On the other hand, ambivalence can produce indecision and paralysis, but it acknowledges the pluses and minuses of real life choices in a complex and rapidly changing world. Control can produce tyranny, but it also provides safety. In contrast, freedom may produce disorganization, chaos, and anarchy, but it also offers opportunity for individual growth, change, and initiative.

Further, intimacy may produce engulfment, but it rewards with love and emotional exchange. And though privacy can produce isolation, it also permits separateness. Similarly, individuality can foster eccentricity, insanity, and criminality, but it promotes self-understanding, creativity, and uniqueness. Conversely, conformity may produce loss of individual identity, but it encourages cooperation and acceptance. And finally, transition can deter resolution of problems and issues, and produce premature abandonment of tasks and undertakings, but it also avoids obsessive overinvolvement and unwarranted commitment. In contrast, continuation can deny endings, impede change, halt progress, and foster stagnation, but it can also produce tenacity, dedication, and completion.

Fortunately, this complex array of dilemmas can be simplified to a very basic set of themes which people use to engage each other when they join together. Upon examination, one can recognize that some dilemmas pit individual self-determination and independence against determination by, and dependence upon, the group. Control vs. freedom, conformity vs. individuality, and intimacy vs. privacy represent this theme.

Further, several dilemmas pit the value of stability against the need and prospect for change in an unstable and inconsistent world. Certainty vs. ambivalence and transition vs. discontinuance represent this later theme. Relief of tension generated around these themes of autonomy vs. dependency, and stability vs. change is achieved through successful resolution of the psychosocial issues as described in Chapter 3.

The chapters in Part II describe how an aggregate of separate individuals, members of the peer group, persons in authority, and people who act as conservators of time-honored tradition form important constituencies for people who participate in groups, organizations, and communities. In these social contexts, the constituencies become prominent for each individual when the themes just described become sources of conflict about participation.

Conflict occurs because the need for dependence and stability is continually at odds with the desire for autonomy and change. Such diametrically opposed longings are mutually exclusive, and therefore, the conflict is unresolvable. The individual can achieve, at best, a reasonable balance of tension between them.

Because this conflict is unresolvable, authority, tradition, the peer group, and individual experience become attractive resources for coping with the tensions it produces. Persons in authority and those acting as conservators of tradition support and protect the individual as he seeks to satisfy the need to be dependent and to see his world as stable and predictable. On the other hand, one's own experience and members of one's peer group contribute to individual autonomy and change, and thus offer support and protection to the individual pursuing independence and growth.

Each constituency offers many forms of support and protection. Among them is material interventions in opposition to threat from other constituencies or the physical environment. Also, each constituency offers acceptance, affirmation, and acknowledgment of the legitimacy of individual attitudes and behavior. These psychological reassurances are of great value.

Unfortunately, a price is extracted for such support and protection. In return, the individual must accept and actively affirm the status and power of each constituency within its active social context. Not unlike the "protection racket" made famous in gangster movies, social constituencies can be coercive, seductive, and corrupt about enlisting individuals as clients and demanding payment from them.

As will be presented in Chapter 4, this occurs because the four constituencies compete for control of the social contexts in which an individual participates. Consequently, each constituency strives to make dominant its own versions of truth and reality, and its definition of acceptable individual behavior. Individual affirmation of this truth, reality, and code of behavior among the aggregate of individuals is the key to such dominance.

Chapter 4 also emphasizes the importance of maintaining an equilibrium of influence between constituencies. Because each holds power to tyrannize the individual through coercion, seduction, or corruption, each constituency must be counterbalanced by opposing constituencies. When a satisfactory balance is achieved, the four constituencies are compelled to pursue the individual's consent and voluntary affirmation.

Educative forms of influence and persuasion then become the only viable means a social constituency may use to sustain itself. In so doing, the constituencies seek to attract individuals with claims and counterclaims about themselves and their world.

To cope with the temptation, opportunity, and danger inherent to such an environment, each individual must confront and evaluate the myriad of competing claims. One must exercise caution because many of the claims have serious meaning about behavior and the quality of one's life.

Thus, the individual must respond in ways that promote his or her own interests and values, preserve access to the four constituencies, and minimize tyranny by any one of them. This is so because, in family and non-family contexts, each constituency is important to the well-being of the individual despite the risks and hazards of engagement.

Since the dilemmas of autonomy vs. dependency and stability vs. change are activated in all social contexts, these risks and hazards are always present, also. In the struggle to resolve the conflict, and manage the risks and hazards, individual internal conflict is outwardly displayed as interpersonal tension. The form and direction of this tension represent the dominant needs of the individual and the social agenda of the constituencies from which he seeks support.

Those seeking stability and dependency will struggle against those seeking autonomy and change. Each will appeal to other individuals, seek to mobilize the peer group, attempt to influence those in authority, and invoke precedent and tradition in ways that promote one's own needs and interests. In exchange for support and protection, the individual must to some degree align himself or merge with the constituencies from which he or she obtains support.

The psychosocial issues described in Chapter 3 are the immediate and practical manifestations of the interpersonal struggle. Thus, relief of tension generated around the intrapersonal issues of autonomy vs. dependency and stability vs. change is achieved through successful resolution of immediate and practical interpersonal concerns.

Most important, each pole is mutually exclusive of and in diametric opposition to its counter pole. Therein lies the recapitulation of the original intrapersonal dilemmas because, to some degree, movement toward one pole invariably requires movement away from the other. However, satisfactory resolution of the immediate and practical issues is essential to social cooperation, keeping the social constituencies at bay, and maintaining individual access to them as needed.

Thus, the heat of conflict between social forces serves to forge education and growth, and to temper one's intellectual and emotional metal. The social force exerted by any constituency is, at once, sustaining and dangerous to the individual. Each is sustaining because it offers security and assistance as the individual pursues stability and dependency or autonomy and growth. But each is also dangerous, because of its potential to extract burdensome costs.

Because the family is the training ground upon which preparation for this difficult balancing act begins, surrogate family experience serves as catalyst and mediator for individual success in nonfamilial social contexts. Therefore, surrogate family relationship maintains the balance of tensions between constituencies, and in so doing, promotes healthy family-like experience for the individual.

The material that follows presents a theoretical perspective on how the surrogate family mediates tensions between the various social constituencies, and then focuses on each constituency and its potential as an agent of education, growth, and healing. Attention to the unique position of each in the individual's life illuminates the powers of persuasion and influence that also are unique to each.

Further, careful consideration is given to dangers inherent to each constituency and to how these potential problems may be avoided or moderated. The nature and direction of each constituency's influence is identified, along with the benefits and risks with which it confronts the individual. In addition to its connection with family experience, the harnessing of the four constituencies to create family surrogate experience may be better understood.

Thus, constructive use of individual experience, the peer group, culture and tradition, and authoritative power is neither automatic nor devoid of risk. As will be clear, educators and other practitioners must be skillful, alert, and sensitive in order to realize the positive potential of each constituency. When such care is exercised, the building blocks of surrogate family experience may be created and put in place.

Chapter 4

A Theory of Education in Groups: Family Surrogate Experience as Catalyst and Mediator

In many ways, joining and meshing with a group has analogues in healthy family functioning. In the family, a child forms attachments with parents and siblings, and accumulates direct experience with the real world. Further, family members act to socialize the child into the family's culture (Fraiberg, 1959; Melson, 1980) so that he or she may participate in recurrent sets of organized activities (Malinowski, 1960) that meet family needs.

Because many family activities are ongoing and their organization acquires stability, they become family "institutions" and lend permanence to relevant values and meanings. As a child matures, participation in these activities in a manner appropriate to age and gender, as defined by family culture, is the price of family membership. Family culture includes religious and spiritual belief, political views, moral positions, artistic expression, traditions and customs, and a variety of existential resolutions to social and spiritual dilemmas of everyday life.

Parallel experiences occur in groups outside the family. One establishes relations with authority and peers, and also interprets one's own idiosyncratic experience as the group develops its own culture within that of the surrounding community (Yalom, 1975). Because parallels between family life and experience in nonfamilial groups are so direct, initial developmental issues reawaken in the latter. These issues pertain to struggles with separation that mark emergence from childhood and the family cocoon as discussed in Chapter 1.

The resolution of these struggles shapes the quality of relationships between maturing children and their parents and siblings. This resolution also is a major determinant of willingness and ability to form attachments in nonfamily groups. In this way, the good things derived from family life serve as pathways to good things to be derived through group participation outside the family. Unfortunately, repeated negative experiences in the family can produce incomplete or badly damaged pathways.

Because attachment and bonding, and acceptance of group culture are the essence of family surrogate experience, a family-like state of tension emerges as issues of dependency and autonomy, and stability and change are balanced again and again. This tension, though distressing at times, serves as a stimulus and vehicle for individual growth.

STABILITY AND DEPENDENCE VS. GROWTH AND AUTONOMY

As described in Chapter 1, basic trust is founded on stability and consistency, but human development occurs through growth and change. By their nature as a dichotomy, the needs inherent to constancy on the one hand and to change on the other create conflict. Thus, one's wish for security and predictability is juxtaposed to one's desire for novelty and adventure.

Because the dependability of those upon whom we are dependent is a source of comfort, the rewards of self-sufficiency and autonomy, as polar opposites to dependency, cause conflict. One's wish "to be taken care of" exists in a state of tension with one's desire for freedom and independence.

Some theorists (Levin, 1987) propose that undependable adults exacerbate children's usual and normal dependency conflict in dangerous ways. To be dependent produces heightened anxiety and conflict for children of unreliable parents, even at times when dependency is necessary and appropriate, and a source of comfort to other children. For some, this continues throughout life because of profound vulnerability to disappointment and assault while dependent at a tender age. Therefore, considerable potential exists for a difficult developmental struggle to be complicated by destructive family influences.

Difficulties of this type are not without serious negative consequence. Stress associated with extreme dependency conflict is thought to increase a child's risk of illness (Hafen, Frandsen, Karren, and Hooker, 1992), delinquency, and other behavior problems. This thinking is supported by observations that the risk of substance abuse, school failure, and delinquency among children is increased when parents' functioning is itself impaired by substance abuse, absenteeism, mental and emotional illness, and marital discord (Brown and Mills, 1987).

SOCIAL CONSTITUENCIES AND EDUCATIVE EXPERIENCE

In work unrelated to the preceding ideas, but instead intended to explain authoritarian-democratic and conservative-radical political attitudes, Eysenck (1954) proposed some understandings relevant to the developmental issues and risk factors just discussed. He theorized that the opposing needs described above (stability vs. change and dependency vs. autonomy) each form a continuum that is perpendicular to the other and intersects at the other's midpoint.

The following narrative applies Eysenck's formulation in proposals that redirect and extend his schema to explain a number of social forces through which educative experience is derived. Some earlier writings addressed the role of these forces in decisions about ethics (Weinstein and Lagudis, 1980) and in knowledge development (Weinstein, 1984).

These earlier works note that four quadrants are formed by the intersection of the needs continuums. They further observe that a social constituency may be attributed to each quadrant, and the four of them compose a paradigm for education. That is, the paradigm defines the limits and exhausts the possibilities of educative experience. In so doing, the paradigm describes these constituencies as the source of all educative experience, and as existing in a state of tension with one another.

Of particular relevance to the present discussion, the four constituencies come into being whenever people join together, whether in families, groups, or communities. These constituencies are (1) participants as unique and separate individuals; (2) participants as members of a peer group; (3) persons in a position of authority; and (4) members as conservators and interpreters of culture, tradition, and custom. Thus, wherever a group exists, its participants experience self and others as distinct individuals, as part of a network of relationships with peers, as part of a structure in which some individuals have special powers and abilities, and as part of an ongoing history of precedents and expectations.

However, the relationship between the constituencies, as aspects of educative experience, is by no means benign. The relationship is dynamic and competitive, and its contentiousness provides energy for educational activity. As with all energy sources, this one possesses potential for good and bad application. Educators and others in human service professions, therefore, face a challenge to harness its potential for education, growth, healing, and other constructive ends.

The narrative that follows describes the individual, the peer group, persons in authority, and custom and tradition in contexts of family, group, and community life. So that educators and other human service providers may use these constituencies for constructive purposes, the material addresses important aspects of their interaction, and potential for positive and negative impact on the individual. Surrogate family relationships emerge as an important tool for control of these powerful forces.

CONTROL OF THE INDIVIDUAL: THE ENERGY BEHIND EDUCATIVE PROCESS

The tension between constituencies becomes observable as they compete with each other to control the individual. They do so by offering various forms of support and protection, and threats of punishment. They also appeal to needs for stability or change, and dependency or autonomy, as described above. In so doing, each constituency presses the individual toward behavior serving its own needs and interests.

Thus, to maintain the legitimacy of its power, authority pushes toward dependence and stability. Through legitimate control of policy and resources, and claims to special knowledge, authority may drive the individual by eliciting fear of sanctions, and dire consequences of error.

Because there is strength in unity, the peer group urges group dependency and conformity of change. Though the peer group may evoke fear by threats of retaliation, a group's preeminent power rests within its potential to reject and ostracize the individual. Shame is a powerful emotional response as the contempt of the group assaults those threatened by personal abandonment.

Similarly, to enhance personal freedom of action, individual need presses for autonomy and individualized change. Inhibition and self-deprivation are the price of self-denial. Frustration and help-lessness threaten those who accept or impose stringent restraints on themself.

Additionally, custom and tradition push toward stability and autonomy to promote a particular set of time-honored values as a monolithic standard for self-assessment. The values, ethics, and morality encoded in written documents (e.g., the Bible, Koran, Communist Manifesto, U.S. Constitution), in oral history, and in culture become the parameters against which the individual is urged to judge himself. Guilt is a driving force for people struggling with a punitive super-ego and seeking to anchor self-assessment to a stable set of principles.

At times, the boundary between tradition and authority, and the peer group is blurred. Then, persons in authority or coalitions of peers aspire to roles as conservators and interpreters of tradition. In these cases, others use tradition to judge the individual. In the community, the issue of separation of church and state addresses the danger inherent in such a blurring of boundaries.

As an illustrative analogy, the four constituencies compete with each other in a manner that may be likened to the genetics of complex organisms. All such organisms contain more genetic potential than they actually display. Geneticists refer to the organism's total genetic potential, regardless of what is visible, as its "genotype." That which is visible is the organism's "phenotype." The phenotype is the product of an interplay of dominant and recessive genetic material. Thus, brown-eyed, dark-haired people may have genes for blue eyes and blond hair in addition to genes for their visible coloration.

Similarly, the various contexts of social existence contain more than meets the eye, as manifest desires, latent wishes, and hidden agenda push members toward greater autonomy or dependency, and stability or change. In group life, each constituency seeks to make its own interests and values dominant, and therefore the phenotype for the family, a group, or the community.

However, the analogy ends here because the mechanism of genetic influence is biochemical action. The script for genetic activity is set when sperm joins ovum. Once set in motion, this action invariably continues to its predetermined conclusion, barring intervention or accident.

In contrast, values, needs, desires, and other motivating factors that drive social existence are not always direct in their actions. Further, social processes are not invariably mechanical, nor are their outcomes consistently predetermined. Therefore, social constituencies must wage a perpetually active struggle for dominance. Dominance means wresting control to define not only the legitimacy and appropriateness of individual behavior, but also truth and reality.

In families, groups, and the larger community, social constituencies do more than struggle in opposition to each other. They also battle within as they fragment, and various segments coalesce in response to emergent issues. In the family for example, "sibling rivalry" is a phrase that aptly describes competition between brothers and sisters for parental affection and family resources. In a group, peers may join together as subgroups in opposition to other subgroups. And in the community, groups of peers may form in opposition to other groups.

Persons in a position of authority often experience similar struggles. Parents may disagree and struggle over child-rearing tactics and strategies. In a group, leaders may argue about goals, methods, or values. In the community, authorities may adhere to one or another competing "school of thought." Similarly, tradition may be interpreted from a position of orthodoxy or reform. Even direct experience may evoke opposing perceptions in one individual.

These tensions within constituencies are clearly visible in the struggle precipitated by the Supreme Court's 1973 abortion rights decision. Community members who polarized around labels of "right to life" and "pro-choice" have formed groups. The purpose of each coalition is to impose on the other its own definition of the status of a fetus as a human being.

The battle has escalated as persons in position of authority, and proponents representing a great diversity of tradition, have actively and heatedly joined the fray. Now, all constituencies are represented and a civil struggle grips the entire nation. Fortunately, the battle has not reached the point of escalating armed conflict, though at times this also seems imminent.

MECHANISMS OF INFLUENCE: THE TOOLS OF EDUCATION

For the present, the abortion struggle employs mechanisms of social influence to control legislation. Some mechanisms are common to education in the more general sense. Others include actions such as persuasion, seduction, corruption, and coercion. Relational tools become part of the mix as some people become "significant others" and some groups and communities acquire "reference" value for the individual.

Persuasion involves presentation of claims about the nature of relevant aspects of the world. Didactic instruction, logic, debate, and intellectual appeal are usually part of persuasive efforts.

The activities and processes of persuasion are the essence of educational ideals and definitions in our democratic society. They presume freedom of choice, rationality, and a commitment to justice on the part of the individual. They also empower by heightening awareness, expanding options and choices, strengthening freedom to act in accordance with one's intentions, and enhancing involvement in processes of growth and change (Barrett, 1983). "Enlightenment" is the purpose of persuasion relative to our educational ideals.

As suggested above, the workings of persuasive activity may be lubricated through interpersonal connection and relationship. Processes of identification and internalization provide windows of opportunity as self-concept, interpersonal relationship, and claims about issues become linked. In this way, attachment and bonding become levers of influence.

Enlightened behavior is thought to be the product of acquisitions in knowledge, understanding, perspicacity, insight, and reasoned choice. Enlightened behavior and attitudes represent highest achievements of the benevolent use of interpersonal relationship and argument as influence.

In contrast, seduction, corruption, and coercion deny freedom of choice and subvert rationality, though they are effective in managing behavior and shaping thought. Exploitation, betrayal, abuse, and neglect lurk within these Machiavellian forms of influence. Thus, people can be taught to behave and think in ways that benefit others to the detriment of self. "Manipulation" is an apt label for these mechanisms of influence because they are usually devoid of the benevolence that is associated with education and other forms of human service.

Seduction becomes part of social influence to the degree that claims, presented as truth, are slanted or distorted to serve the interests of the claimant. For example, the child whose bedtime is nine o'clock, responds to an exhausted mother's 8:45 p.m. statement: "It is nearly nine o'clock and time to get ready for bed!" by saying: "Its just a little past 8:30! Can't I finish watching my TV show?" In this way, each presents the glass as "half full" or "half empty."

Though no mistruth is stated, the credibility of each claimant is arguable as personal agendas are pursued in soft areas around hard facts. Such behavior is seductive because it is an attempt by one or more individuals to extract benefits from another by influencing that other to disregard his or her own interests, perceptions, and principles. Persons in authority, the peer group, custom and tradition, and one's own neediness are capable of seductive influence.

Corruption plays a part to the degree that the individual is exploited through temptation of extrinsic reward. Parents may offer material rewards to induce children to do chores or to achieve in school. Though candy, toys, and other treats may be effective enticements for good behavior, they are also lures for sexual molestation and other forms of victimization of children. Thus, corruption is behavior in which any constituency offers individuals tempting incentives to violate their own needs, wishes, or principles.

In the community, favored treatment is extracted with a variety of tempting rewards. We say that individuals who accede to these temptations are "prostituting" themselves, and we use labels such as "graft" and "bribery" to express outrage about corrupt behavior. That many people are vulnerable, and therefore corruptible, is clear in indictments against political figures secured in police "sting" operations, "insider" stock trading convictions, and sensitivity about "conflict of interest." However, the power and ambivalence associated with corruptibility is acknowledged in subsequent defense claims of illegal entrapment.

Coercion influences by threat of negative consequences for noncompliance. These consequences usually take form dictated by the position of a constituency in the life of the individual. Accordingly, the peer group can threaten with shame and ostracism. Authority may evoke fear through legitimate power to impose aggressive forms of punishment. Since custom and tradition act as standards by which the individual may evaluate himself, self-mediated punishment or guilt becomes a coercive force. Self-denial of personal wishes and needs, and rejection of one's own experience threaten one with frustration and self-deprivation. Hence, coercive potential may be realized as the peer group imposes conformity, authority requires obedience, tradition demands adherence, and the individual begs indulgence.

Unfortunately, the social constituencies struggle against each other continually, and fight with all the tools at their disposal, including those just discussed. However, within this struggle for dominance and the processes through which it is waged lives the educative potential of group experience. The individual constantly faces claim and counter-claim about the nature of the world. In addition, he is pushed and pulled by his own needs as well as those of claimants.

For instance, authority figures may say one thing and peers may say another about the same object or event. One's own experience with the object or event may lead to still other conclusions, and tradition may say nothing at all. In many instances, one may receive contradicting reports from authorities and/or peers about objects or events that one will never observe directly.

Subsequently, to some individuals and their friends, the moon appears to be made of green cheese, but most of us accept astronomers' reports that it is made of rock. This is so even though kindly Aunt Mathilda told us what Granny told her: "We are really seeing the face of the man who lives there."

SELF-INTEREST: INDIVIDUAL MOTIVATION TO SEEK EDUCATION

The example just cited with tongue in cheek is of minor concern to everyday life. However, claims are made about other issues which include many serious implications about how to live life, treat people, and organize the community. The battles over such issues occur in areas which range from the insular and abstract domain of academic debate to death struggles over food, shelter, resources, territory, and ideology in the real world.

Therefore, self-interest is a powerful incentive to engage in dialectic that is part of everyday social existence. Student demand in the 1960s for "relevance" in educational experience was a manifestation of needs to satisfy self-interest.

Self-interest demands informed and educated decisions about personally relevant claims and issues. To make informed and educated decisions, the individual must be exposed to the content of claims and issues. One must evaluate the logic and evidence of each case. Moreover, one must assess the credibility of sources whether they be the peer group, authority, one's own experience and intuition, or traditional writings.

Thus, a hormonally supercharged adolescent may be told by parents and religious sources that masturbation is sinful and leads to blindness. Because he notes that his vision is excellent, and sees himself as a kind and decent person, he must contemplate the divergence between these claims and his own experience. He may discuss the problem with close friends if neither he nor they are too embarrassed to do so. In any event, he inevitably must make a decision that has meaning and consequences for his own behavior. For him, the degree to which his sexual needs are gratified or frustrated hangs in the balance. The sorting out of one's own self-interest is basic to educative process.

FAMILY SURROGATE EXPERIENCE:
EDUCATIONAL CATALYST AND MEDIATOR

As has been stated repeatedly throughout this writing, trust is a fundamental ingredient for healthy family functioning and family surrogate experience. When one trusts others, anxiety and other discomforts are minimized at the prospect of being vulnerable to or depending upon them (Northouse and Northouse, 1992, p. 39). Consistency, stability, and benevolence are building blocks of trust basic to credibility (Giffin, 1967). Credibility is the catalyst for joining self-interest with educational opportunity.

To be credible, statements and behavior must display an internal consistency of logic and meaning, be faithful to experience and observation, have predictable constancy, and be devoid of dangerous narcissism. The individual assigns credibility to those attributed the basic honesty to say what they mean and mean what they say. That is, others must be seen to share their truths as they believe those truths themselves.

Further, these others must be seen as competent in order to offer meaningful statements. They must also temper inclinations to stretch truth immoderately, and avoid use of truth in hostile and insensitive ways (Fields, 1992).

Frequent and profound disappointment damages or destroys both trust and credibility. We are reluctant to engage in meaningful dialogue with those who have confronted us with deceit, hypocrisy, and misrepresentation. Such dishonesty portends betrayal, neglect, abuse, exploitation, or abandonment.

If there is trauma and disappointment, we will continue dialogue, but primarily as a vehicle for protest. If the trauma and disappointment continue, dialogue will become a vehicle for voicing despair. Eventually, we withdraw and discontinue dialogue. Thus, group experiences offer dialogue and interaction with all social and educative constituencies discussed above. But without constructive family-like connections, the individual is to a degree closed off from the educational opportunity afforded by each.

In the presence of indifference or danger, the individual will expect threat rather than opportunity for stimulation and growth. Gifts of insight and meaning are overlooked because self-protection becomes the important priority. Dialogue, messages, and ideas become Trojan Horses to be viewed at a distance and with suspicion. Skepticism, pessimism, and cynicism color an atmosphere in which exchanges are examined for tricks and traps rather than truths and utility. Under such circumstances, social isolation prevails over social integration, consciousness of the connection between behavior and outcome is jeopardized, a sense of freedom to be creative is lost, and self-doubt replaces self-awareness and confidence.

DISEQUILIBRIUM OF CONSTITUENCIES: A THREAT TO SAFETY AND GROWTH

The concerns discussed in the section immediately above are about obstacles to joining with others or permitting others to be significant to us. They address such questions as "Can authority be trusted?", "Do my friends really care about me?", "Do the values and traditions with which I have been raised tell the truth about the meaning of existence?" and "Can I rely on my own perceptions and feelings to accurately evaluate the events of my life?" Though a lack of attachment and failure to bond may produce negative replies to these questions, an unbalancing of social constituencies may produce similarly negative answers.

Because of the coercive potential of each constituency, a healthy balance of tension is required so that no one dominates. In the community, history is replete with disaster attributable to disequilibrium between these forces. The stultifying conformity and lynch mob mentality that lurk beneath extremes of collective thought are no less dangerous than the criminality, social fragmentation, and isolation that reside within excessive individualism. The rigidity and dogmatism that emerge from literal interpretation of tradition, and the infantilizing dependency proffered by autocracy are also very destructive.

DISEQUILIBRIUM AND EQUILIBRIUM IN COMMUNITIES AND GROUPS

The dangers of authoritarian dominance were clearly demonstrated by Hitler's fascism in Nazi Germany, and the disasters that befell Saddam Hussein's Iraq during and after the Persian Gulf War. On a less grand scale, notorious examples of frenzied peer group action include death and injury due to college fraternity hazing, and the "wilding" episode in New York City in which a gang assaulted and raped the Central Park jogger. Tradition taken to extreme shows itself through religious inquisition, the Jonestown, Guyana and Waco, Texas disasters, the Salem witch-hunts of 1692, Senator Joseph McCarthy's search for communists in the early 1950s, and the current hysteria about child molesters. And the bizarre criminality of Gary Gilmore, Jeffrey Dahmer, and David Berkowitz (Son of Sam), provide ample evidence that individualistic isolation from others in one's community is still another danger.

Despite some of the occasional aberrations as cited above, a successful balance of constituencies is a major identifying characteristic of governance of American communities. Government in the U.S. is noted for its system of checks and balances that provide platforms for each of the constituencies, protection against tyranny by any one of them, and a history of stability.

The community of peers finds representation in the Congress, and uses the jury system to resolve civil disputes and criminal cases. Authoritative views find expression through the executive branch with diversity reflected in the cabinet and subordinate departments. Individual experience is given voice at the polling place, and public hearings. The time-honored tradition of the Constitution is made palpable through the courts. Finally, recognition of diversity of tradition inherent to religious and cultural heterogeneity is apparent in separation of church and state, with governmental focus on secular rather than religious matters.

The inherent tension between constituencies is operative perpetually in the system of checks and balances which has been a battlefield since its inception. Many presidents seeking support for their own views have been blatantly selective in replacing retiring U.S. supreme court justices. Presidents also have a long history of campaigning on behalf of congressional candidates whose views are in concert with a presidential agenda. In return, members of congress have provided similar support for presidential candidates.

Fortunately, the "opposition" from Congress, the administration, the judiciary, and the electorate have provided active counterforces in keeping government from tipping in extreme ways. Clearly, even grand systems of long standing are vulnerable to disequilibrium and require active vigilance to maintain a healthy balance.

The trustworthiness of the government is confirmed by its ability to withstand the test of time and its unquestionable stability. It is a model for organizations and groups of all sizes and purposes throughout society, proving its effectiveness. The more formal organizations have executive officers, policy-making boards, constitutions, meetings, and elective processes. Less formal and usually smaller groups involve members in roles that are analogous to these elements.

Unfortunately, the same dangers exist for small groups as well as larger organizations. Autocratic tyranny, scapegoating by the peer group, chaos and disorganization, and Machiavellian and/or Darwinian values are among the many potential dangers attributable to an imbalance of tensions, regardless of group size.

Opportunities for family surrogate experience become jeopardized when a disequilibrium of influence develops and members lose touch with peers, authority, self, or culture. Hence, educators and other professionals who provide surrogate family opportunities must exercise great care in preserving members' access to these sources of educative energy. Simultaneously, the practitioner must work to maintain an equilibrium so these influences do not endanger participants.

REFERENCES

Barrett, E. (1983). *An Empirical Investigation of Martha E. Rogers' Principle of Helicy: The Relationship Between Human Field Motion and Power.* Unpublished dissertation for the PhD, New York: New York University.

Brown, B. and Mills, A. (1987). *Youth at Risk for Substance Abuse* (DHHS Publication No. ADM 87-1537). Rockville, Maryland: U.S. Alcohol, Drug Abuse, and Mental Health Administration.

Eysenck, H.J. (1954). *The Psychology of Politics.* London: Routledge and Kegan Paul Limited.

Fields, R. (1992). *Drugs and Alcohol in Perspective.* Bellvue, Washington: W. C. Brown Publishers.

Fraiberg, S.(1959). *The Magic Years: Understanding and Handling the Problems of Early Childhood.* New York: Charles Scribner's Sons, pp. 186-273.

Giffin, K. (1967). "The Contribution of Studies of Source Credibility to a Theory of Interpersonal Trust in the Communication Process." *Psychological Bulletin,* Vol. 68, pp. 104-120.

Hafen, B., Frandsen, K., Karren, K., and Hooker, K. (1992). *The Health Effects of Attitudes, Emotions, and Relationships.* Provo, Utah: EMS Associates.

Levin, J.D. (1987). *Treatment of Alcoholism and Other Addictions.* Northvale, New Jersey: Jason Aronson, Inc.

Malinowski, B. (1960). *A Scientific Theory of Culture.* New York: Oxford University Press.

Melson, G. F. (1980). *Family and Environment: An Ecosystem Perspective.* Minneapolis, Minnesota: Burgess Publishing Company, p. 22.

Northouse, P. G. and Northouse, L. L. (1992). *Health Communications: Strategies for Health Professionals,* 2nd ed. Norwalk, Connecticut: Appleton and Lange, pp. 37-44.

Weinstein, S. "Social Realities and Measurement in the Scientific Study of Sex." *Journal of Sex Research,* Vol. 20, No. 3, August, 1984, pp. 217-229.

Weinstein, S. and Lagudis, M. (1980). "Health Ethics." In G. B. Dintiman and J. S. Greenberg (eds.), *Health Through Discovery,* 1st ed. Reading, Massachusetts: Addison-Wesley Publishing Company, pp. 505-518.

Yalom, I. (1975). *The Theory and Practice of Group Psychotherapy, 2nd Edition.* New York: Basic Books.

Chapter 5

The Individual Among the Aggregate: Growth Through Vigilance, Exploration, Contemplation, and Testing

An aggregate is a collection or assemblage of individual people who share no social ties and are psychologically separate from each other. For example, individuals among an aggregate of people in a theater each may come to a movie alone, watch the show with only minimal awareness and concern about the presence of others, and leave alone when the movie ends.

Even when social ties are established, most people will display a degree of psychological separateness so they do not lose touch with their own subjectivity or individual identity. Thus, for those who come to the theater with and sit among friends and family, each, for a time, is alone in the dark. During that time, each focuses his attention on the screen, shuts out distraction, settles in to watch the movie, and feels the impact of his own individual experience.

Therefore, to the degree that individuals maintain such separateness, any grouping or social context is to some extent an aggregate. As a social constituency, the aggregate is a very human statement about the need to maintain a degree of separateness from others and to preserve individuality.

Thus, individual experience refers to one's own sensory contacts with people, objects, events, and processes in one's environment. It is the subjective experience of personal involvement and doing.

Though the encounters through which these contacts are achieved may be controlled or mediated, and their meaning influenced by others, the moment of contact and subsequent engagement is a bridge linking environment with individual physiology. In this way, individual experience is the rapt attention, the quickening pulse, the widening eyes, or the gasp that signals emotional and physiological arousal. Or, it may be the sigh, the heavy and drooping eyelids, and the slow breathing of a euphoric and settling calm. Hence, the physiology of individual experience finds outward expression in many forms including laughter, a yawn, a frown, and the physical signs of fear, anger, and sexual arousal.

While individual experience is a product of behavior that addresses the needs of the individual, this writing concentrates on learning that occurs, rather than needs that are satisfied. Of particular importance are changes and growth in outlook about self, the social contexts of one's life, and the physical environment.

For example, a child may satisfy his hunger by making a peanut butter and jelly sandwich while mother is busy with other chores. The experience may be merely a repetition of a long-standing routine with no particular significance beyond its heuristic and entertainment value. However, if it is a first try or involves some experimentation, the child will not only enhance his mastery of the art of peanut butter sandwich making, but will add to his sense of self-sufficiency, independence, and freedom. It is these later possibilities that are of concern in the narrative that follows.

EVOLUTION, THE DRIVE FOR EXPERIENCE, AND LEARNING

Our capacities and needs for subjective experience emanate from the beginnings of animal life on our planet. The simple creatures of early biological times relied upon immediate physical contact, the sensitivity of their protoplasm, and physiologic response for individual survival in a liquid environment. There were no social linkages, no communication, or tools to aid our early evolutionary ancestors as each struggled to avoid inevitable death in isolation from others of their kind. The self as embodied in the physical was the only instrument available as each moved about its world alone, extracting sustenance and reacting to danger.

This remains so for many creatures whose evolution has ceased or progressed in a direction different than ours. Ninety-nine percent of the animals alive today rely primarily on their sensitivity to the chemistry of their surroundings for survival (Wilson, 1992). The chemical traces left as scents and odors on the ground, wafted by wind, or borne by water arouse these creatures to feed, mate, fight, or flee.

However, the survival value of beforehand recognition of opportunity and danger pushed our own evolution in directions that planted the anatomical, physiological, and neurological seeds of our current nature. For example, we have evolved to rely primarily on sight and sound rather than odor or scent to make our way. This is important because vision and hearing are the evolutionary tools underlying intelligence (Wilson, 1992).

Clearly, intelligence became central to adaptation and survival for our species in our evolutionary history. For example, our earliest ape-like ancestors had cranial capacities less than one-third that of modern human beings. Not only did the size and complexity of our brain increase over the millennia, but the development of elaborate nerve centers for speech control set the stage for symbolic language and semantic memory (Wilson, 1992).

Eventually, our evolving neuroanatomy supported the intelligence to generalize sensory contacts and to anticipate the workings of our environment. As a result, we relied less and less on immediacy and reflexiveness for survival. Thus, the primeval mandates of eat or be eaten, and kill or be killed perpetuated instincts and capacities to comprehend and anticipate the potential dangers and resources of our territories.

Natural selection strengthened the genetic foundation of these emergent instincts and capacities. Increasingly, we used cunning rather than brute strength and speed to survive and seize opportunity in a predatory world. A canny ability to predict the actions of adversaries, predators, and prey, and a shrewd appreciation of naturally available materials, became powerful evolutionary assets. However, other anatomical traits permitted us to apply our intelligence actively to augment our relatively puny physical power.

Principal among these are our erect posture and bipedal locomotion. These enabled us to transport ourselves, and to carry objects in forelimbs that evolution transformed into arms and hands. The apposition of forefinger and an elongated thumb appear to be the finishing touches that enabled us to carry objects and to fashion and manipulate them as tools. Accordingly, we acquired anatomical means to focus and multiply the force of our efforts and to harness energy from sources other than our bodies.

Still, our inborn intelligence was insufficient to use these anatomical appendages in an intelligent manner. To make them real assets, we had to discover and understand the potential of objects and events in our environment. The process of discovery and comprehension was founded on traits that are suggestive of both ability and instinct. That is, the process of discovery was predicated on both the capacity to discover and comprehend, and on a readiness to take the necessary action to do so.

This evolving readiness carried us beyond the instinctive alertness, curiosity, and survival-oriented learning of other creatures. Beyond being merely alert, we are vigilant. We react to danger and opportunity while also actively looking for trouble when no danger is present, and seek gratification when not driven by need. Beyond being merely curious, we are inquisitive. We examine our environment for immediate opportunity and danger and often continue our examination long after we have concluded that neither danger nor opportunity are at hand. And finally, we do not merely learn, we contemplate our discoveries. We reflect upon and examine within our minds what we remember of the real world.

In these ways, we aggressively pursue discovery and comprehension before, during, and after events that are important to us. Eventually, vigilance, inquisitiveness, and contemplation superseded the ferocious and raw reactivity that characterizes the lives of other creatures and our own earlier, preintelligent existence.

Though trial and error certainly played an important part in the process of discovery, our ability to remember seemingly random events and to generalize from them was only the beginning in our mastery of our world. The doors to true mastery opened as we began to exploit our developing capacities for recreating the world in our own minds through symbols and images.

With these more sophisticated capacities of applying our intelligence came realizations that there was method to the madness and violence of primitive experience. Our sophistication grew as inductive reasoning permitted us to broaden our recognition of the workings of experienced events, and to then use symbols and images to deduce the future.

Unfortunately, the ferocity and aggressiveness that served our carnivorous primate ancestors so well during an earlier era remain within our genes. These traits, when linked as an emotional force to the power of our intelligence place us at great risk. The drive and the wherewithal to realize our ambitions and subject the world to our will may gratify in the short run. But those who witness the long-term environmental consequences of our actions cry out for control and restraint in the use of our power (Wilson, 1993).

As we are slowly finding, such restraint is possible because our technical and social development has reduced the survival value of aggressive and all-consuming acquisitiveness and dominance. We have reshaped our environment to the extent that few modern encounters levy ferocious demands on muscle and blood.

Despite our unprecedented security, internal pressure for vigilance remains a genetic imperative. Exploration continues to whet our curiosity, and our discoveries give pause for contemplation.

As a result, our current evolutionary stage presses us to seek a level of external stimulation below which we suffer the discomfort of boredom and the dangers of inattentiveness. Subsumed under such labels as environmental variety (Kagan, 1976), drives for altered states of consciousness (Weil, 1972; Fields, 1992), and optimal levels of emotional arousal (Duffy, 1962; Easterbrook, 1959), such very human experiences as boredom, tediousness, repetitiveness, or just plain being in a rut have long been recognized as painful and destructive absences of stimulation.

Because we act and move about to seek needed stimulation, the complexity of our world forces inevitable and repeated confrontation with the unknown. Such confrontation summons further individual exploration because tension associated with ambiguity evokes primitive physiological readiness for fight or flight as it did in the wild. In this way, genetic vestiges of our past are activated (Hafen, Frandsen, Karren, and Hooker, 1992), and the human organism physiologically prepares for survival. Thus, even when people feel safe and satisfied, they do not just curl up and go to sleep while awaiting the next crisis.

As the above observations indicate, the very core of individual experience contains traits bred into us because of their survival value. Needs for stimulation and inevitable confrontations with the unknown continue to engage these traits. Their modern manifestation is observable in the blend of risk-taking and caution people exhibit as they encounter threats to and opportunities for social and economic advantage.

Consequently, physiological survival is less often at stake, though vigilance, inquisitiveness, and contemplation continue to enhance the quality of life. They enable us to predict and control our environment, infuse wisdom into the exercise of power, and reduce tension about that which we cannot control.

THE FUNCTION OF INDIVIDUAL EXPERIENCE

Human beings are creatures for whom processes of natural selection perpetuated a readiness to explore and to comprehend their world. More important, these evolutionary characteristics continue to serve the individual in modern times even when they are not so necessary to physiological survival. As will be discussed, readiness to explore and to comprehend are tools that have universal applicability to social as well as physical environments.

The gathering of individual experience is a process through which these tools are honed and techniques for using them are perfected. Vigilance and inquisitiveness lead to recognition which, upon contemplation, grows into understanding. In turn, this understanding leads to analysis, creativity, and finally the exercise of sound judgment (Bloom, 1956).

Individual experience also stimulates growth and strengthens reciprocity between reasoning and behavior. When enough experience is gathered, intelligence broadens into perspicacity, insight, enlightenment, and wisdom. With constant use, vigilance, inquisitiveness, and contemplation become increasingly functional as basic implements for meeting individual needs.

This occurs, in part, because people's needs appear to occupy a hierarchy that extends from the basics of physiological security to the realization of individual personal potential (Maslow, 1962). Some argue that higher level self-actualization needs might be better understood to be one's achievement of personal freedom, happiness, and successful adaptation despite unmet lower order survival needs (Sumerlin and Norman, 1992; Sumerlin, Privette, and Bundrick, 1993).

This latter proposal appears to have important meaning about the role of individual experience in the surrogate family. In essence, the surrogate family offers an alternative environment where the individual may seek freedom, happiness, and successful adaptation despite the deficiencies of real family. Suitably, the surrogate family becomes a safe haven for individual experience and learning that are functional to the satisfaction of personal needs.

Individual experience strengthens five functions that satisfy these needs. The functions are hierarchically ordered around protection and self-maintenance at lower levels, and self-enhancement at higher levels. They serve individual experience as follows:

1. Developing expertise about the physical and social environment.
2. Applying expertise to protect self from environmental assault and social tyranny.
3. Using expertise to derive benefits from environmental opportunity and social participation.
4. Shaping and confirming identity and self-concept.
5. Resolving existential problems and issues.
6. Securing emotionally nourishing stimulation.

The first function refers to the acquisition of knowledge and skills used as intervention on one's own behalf into the events and processes of one's social and physical environment. The second deals with the exercise of judgment and selectivity in the use of skills and knowledge for self-protection. The third refers to similar exercise of selectivity and judgment for positive self-benefit. These three functions serve lower-order needs for social and physical security.

The fourth function refers to the acquisition of insight and understanding about one's own personality, character, and capabilities. The fifth directs attention to construction of a mental and emotional frame of reference which gives meaning to life and its impinging events. And finally, the sixth deals with one's use of remaining personal resources to pursue other values once lower-order functions have been served.

MECHANISMS OF INDIVIDUAL EXPERIENCE

As discussed above, the primary material of individual experience is provided by the sensory organs. Still, raw sensation remains diffuse and undifferentiated in the absence of a secondary overlay of organization. Though we are born with much of our sensory equipment in place, along with some aptitudes and inclinations that may influence their use (Gardiner, 1983), we are not born with such a secondary overlay.

No doubt, we see and hear cats, dogs, and automobiles almost from birth, but we cannot respond in self-serving ways to such stimuli and their place in our existence until later. Because such self-serving response is vital to survival, we are dependent on the family to support and protect us until stimulation, sensation, and physical development provide us with neurological anatomy, a reservoir of experiences, and an assortment of psychological tools. These anatomical developments, real-world experiences, and the tools for organizing them are necessary to creating a secondary overlay of organized response. In turn, the experience of dogs, cats, and automobiles evolves from unlabeled sensations of soft, warm, loud, and frenetic into systematic reactions to "doggie," "kitty," and "Daddy's car."

The genetics that permit raw, primary individual experience are perpetuated by the very blood ties that define family. In addition to creating the child and keeping it alive, the family takes an active role in promoting and shaping the child's capacity to respond adequately to experience. As described in Chapter 1, a healthy family does not provide stimulation and exposure in a random or haphazard way. The family shelters the child from dangerously aversive experience, and provides stimulation and exposure for the child in a highly selective fashion. In fact, the stimulation and exposure through which each family attempts to shape its childrens' social and psychological development are analogues to the food, shelter, clothing, and health care which families use to promote their childrens' physical development.

From a functional perspective, this selectivity not only protects the child, but shapes secondary organization so the emergent adult may meet his own needs, satisfy the requirements and demands of social existence, and enjoy living. However, beyond the notion of functionality, many families adhere to the belief of "an ideal, best adult" and a best set of exposures and stimulation to produce the ideal grown-up person (Kagan, 1976). Thus, social influences on the content and organization of individual experience begin to operate at very early stages of life.

SPECULATION ABOUT SECONDARY PROCESS AND INDIVIDUAL EXPERIENCE

Because we directly observe the machinations of the central nervous system through limited points of access, there has been considerable speculation about secondary organization of sensation. Studies of animal neuroanatomy, observations subsequent to accidental head injuries, and recent development of instruments sensitive enough to detect minute variations in the brain's electro-magnetic activity and temperature have provided some opportunities.

We have identified several locations in the brain where neurological control of some activities is centered. Further, we have some understanding of brain chemistry, and the impact of experience on neuroanatomy. We have been able to identify such neurochemical substances as endorphins, phenylethylamine, dopamine, norepinephrine, and oxytocin. All seem to be involved with mood, and a variety of feeling states such as fear, anger, joy, and sexual arousal (Gray, 1993; Toufexis, 1993).

Additionally, our knowledge of the physiology of the nervous system is, in some ways, fairly well developed with regard to workings at the cellular and synaptic levels. Yet, despite these gains, we have limited understanding of how the human brain operates at a behavioral level, particularly with regard to its chemistry (Avis, 1990; Cooper, Bloom, and Roth, 1986). Therefore, the events and processes that constitute secondary organization are topics of continuing controversy and debate. In most basic terms, the question has been about what happens inside people between the time of exposure to environmental stimuli and the time they display behavior apparently in response to those stimuli.

Earlier in human history, when we began to suspect that there was more to behavior than was observable, many people explained insane, criminal, virtuous, or saintly behavior in mystical terms. Such behaviors were thought to be produced by invasions of one's soul by devils, demons, evil spirits, or divine inspiration. The myth and folklore that served to explain the workings of the physical world were understandably put to use in explaining human behavior.

As a result, education and mental health care often resembled religious exorcism. Ritual, prayer, punishment, penitence, and sacrifice were common solutions to a range of educational and health problems. Interestingly, these methods, employed by a witch doctor, shaman, medicine man, or healer often produced desired results. Though some individuals, groups, and communities still accept such explanations and practices, mystical accounting of internal events and processes continue to be increasingly removed from the mainstream of behavioral understanding.

Later, as humans developed more mechanistic explanations of the world, the claims of Sigmund Freud were among the first to appear to offer useful psychological understandings (Fine, 1979). Although much of Freud's original theory is superseded, one fundamental proposition remains at the core of our beliefs about what happens between stimulus and response. This proposition is that internal events and processes that occur between stimulus and response are in large part a product of past experience (Combs, Avila, and Purkey, 1971).

Controversy continues, though, about the nature of these internal events and processes. According to behaviorists, adaptation to external stimuli produces reflex-like responses. Response is reinforced through reward and punishment that results from encounters with one's world. Thus, immediate behavior, and personality itself, are thought to be sets of reflexes and habits produced by positive and negative outcomes of previous experience. Behaviorists perceive the individual as a passive and unconscious participant in the process of acquiring these reflexes and habits (Allport, 1955).

In accordance with advances in information-processing technology, some modern thinkers extended ideas about secondary process in terms analogous to programming a computer (Maltz, 1960). Just as one programs a computer by imposing electronic instructions to which the computer must rigidly respond, human beings are programmed through reciprocal interaction with environmental stimuli. Yet, although computers are locked into their pattern of response until someone changes the program, human beings' patterns of response, and likewise their programs, change as environmental contingencies change. One emergent question, then, is whether the conditioning or programming process is psychological or physiological.

Obviously, the silicon chips and electrical circuits of a computer's internal workings differ from the neural pathways and brain chemistry that are mechanisms of inner events and processes in people. We are only beginning to understand the latter, but accelerating interest in and study of physiology and behavior has begun to reveal the intimate connection between body and mind. Thus, the cybernetic analogy between people and machines has progressed toward contemplation of people as machines.

Modern psychiatry appears to have productively integrated some of these lines of inquiry to treat mental illness. Many psychiatrists practice from the perspective that an individual's genetic predispositions and interactions with external environmental stimuli produce a secondary overlay of conditioned organic events that drive behavior (MacIver and Redlich, 1959). Efforts to treat illness and modify behavior include direct intervention into this physiological overlay through administration of drugs, electrical stimulation and shock, surgery, hypnosis, and conditioning regimens.

However, invasive methods prominent among these are relegated to the medical profession for treatment of seriously debilitating illness. Illicit drug use not withstanding, these methods present dangers to which normal, functional, reasonably healthy individuals would not voluntarily and knowingly subject themselves. Because of the risks, they rarely, if ever, fall into the domain of educators, social workers, clergy, and other human service providers to whom this writing is addressed.

SECONDARY PROCESS, CONSCIOUSNESS, AND INDIVIDUAL EXPERIENCE

Some powerful theory and interesting science argue convincingly in support of important aspects of behavioristic views (Skinner, 1953). However, neither classical conditioning, cybernetics, nor physiological explanation address consciousness as an important determinant of behavior.

Nevertheless, individuals, families, social groups, organizations, and communities organize activity as though consciousness exists and is important. At this time in human history, the mainstreams of family life, education, religion, business and industry, the arts, legal systems, and psychotherapy are predicated on the existence of an inner world of conscious experience. Not only do these enterprises presume consciousness, but their activities make explicit the view that consciousness includes meaning as well as sensation.

The above enterprises are in the business of creating, expanding, judging, and altering meaning and, as a result, consciousness. They do so through sensory contact, words, symbols, imagery, interpersonal relationship, and activity. Regardless of the validity of presumptions that guide them, these enterprises maintain the fabric and continuity of society.

Perhaps even more important, the presumption of consciousness serves as a guide to shape the quality of social existence. Important social values such as free will, choice, democracy, spirituality, and personal responsibility are considered central to positive social experience. They are also tacit acceptance of the view that the individual has an active role in creating the consciousness and meaning that are at the core of these values.

Prominent supporters of the secondary overlay as a psychology of consciousness and meaning in which the individual is an active participant are phenomenologists, gestaltists, and symbolic interactionists. Interestingly, this thinking emerges from such diverse disciplines as philosophy, psychology, and sociology. The phenomenologists address the issue of the validity of individual subjective experience as a definition of reality in view of the varying states of awareness to which we are subject (Allport, 1955, p. 5). The gestaltists attend to problems of attention and perception in the subjective experience of objects, events, and people in one's physical and social environment (Perls, 1973; Kepner, 1980). Symbolic interactionism confronts the question of how the individual attributes symbolic meaning and value to objects, events, people and self, and the manner in which interaction with others produces and changes these meanings and values (Blumer, 1969; Shaver, 1981, p. 248). The narrative that follows joins these separate theoretical explorations in a manner that exploits and expands upon their relevance to individual experience and the surrogate family.

According to this thinking, to live and function we develop a very personal state of awareness or consciousness that serves to guide our response to our world. To achieve the transition to a secondary level of experience, we must organize sensation in order to bring some kind of meaning to it.

Acquisition of tools that permit secondary mental process begins as the infant's awareness expands beyond a limited focus on the pleasure or pain of immediate experience. Growth permits control of the chaotic stream of primary consciousness and forces it to yield to the logic and language of secondary awareness. More mature experience gradually achieves broad and increasingly complex meaning beyond mere sensations of the moment. Thus, secondary organization is an overlay of consciousness that incorporates numerous skills, understandings, and an awareness of internal stimuli. When this overlay is in place, the individual may manipulate symbols and derive meaning.

Such psychological development, through which the tools of secondary awareness are acquired, begins in the context of the family. As discussed earlier, the family provides an environment in which development may safely occur, and teaches and models tools such as language, logic, expectancies, and attributions.

The family not only provides the tools, it shapes their form and the way they are applied. Language and observation of behavior of other family members provide a young child with indirect experience that begins to shape the world he has yet to touch. These indirect experiences become formative molds that cast and recast more direct experience with objects and events in the child's rapidly expanding environment.

Once they are acquired, the tools of secondary process are used to construct an orderly and usable awareness in one's own mind. In this way, the individual not only accumulates direct and indirect experience, but also shapes that experience to suit his needs.

These shaped and reshaped experiences are then integrated into a mosaic of broader images of self and others, and objects in one's world. Emotional-visceral response and rational-intellectual explanation are assigned to each image. Together, affect and thought blend objectivity and subjectivity in remembrance of past encounters and integration of new experience. In this way, qualitative elements of experience intrude upon pragmatic and utilitarian concerns about existence.

In consequence, the mosaic represents more than mere mental approximation of reality. It has further meaning beyond the symbolic and abstract, and is more than a definition of experience for the individual as a passive recipient of such experience.

More accurately, the mosaic is an active force in one's life as it shapes intentions behind behavior (Perls, 1973). It exerts powerful internal pressures to seek congruence between that which exists in one's mind and that which one displays to the outside world (Festinger, 1957). This includes not only overt instrumental behavior, but also one's ideals, choice of others with whom to establish relationships, and behaviors displayed to maintain these relationships. In the end, the imagery within our own mosaic defines our personality and is the basis upon which others judge our sanity.

THE UNCONSCIOUS AND INDIVIDUAL EXPERIENCE

A second major contribution of Freud defines the potential for the individual to tyrannize self. He was among the first to stress the importance of the unconscious in forming the mosaic and shaping its influence on behavior and quality of experience (Combs, Avila, and Purkey, 1971).

Thus, potential for tyranny exists because the mosaic is established at both conscious and unconscious levels of awareness. Even though many unconscious expectations and impulses are reasonably healthy and functional, individuals are deprived of choice if they behave in ways and are driven by that of which they are unaware (Flynn, 1980). Danger exists in unconscious pressure to act or react when action is not in one's best interest, to remain passive when action is necessary and appropriate, or to choose courses of action that are inappropriate to the demands of the moment.

Just as truth can be withheld, and one can be deceived by the conscious and unconscious manipulations of others, one can also be controlled or manipulated by self-imposed illusions (Miller, 1981).

Even the most conscientious and thorough individual explorations can produce distortion if experience collides too painfully with the needs of the explorer. Therefore, a duplicitous self may seduce, corrupt, or coerce from the hidden reaches of unconscious needs.

For example, the person whose childhood world was unresponsive to his efforts and behavior may see himself as incapable of control rather than acknowledge his rage toward his negligent parents. He may unconsciously assume a posture of passivity and helplessness rather than angrily risk the loss of what little love his parents can offer.

Similarly, the child whose world was vengeful and vindictive may, as an adult, unconsciously deny himself freedom to take risks, exercise creativity, and try new perspectives. By protecting himself this way he need not face his fears and suspicions of personal inadequacy. If he grows to see his adult world to be manageable, he may become active and seek to better his circumstance.

An individual whose self-view is stable, comfortable, and realistically positive is not likely to unconsciously pursue the narcissistic self-aggrandizement that temporarily soothes deep wounds to the ego. In the absence of profound need to avoid anxiety and depression about self, one is better able to develop deep and meaningful relationships with others. Additionally, a person who sees others as accepting, empathetic, and genuine is not likely to display the anger of alienation, nor the sadness and depression of isolation.

And finally, people who define their own feelings as healthy sources of information about the impact of relevant life events will display greater consistency between word and deed. They tend to present a truer picture of identity to self and others. An individual becomes a gauge of one's own personal experience and may exploit valuable intangibles such as intuition, insight, aesthetic experience, and artistic expression. In so doing, one enhances access to the unconscious and reduces its potential for tyranny.

If, on the other hand, an individual defines feelings as signs of personal deficiency, or as experiences to be feared, their relegation to the unconscious offers tenuous relief. Subjective experience becomes unstable and inconsistent, and one's own feelings are regarded with distrust and anxiety. One may present self to others in a manner that conveys defensiveness at best, and emotional lifelessness at worst.

INDIVIDUAL CONSCIOUSNESS AND SOCIAL MEANING

From a broader perspective, one's world view is important not only to self, but also to others. Socially, changes in one's subjective world can represent sacrifice of established and comfortable ways of living, and painful acquisitions of new behavior for others, and vice versa. This is especially so in the family, but also is true in other settings marked by high levels of social interdependence. Hence, the individual as the irreducible element and beginning of all social contexts, is the focus of the energies and efforts of many others seeking to influence or control him.

Despite the processes through which one's view of the world develops, and the forces that seek to shape and modify it, each individual achieves a perspective that reflects his own unique mix of genetics, direct experience, and indirect experience. From the perspective of the individual, the major concern is about whether or not that perspective is functional. In other words, does it work effectively to meet the personal needs and social demands of one's life?

Certainly, some aspects of personal perspective are unequivocal and basic to survival. Nevertheless, in most areas of living there are many ways to skin the proverbial cat. Therefore, the quality of one's experience and one's view of the world may be, at times, idiosyncratic to the extreme, yet still functional.

Such idiosyncrasy may represent needed creativity and adventurousness for progress to higher levels of function. But despite the potential value of such progress, the social risks of idiosyncrasy are often high. In the eye of others, the gap between an individual's eccentricity and the threat posed by his social deviance is narrow.

PROCESSES OF INDIVIDUAL EXPERIENCE: PERSONAL REALITY IN THE MAKING

Christopher Columbus's epic voyage beyond the horizon, which forever changed the shape of the earth, is not unlike a child's examination beyond the horizon of his own much smaller world. The child is ambitious to see, smell, taste, feel, and hear for himself all he has heard so much about from his parents and siblings. His purpose is not just to experience what he was told, but to confirm the ideas and grand fantasies evoked by such stories. Consequently, he sets out to exercise his own vigilance, inquisitiveness, and powers of reflection to verify, expand upon, and discover new meaning.

Under ideal circumstances, his return from a backyard adventure will be filled with tales of experiences among the rose bushes, under the apple tree, or in the vegetable garden. Under more difficult circumstances, he will return from the streets or a littered and dangerous vacant lot, and will talk of abandoned autos, broken home furnishings, and discarded bottles and cans.

In either case, he will tell of things he thought to be true that in fact were. He will tell of objects or events he truly believed were real only to discover they were not. He also will share information about which he no longer holds doubts, and he will tell of strange new things that attracted his attention and aroused his curiosity. And most important, he may tell of ideas and perceptions that are uniquely his own.

If these children are adequately prepared for the hazards of their adventure, they will return without cuts and scrapes or other injury. Such preparation would also serve to restrain them from doing damage to the interests of others, whether those interests be the flowers in mother's garden or the cardboard shelter of a homeless person. Thus, values such as personal safety and social responsibility restrain the process of discovery and the gathering of individual experience.

No doubt, the pictures imprinted on the mind of a child under ideal circumstances will differ from those produced in the slums because these experiences take place in settings that are so alien to one another. In addition, they will differ as a function of the strength of concerns about personal safety and social responsibility. However, in either setting, and regardless of restraint, the beholder will recognize the congruence and discrepancy between what he was told and what he observed. He will notice as well, things that no one ever mentioned to him.

On future trips, some repetitions of old observations may provide confirmation of initial impressions and others may not. Each child's mosaic of mental images will be altered and broadened as old meanings are adjusted, expanded, or discarded, and new meanings are acquired.

INDIVIDUAL EXPERIENCE, AND THE ART
AND SCIENCE OF LIVING

These simple scenarios represent more than aimless wanderings of a child seeking serendipitous stimulation. They are a prototype of individual human inquiry at all levels of sophistication. Such inquiry begins when one's attention is attracted to an object or event, and one's curiosity is aroused. The arousal may be a product of reports by others, or of direct observation by the individual.

Individual attention and curiosity may be aroused for a variety of reasons. The object or event may be novel and, therefore, stimulating. In some cases, inquiry becomes a form of play, and the object a toy. Or, an event may hold special meaning because it offers opportunity to calm unrest about experience and issues of the past. Further, curiosity may be the handmaiden to pragmatism as one examines the world for utilitarian solutions to practical problems of the present.

Some objects arouse curiosity simply because their novelty creates uncertainty and, therefore, poses a threat to security. One seeks to discover whether or not the object is dangerous, has some positive value, or is merely a benign presence. Subsequent action will inevitably either remove the object, exploit it, ignore it, avoid it, or accept it as a passive presence in one's way of doing things.

This process of acquiring personal experience is much like that of generating knowledge in the more formal scientific sense. Attention and curiosity are aroused as described above, and exploration then begins. Usually, exploration starts by examination of a first case–an example that constitutes the initial encounter. The effort is to gather enough information to permit plausible speculation about what the object or event is, the category or class it may fit within, outcomes of its actions, the dangers and benefits it may portend, and the purposes it may serve.

If initial exploration stimulates further curiosity, then other cases may be collected and surveyed. In the process of examination, simultaneous occurrences may be noticed (e.g., blond hair and blue eyes, wet wood and smoky campfires, cool breezes and goose bumps, stagnant ponds and mosquito bites, frogs and fewer mosquito bites, more butter and better tasting cookies). From there, in an effort to comprehend the object's inner workings, contemplation begins about the nature of the relationship between those events. Of primary interest is the possibility of a causal connection between them, but other possibilities demand consideration. Are such simultaneous occurrences purely accidental or random coincidences? Is something else going on beneath the observable surface that causes the otherwise unrelated events to occur together?

As observation and contemplation produce speculation, one seeks to test the truth of one's ideas. One may open an external covering to see inside. One risk of such an approach is destroying the entire object, as in the case of "the goose that laid the golden egg." Another is the danger of unleashing troublesome forces from within, as in "Pandora's Box." Even in cases where an object remains intact, and no dangers may be turned loose, there is the possibility that an object's contents may be incomprehensible, as in the proverbial "can of worms."

In cases where such risks violate concerns about personal safety and social responsibility, the object may be untouched and watched throughout the course of its natural existence. Or it may be manipulated from the outside. If the object of interest is some inner working of a person, that person may be questioned about his experience of it. These strategies permit the examiner to seek answers to his questions, observe outcomes of natural processes, or record results of purposeful manipulation.

Thus, the process of discovery through which one's history of individual experience is acquired begins with vigilance and inquisitiveness at all levels of sophistication. An object is encountered and is scrutinized. It is seen to have buttons, levers, and whistles, but its actions and purpose are undetermined. The curiosity that killed the cat is alive and well in the exploratory question: "What happens if I push this button?"

PERSONAL, SOCIAL, AND ENVIRONMENTAL RISKS OF INDIVIDUAL EXPERIENCE

The world of fiction is rife with sensational outcomes of premature testing and careless experimentation gone awry. Engaging the unknown prior to determining potential consequences, or in ways that jeopardize self or others, is equivalent to a dive into a pool of unknown depth. The Frankenstein Monster, the Incredible Hulk, and The Fly are but a few of the more popular fictional characters spawned in these scenarios.

Clearly, the idea of risking self, others, or one's world to "try something to see if one likes it, if it works, what it does, or simply if one can do it" has implications that range from harmless and frivolous to potentially dangerous and tragic. From a physical perspective, many reckless encounters produce only skinned knees, a bump on the head, or singed eyebrows. However, others produce illness, disfigurement, crippling injury, and death. From a social perspective, recklessness may only produce momentary embarrassment or it may lead to ostracism and serious recrimination.

On the other hand, adequate preparation yields a more advanced level of examination with questions such as: "Will this or that happen when I push this button?" The idea of making reasoned predictions based on carefully gathered experience and understanding, and then testing to see if they come true, represents the best of our capabilities as gatherers of experience. The inevitable risks of inquiry are addressed most adequately in carefully choreographed interactions between sound inductive reasoning and cautiously tested deductive extensions of that reasoning.

Even more so, personal safety and social responsibility are important concerns at the most sophisticated levels of inquiry. Institutional review boards in universities and other centers of scientific exploration try to "childproof" investigatory activity. These panels scrutinize research plans for impact on human subjects, animals, and the environment. For example, to discover a better mouse trap has long been recognized as an admirable goal, but to test or play with it capriciously portends painful possibilities for self and others.

INDIVIDUAL EXPERIENCE IN THE SURROGATE FAMILY

Similarly, responsible parents "childproof" the home against risks of exploration by naive and immature children. However, such parents provide more than protection when they support and guide childrens' healthy and appropriate exploration. These parents not only encourage and help children to safely gather experience, but also supervise training so that future independent explorations may be carried out responsibly and safely. This support, protection, and supervised training are at the heart of individual experience in the surrogate family.

For individuals emerging from healthy families, the surrogate family provides additional opportunity for growth-promoting personal experience. For such individuals, a surrogate family may be viewed as a family-like extension of real family rather than as an alternative to it. Unfortunately, the disrupted or impaired family is a potent source of significant and enduring damage to the exploration of one's world, organization of individual experience, and discovery of personal meaning. This happens because of disturbance or impairment of support, protection, and supervision.

Many problems are created by parents who are negligent about providing adequate support for their adventurous children. In some cases, these children are deprived of needed experiences because they cannot pursue them without parental assistance. In others, these children take risks they are ill prepared to handle without adult protection. Such children are forced to make their own way by inappropriately assuming adult levels of responsibility for their own care in day-to-day life.

Though inadequately supervised, these children may be abused in response to forbidden exploratory behavior. Further, negligent parents frequently abandon them to the painful consequences of risky initiatives gone awry. Because these children are inadequately supported, protected, and prepared, they are deprived of important individual experiences of childhood. In the absence of these experiences, they emerge into adolescence and young adulthood with incomplete and distorted awareness of self, social existence, and the environment.

At the other extreme, some families are overly protective to the point of actively depriving their children of needed experience. Such overprotectiveness may be symptomatic of parental anxiety about issues unrelated to experiences their children are seeking. As described in Chapter 1, these parents may view their childrens' longings for developmentally appropriate new experience as threats to parental control and the integrity of the family. Other parents may be narcissistic to the point that their own demands leave little room for their children's needs (Weinstein, 1991). In either case, developmentally appropriate experience is missed, and children are deprived of the sense of control, self-esteem, and new perspectives that come with experience and mastery.

Therefore in the problematic family, members' innate capacities and instincts for vigilance, curiosity, and thoughtfulness are subverted and distorted. The hypervigilance spawned by abuse, disappointment, and, ultimately, distrust leave little time and energy for curious explorations and patient contemplation.

As a result, the process of exploration is misdirected and loses its efficacy. This occurs in some cases because curiosity is dulled. Exploratory behavior lacks focus and has an aura of listlessness. Some such exploration may be chaotic as it is disorganized by distractibility, inattentiveness, and impulsivity.

In other cases, curiosity may be so highly mobilized in service of self-protection that exploration is limited by defensiveness, and distorted by overreaction. Still other explorations may convey obsessive-compulsive qualities as their exaggerated intensity betrays the desire to escape from self.

Thus, the questions of whether or not Johnny should climb the apple tree, hang up-side-down from the monkey bars, or take boxing lessons have many meanings beyond the acts they portend. The same is true for the newly licensed adolescent seeking his first solo drive in the family car, or to drink a bottle of beer while attending a party with others his own age. Similarly, the young adult contemplating a first sexual encounter with a new partner faces complex issues, too.

The fact that the apple tree is in a neighbor's yard and has climbable limbs extending thirty feet above the ground presents several very different risks. The reality that the earth beneath the jungle gym in the schoolyard has been packed hard as concrete is also potentially problematic. The fact that the boxing class at the local recreation center attracts rough boys from the other side of the tracks presents a different set of problems. The scenarios presented above for the adolescent and the young adult suggest physical and social risks that parallel those presented for younger children.

The negligently unsupervised child will or will not engage in these activities in accordance with the resources they require, their attractiveness, and his own immature judgment about his abilities to safely participate. He will not be prepared or assisted, and, except for the limits of his resources, no restrictions will be imposed on the extent of his engagement. Though his own anxiety may serve as a guide, there are no controls on the recklessness of his behavior as he seeks to satisfy his curiosity and test himself and his world.

He may then become the abused child who is assaulted from time to time. This happens when his forays into forbidden realms of new experience occasionally catch the eye of an otherwise inattentive parent. At other times, he is the abandoned child when exploration turns sour, and he is left unassisted to lick his own wounds and heal himself.

The inconsistency of his parents exaggerated reactions leave him unsure of what he has done wrong. But he discovers with certainty that individual initiative and spontaneity are very dangerous. As a result, fearfulness about the potential consequences of misadventure may become a formidable deterrent to appropriate exploration.

Some children, fueled by disappointment and anger toward their parents, respond explosively to the opposite extreme. In these cases, children may recklessly and suicidally cast caution aside. They may do so in reactions against their own fear, or in unconscious attempts to fulfill a parent's implicit wishes to be rid of his or her children (Farberow, 1980).

As implied above, the gathering of individual experience may be described as occurring along a continuum. The polar opposite extremes of the continuum define the level of restraint with which individual experience and exploration are pursued. At one extreme, one is confined to very narrow experience and is imprisoned within a limited perspective. At the other, there is nihilism, grandiosity, and impulsiveness as experience is sought in ill-considered and dangerous ways. Eleanor Rigby of the Beatles and Evil Knevil, the motorcycle daredevil, are symbols of these two extremes.

Thus, individual experience in the surrogate family addresses needs to expand or alter aspects of consciousness created in the family. The overly naive, sheltered, or protected may be supported and assisted to broaden awareness and outlook through acceptance of reasonable risks. On the other hand, the overly cavalier may be assisted in controlling dangerous nihilism and understanding the potential impacts of actions on self, others, and the environment.

For individuals emerging from unhealthy families, the surrogate family is an opportunity to recreate personal history in a healthy, alternative social context. The surrogate family accomplishes this by providing support and protection for individual exploration that parallels the provisions in the healthy family. That is, the surrogate family supports healthy individual experience, protects the individual from unreasonably risky exploration, and provides assistance at times when adventure turns sour.

As described in Chapter 4, and in the introduction to Part II, healthy individual development occurs in an environment that is reasonably responsive to needs for dependency, autonomy, stability, and change. When one or more of these needs are repeatedly and dangerously neglected, vigilance, curiosity, and contemplativity are put to different uses then when they are met. In the former case, these traits are organized for purposes of defense and self-protection. In the latter, they are organized to respond to opportunity.

Accordingly, surrogate family experience is one that provides an environment in which the individual's inherent vigilance is acknowledged and supported, natural curiosity is aroused and encouraged, and patient contemplation is assisted and valued. Not only are these traits to be supported and encouraged, but the surrogate family environment must provide freedom to use them to pursue opportunity rather than to defend self.

Thus, in the context of the surrogate family, focus, organization, realistic personal investment, openness, idealism, self-awareness, self-enhancement, and discipline are qualities to be promoted in the gathering of individual experience. Surrogate parents provide support, protection, and supervision. The surrogate siblings of the peer group provide assistance, feedback, and dialogue. And, the culture and traditions of the surrogate family provide a stable set of values and norms to guide individual exploratory activity.

REFERENCES

Allport, G. (1955). *Becoming: Basic Considerations for a Psychology of Personality*. New Haven, Connecticut: Yale University Press.

Avis, H. (1990). *Drugs and Life*. Dubuque, Iowa: W. C. Brown.

Bloom, B. (ed.). (1956). *Taxonomy of Educational Objectives: The Cognitive Domain*. New York: David McKay Company, Inc.

Blumer, H. (1969). *Symbolic Interactionism: Perspective and Method.* Berkeley, California: University of California Press.

Combs, A., Avila, D., and Purkey, W. (1971). *Helping Relationships: Basic Concepts for the Helping Professions.* Boston: Allyn and Bacon, Inc.

Cooper, J., Bloom, F., and Roth, R. (1986). *The Biochemical Basis of Neuropharmacology.* Oxford: Oxford University Press.

Duffy, E. (1962). *Activation and Behavior.* New York: John Wiley and Sons.

Easterbrook, J. A. (1959). "The Effect of Emotion on Cue Utilization and the Organization of Behavior." *Psychological Review,* Vol. 66, No. 3, p. 183.

Farberow, N. (ed.). (1980). *The Many Faces of Suicide.* New York: McGraw-Hill Book Company.

Festinger, L. (1957). *A Theory of Cognitive Dissonance.* Stanford, California: Stanford University Press.

Fields, R. (1992). *Drugs and Alcohol in Perspective.* Bellvue, Washington: W. C. Brown Publishers.

Fine, R. (1979). *A History of Psychoanalysis.* New York: Columbia University Press.

Flynn, J. D. (1980). "Educating for Autonomy: A Gestalt Approach to Higher Education." In Feder, B. and Ronall, R. (eds.), *Beyond the Hot Seat: Gestalt Approaches to Group.* New York: Brunner/Mazel Publishers, pp. 133-154.

Gardiner, H. (1983). *Frames of Mind: The Theory of Multiple Intelligences.* New York: Basic Books.

Gray, P. "What is Love?" *Time,* Vol. 141, No. 7, February 15, 1993, pp. 47-49.

Hafen, B., Frandsen, K., Karren, K., and Hooker, K. (1992). *The Health Effects of Attitudes, Emotions, and Relationships.* Provo, Utah: EMS Associates.

Kagan, J. (1976). "The Psychological Requirements for Human Development." In Nathan Talbot (ed.), *Raising Children in Modern America: Problems and Prospective Solutions.* Little, Brown and Company, Inc., pp. 86-97.

Kepner, E. (1980). "Gestalt Group Process." In Feder, B. and Ronall, R. (eds.), *Beyond the Hot Seat: Gestalt Approaches to Group.* New York: Brunner/Mazel Publishers, pp. 5-24.

MacIver, J. and Redlich, F. C. (1959). "Patterns of Psychiatric Practice." *American Journal of Psychiatry,* Vol. 115, pp. 692-697.

Maltz, M. (1960). *Psycho-Cybernetics.* New York: Simon and Schuster.

Maslow, A. (1962). *Toward a Psychology of Being.* New York: Van Nostrand.

Miller, A. (1981). *The Drama of the Gifted Child.* New York: Basic Books.

Perls, F. (1973). *The Gestalt Approach and Eye Witness to Therapy.* Ben Lomond, California: Science and Behavior Books, pp. 2-4.

Shaver, K. (1981). *Principles of Social Psychology.* Cambridge, Massachusetts: Winthrop Press.

Skinner, B. F. (1953). *Science and Human Behavior.* New York: The Macmillan Company.

Sumerlin, J. R. and Norman, R. L. "Self-Actualization and Homeless Men: A Known-Groups Examination of Maslow's Hierarchy of Needs." *Journal of Social Behavior and Personality,* Vol. 7, No. 3, September 1992, pp. 469-481.

Sumerlin, J. R., Privette, G., and Bundrick, C. M. "Black and White Homeless Men: Differences in Self-Actualization, Willingness to Use Services, History of Being Homeless, and Subjective Health Ratings." *Psychological Reports,* Vol. 72, June 1993, pp. 1039-1049.

Toufexis, A. "The Right Chemistry." *Time,* Vol. 141, No. 7, February 15, 1993, pp. 49-51.

Weil, A. (1972). *The Natural Mind, a New Way of Looking at Drugs and the Higher Consciousness.* Boston: Houghton Mifflin.

Weinstein, S. "Prevention of Emotional Distress, and Drug and Alcohol Abuse Among Musicians and Other Arts Performers and Students." *Canadian Band Journal,* Vol. 15, No. 4, Summer 1991, pp. 39-40.

Wilson, E. O. (1992). *The Diversity of Life.* New York: W. W. Norton.

Wilson, E. O. (1993). "Is Humanity Suicidal?" *The New York Times Magazine,* May 30, pp. 24-26, 27, 29.

Chapter 6

The Peer Group: Education by Consensual Validation

The term "peer" as noun and adjective means equal standing between individuals, or membership in a group based on an identifiable category of standing (Webster, 1973). Peers include those who face situations in common, such as a similar physical or social environment, or whose experiences and needs are alike (Clark, 1972). Also, individuals may be peers because they hold generically similar attitudes about significant persons, events, and activities (Secord and Backman, 1964; Sullivan, 1955). In short, peers are seen to be of a kind in one or more areas of description by self and others. Because of such similarity, they may be classified or grouped together.

"Consensual validation" describes peers' capacity to affirm each other's ideas about objects, events, and self (Bennis and Shephard, 1956; Alexander, 1964). As peers interact in a group, their opinions and perspectives tend to become increasingly similar and affirming to each individual member (Asche, 1952; Newcomb, 1956; Thibaut and Kelly, 1961; Cartwright and Zander, 1962; Sampson and Marthas, 1990). Through ever-expanding agreement, peers seek to achieve consensus which validates individual conceptions of truth, reality, and behavior.

This affirmation is important beyond the resolution of conflict between individuals and the achievement of consistency in social relations. It addresses the very important need to differentiate between reality and fantasy (Sullivan, 1955). Autistic thinking is an example of a failure to meet this need, and results in both physical and social penalties. Thus, to have one's behavior, perspective, and values judged by a "jury of one's peers," and to have them validated by consensus, serves many functions (Clark, 1972).

Despite powerful needs for validation, peers may not necessarily join with one another. In many instances, peers come together as unrelated aggregates in which interaction and intimacy are limited, interpersonal relationships are devoid of friendship, and individuals do not identify with each other. The coincidental presence of peers at a given location may create an illusion of togetherness even though no links exist.

Without interaction, intimacy, friendship, and identification, trust becomes a prominent and unresolvable issue. Social ties founded on trust are necessary to the achievement of consensus about and validation of individual and group answers to personal, social, or environmental issues. In the absence of trust, the creation of peer relationships from which significant personal meaning may be derived is frustrated.

Unfortunately, many individuals struggle internally with the problem of trust. They are reluctant to relinquish individual autonomy in defining themselves or their world. Because of their ambivalence and internal conflict about issues of authority, intimacy, and loss of individuality, interdependent participation in the peer group exacts an unacceptable emotional price (Bennis and Shephard, 1956).

At the opposite extreme, some cope with this same conflict by seeking anonymity and engulfment in the ethos of the peer group. These individuals appear to display no mind of their own as they attempt to create and pursue an illusion of the peer group as an undifferentiated mass. Safety and comfort are primarily sought in a pretense that the individual is invisible and will attract neither the attention nor the ire of untrustworthy peers (Bennis and Shephard, 1956).

Still other individuals deny the congruences, similarities, and status of others as peers, and some reject the significance of the peer group. In doing so, they may seek validation from authoritative sources outside the peer group. Or, in cases of extreme social isolation, some individuals attempt to self-validate by using standards and traditions of the surrounding culture, and their own idiosyncratic experiences.

In consequence, the push and pull of the four social constituencies described in Chapter 3 are active in the formation of the peer group. Because the emergence of a peer group is so heavily contingent upon the volition of the individuals forming it, the tolerance of authoritative figures, and sanction by culture and community, its potential as a source of positive social influence and as a component of surrogate family opportunity is often underutilized.

PEERS AND UNRELATEDNESS

As implied above, the most mature adult peers' activities can more closely resemble the parallel play of early childhood than reciprocal social exchange. Very young peers come with pail and shovel to share a sandbox, and adults are attracted to more mature activities. But, in both cases, discussions and activities may proceed as simultaneous soliloquy rather than interactive dialogue.

At such times, some participants are very willing to talk, but are unwilling to listen. Others are willing to listen, or act as though they are listening, but are unwilling to talk. The potential of each participant doing both in reciprocity with his counterparts is notably unrealized. As a result, one may question whether participants have truly joined one another or are merely sharing time and space.

To further illustrate, when the band plays fast music at a dance, people pair off to become partners. But each gyrates and whirls independently around the other with little, if any, cooperative following and leading. In fact, if the dance floor is large enough, several hundred may be dancing, but not a single individual is touching or in step with another. The only true cooperation is the occasional effort to avoid collision.

No doubt, most are having a wonderful time despite the fact that each individual's dancing is an isolated solo performance among the many going on around the floor. Thus, people can and often do join with their peers in ways that satisfy individual needs, but in which the give and take necessary to coordinated social interaction is limited or nonexistent.

Further, no one need identify with or attribute significant personal meaning to other participants, individually or in total. For example, workers may join a labor union as the cost of getting a job at a unionized work site. They pay their dues, but may work out of sight and independently of one another. More important, they may rarely participate in union activities with other members, and simply rely upon officers and representatives to deal with management.

Similarly, in many traditional educational settings, students gather as class members, busily take notes, and pass exams to achieve academic standing of one kind or another. Though some small groups of friends may find their way into a large class and sit together, neither they nor others in the room engage each other in dialogue.

The contribution of mutual interest to each dancer, labor union member, or student is the fact that neither the dance, union, nor the class can exist if others do not subscribe in sufficient numbers. As these examples demonstrate, many groups of peers may serve practical purposes without members interacting, caring in any personal way about one another, or holding dear their status as a peer. Participants need not become friends or identify with each other for such purposes to be met.

In some instances, peers enjoy intense group interaction, but the group does not acquire personal meaning for the participants nor do any of its individual members become intimate. A spontaneous ball game among strangers at a local playing field, the activities of a chess club, or the rehearsals of a concert band are usually filled with intense interaction. After all, games cannot be played without others to serve as teammates and opponents, and musical chords and harmonies must be produced by groups of musicians playing in time with one another. It follows that highly cooperative interaction around enjoyable tasks is the nature of participation. But when the activity is completed, people go their separate ways with little or no knowledge about one another and without a second thought.

In some cases, however, organizations of peers may acquire significant personal meaning despite the fact that they have no social interaction. This might occur if the college lecture course, described above, was offered to students on a highly selective basis as an "Honors Class." Interaction between students may remain limited, but new personal meaning may be derived from the experience and attributed to the others who attend.

On a broader scale, many people join interest groups that never meet except for the involvement of a dedicated and active few. Members receive literature and other communications that create significant meaning, and instill the organization with important value as a reference group. Environmentalist organizations such as the Sierra Club, or human rights organizations such as the NAACP or NOW are prominent examples.

To be sure, many of the peer arrangements described above are of great value to the participants. Unfortunately, in the absence of meaningful interpersonal relationship, or as aggregates who are socially remote to one another, peers cannot contribute to family-like experience. This is so, even though they have personally significant characteristics or interests in common.

Therefore, the situations described above and the simple definitions presented in the first paragraph of this chapter are inadequate to explain peers as a component of the surrogate family. If anything, the preceding narrative describes what is not family-like about many peer relationships.

BROTHERS AND SISTERS:
FAMILY LINKS TO PEER GROUP INFLUENCE

For peers to become family-like, social interaction, intimacy, and reference value to individuals forming the group are necessary preconditions. These preconditions must be met if peers are to have meaningful interpersonal relationships as they share the commonalities that make them peers.

Thus, one may join an organization or club by clipping an application from a newsletter and submitting a dues payment by mail. However, there must be meetings or other social activity for surrogate family opportunity to exist. In this way, peers get to know each other and develop friendships. And more important, they are the means through which the group's relevance to self-perception is actively confronted.

Many situations are rife with opportunity for surrogate family experience, but those in need may have difficulty taking advantage of it. This is so because participation with peers in a surrogate family is not a passive activity. It demands assertiveness and skill, and a willingness to take some risks.

Particularly scary among these risks is the potential that personal differences may be judged and one might be rejected by others.

Another risk is the possibility that any lack of unanimity will lead inevitably to unresolvable conflict, and a great deal of frustration. Suspicion that others may be unaware of or uncaring about their involvement in the peer group's activities and processes can be very troubling, as well (Bennis and Shephard, 1956).

As discussed at length in Chapters 1 and 2, the development of assertiveness and skills, and preparation to accept the above risks has origins in past experience with siblings in the family. Just as with brothers and sisters in a true family, social interaction in the surrogate family requires that peers speak and listen to one another, face to face, and do so amid a sense of belonging. In its most basic sense, interaction among siblings in the family, or sibling surrogates in a peer group, means talking about and doing things together in concert with reasonably organized and defined sets of values and norms.

Thus, effective communication between peers is necessary and important to surrogate family activity. Some communication addresses issues and tasks that are important to practical matters of interdependence. This is so because, inevitably, there are chores to be done, tasks to be completed, and contributions to be made. The greater benefits of sharing resources and combining efforts are derived through these costs.

Because all work and no play make Jack and Jill dull people, other communication between peers occurs in contexts of shared experience, companionship, and play. Thus, surrogate family opportunity in a peer group emerges through communication while "doing" and "being" together. Just as in the family, the resultant dialogue is one avenue through which beliefs and values emerge and are transmitted as peer groups become family-like to their members.

PEERS AS SURROGATE FAMILY
AND A PRIMARY REFERENCE GROUP

Reference value is important to individual acceptance of and adherence to the beliefs and values of peers, and is thus at the core of the influence of a peer group. The notion of reference value acknowledges that the opinions, attitudes, and outlook of some groups of peers have special meanings for the individual (Clark, 1972). These same opinions, attitudes, and outlook expressed by other groups of peers may not have such meaning. Hence, reference value is not equivalent for all the potential groups of peers to which the individual is exposed.

One special meaning is acceptance of a peer group as a point of reference or standard of comparison in judging oneself. When an individual accepts a group in this way, peers become yardsticks against which to assess the fairness of outcomes of one's own behavior, and the legitimacy of one's own attitudes and actions. Peers may also serve as gauges for judging the adequacy of one's own performance, and the appropriateness of one's responses to the behavior of others (Kemper, 1968).

A peer group acquires another special meaning when it serves as a means to achieve desired social status. Subsequently, the individual's narcissistic needs for status, prestige, and privilege often are important motives that undergird the attractiveness and reference value of a peer group.

In addition, the group may provide values and norms that serve as a guide to living, and to making personal decisions for its members. In this way, the peer group again serves as a point of reference as it lends reassurance and validation to the personal judgments and choices made by individual members.

At a deeper and more profound level, the reference value of the peer group extends well beyond its usefulness as a source of standards, status, and norms. More important is a peer group's viability as a choice of other people from whose perspective one may view self. Thus, when the peer group has reference value to the individual, it serves as a mirror. The opinions and attitudes of other members about their peers sustain or alter for each an image of self.

Because they are composed of people whose perspective is important in just this way, peer groups with whom one identifies, and from whom one seeks acceptance, have powerful potential to exert influence (Glaser, 1956). The concept is analogous to the "significant other" in one-to-one relationships. Such groups of peers have considerable potential to make real a sense of "kindred spirit." The realization of this potential converts friends and acquaintances into brothers and sisters outside the family.

TRUST AND LOYALTY:
CATALYSTS TO PEER GROUP INFLUENCE

Thus, interaction and reference value describe conditions under which peers may develop sibling-like relationships in a primary group. However, just as in the family, trust is a requisite to intimacy, and an important ingredient in the exercise of influence in peer relationships.

Just as one may seriously question honor among thieves, trust is not to be presumed as a given among peers. Betrayal, neglect, abuse, exploitation, and abandonment are common themes around which peers struggle with one another. Moreover, some untrustworthy peers may tyrannize their fellows through coercion, corruption, or seduction as described earlier in Chapter 4.

Under these dangerous conditions, the influence of the peer group is compromised. For example, an individual may comply with the will of the group, but compliance may be limited to overt behavior necessary for survival in the group. In part, this occurs because oppressive tactics have little or no impact on private attitudes and beliefs (Clark, 1972).

In contrast, private attitudes and beliefs are subject to confirmation or change as trust permits interpersonal or relational aspects of peer group participation to be valued by the individual. Under such circumstances, the individual has the safety and freedom to begin revealing information he would otherwise keep to himself, and to seek acceptance as an authentic person. In this way, trust promotes loyalty, and vice versa, as members display trust of and trustworthiness to each other.

Both trust and loyalty are catalysts for deeper levels of peer group influence. Openness to the messages of the group is enhanced in the absence of suspicion and defensiveness. Potential for influence reaches its peak when an individual identifies with the peer group, trusts its members, and is loyal to them.

Identification links self-perceptions to others, and one accepts others' influence, in part, to establish and maintain desirable relationships with them. In contrast to the family in which blood, law, and tradition keep people together, trust and loyalty make relationship possible between those drawn together by identification with one another. Thus, identification is the psychological blood tie, and trust and loyalty the glue of desirable relationships between peers in the surrogate family.

When this glue is present, the stage is set for the messages of the peer group to be internalized by the individual. That is, one accepts the values and beliefs contained within these messages as one's own. One not only accepts them as truth, but also seeks to live in congruence with such truth. One does so in associations with others within and outside of the group, and through changes in personal behavior. Dialogue with valued and trusted peers, and consensus with them, results in perceptions of self and one's world that may be shaped, expanded, and validated.

BARRIERS AND OBSTACLES
TO PEER GROUP PARTICIPATION

As emphasized in earlier chapters, the transition from the family cocoon into the community and life with the peer group may not be smooth and easy. Under the best of circumstances, peer groups offer no guarantees of positive and constructive experience or influence.

However, the more troubled and disrupted an individual's family may be, the more prominent the peer group becomes as an alternative resource (Kohut, 1976). In part, this holds true because the social and emotional deprivation that characterizes life in some disturbed families leaves a residue of unmet, but nevertheless powerful, needs.

As a result, needy family members are strongly attracted to sources of emotional supply outside of the family. Just as a moth seeks to escape the darkness and is drawn to a flame, needy individuals are drawn to the peer group and become vulnerable to its negative and destructive potentials. For such individuals, the fear of being alone distorts and far outweighs the risk they may sense about a particular group of peers.

Furthermore, some family circumstances provide disturbed or inadequate preparation for peer group participation. Growing up as an "only child" or as a "first born," and inadequate parenting are examples of problems separate from those created by general family disruption.

Children who have no siblings experience the family differently than other children. These children neither face the demands nor enjoy the benefits of life with brothers and sisters. Most important, they never relinquish the primacy anointed to status as the sole child in a family.

Though first born children temporarily enjoy this primacy, they eventually pay the price of losing it, and encounter similar struggles with siblings as do later born. The intrusion of new brothers and sisters imposes problems of sharing resources and responsibilities, maintaining communication and privacy, and finding a balance between participation in the family culture and individuality.

Thus, the threat of isolation on the one hand, and loss of identity in an "undifferentiated ego mass" (Bowen, 1966) of siblings on the other, is a major challenge to family life among children. Despite its difficulty, this challenge offers important preparation for inevitable encounters with peer groups outside the family.

Though children without siblings are spared the trials and tribulations listed above, the benefits of life with siblings appear to outweigh the disadvantages, especially for later born. The only child and the first born appear to be more susceptible to the hazards of peer group participation outside the family than are other children. They emerge from the family with greater needs for love, protection, sympathy, advice, and reassurance from others (Olson, 1979). As a result, they tend to be more vulnerable to peer pressure (Hines, 1973; Andrews and Brown, 1974; Johnson, 1973), more troubled by conflict of opinion between themselves and others (Warren, 1966), and more dependent on and influenced by the social evaluations of others (Schachter, 1974). Peer pressure, conflict of opinion, and social evaluation are omnipresent elements of peer group experience.

Inadequate parenting may also retard or disturb preparation for joining peer groups outside the family. For example, an overwhelmed mother in a single-parent family may demand child care assistance from an eldest child. To some degree, this "parental child" is forced to grow up too fast and is deprived of some of the growth afforded by lost time that should be spent with peers outside of the family. He or she is also deprived of learning that comes from relating to siblings as the brothers and sisters they really are.

Because she is so drained by the demands of her life, this same mother may relate to her children in ways that fail to acknowledge individual differences between them. She is too exhausted to give the time and energy required beyond that of managing them as a group of siblings. Maintaining appropriate individual relationships with her children addresses many of the separation and individuation issues discussed in Part I of this book. Most important, it shapes sibling relationships in ways that support eventual entry into the peer group.

In extreme instances, such as those precipitated by parental alcoholism, siblings may be forced to relate in ways that avoid confrontation with a difficult and embarrassing family problem. Thus, rather than living as an authentic child and expressing genuine personal needs appropriate to childhood, each sibling accepts a role in which self is sacrificed to an illusion. The illusion is that all is well in the family.

In the classic codependent family of an alcoholic, one sibling may become a family "hero" to maintain appearances of normalcy to the outside world. Another may be a "scapegoat" to draw attention away from issues created by the family drunk. Still others may take on a role as "lost child" and/or "mascot" to serve as a foil to the scapegoat or further draw attention away from the real problems of the family (George, 1990). The siblings do not have access to each other as real people because each is trapped in his or her role. The real person is hidden behind his role as he accedes to demands that he not talk or feel, and therefore cannot trust.

Despite such difficult problems that interfere with the development of health-promoting relationships with siblings, positive relationships with peers are possible and necessary. Surrogate family experience is a vehicle for fulfilling this need and capitalizing on opportunities inherent to a variety of human service settings.

THE PEER GROUP UNCONSCIOUS

As discussed above, the social interaction and reference value of a primary group of peers has many benefits for the individual participant. However, without personal caution and self-protective vigilance, the risks of participation are very dangerous. Have no doubt that the peer group can be merciless in its treatment of individual members, and that an entire membership can be swept into very destructive emotional acting out.

Typically, such dangers manifest themselves as extremes of competitiveness and rivalry, and/or rebelliousness and defiance. In large part, they emanate from unconscious needs and motives as well as rational conflict. Among the unconscious are hidden agendas created by unresolved feelings, habitual behavior, and fears of vulnerability (Sampson and Marthas, 1990). These unconscious feelings, fears, and behaviors are thought to be fueled by developmentally primitive anxieties about isolation or estrangement on the one hand and engulfment on the other. The roots of this distress were discussed at length in Chapter 1.

In an attempt to allay these primitive anxieties, peers may fight with or run from each other, seek assistance from outside the group, or break up the group (Thelen, 1959). They also may deny the existence of anxiety-evoking problems, or attempt to solve a problem indirectly, by attacking symbols that represent it (Sampson and Marthas, 1990).

The possibility that whole groups of people are capable of acting on motivations of which they are unaware and without conscience is distressing, if not surprising. Nevertheless, just as stampeding cattle trample everything in their path, lemmings march to their own demise, and sharks victimize each other in a blind frenzy of feeding, so may a peer group damage its environment and the surrounding community, victimize its members, and destroy itself when it is aroused. Thus, the "scapegoat" and the "rampaging mob" represent the worst of a peer group's destructive potential.

In both cases, the peer group takes action against a problem it cannot or will not face directly. Members attempt to destroy the problem, or some symbol of it, in order to avoid the threat it may pose to the group's security. The group hopes that these tactics will serve to keep the threat safely hidden in the collective unconscious of the membership. Unfortunately, in so doing, the group is as headless as the proverbial chicken running about the barnyard, but far more destructive in its raging nihilism.

Such threats can emerge from within the peer group or from outside it, and the resultant emotion can be vented inwardly or outwardly. Persecution of a scapegoat is one form of avoidant response in which the group's frustration is turned inward against one or more of its own members. In this case, unfortunate individuals serve as sacrificial lambs so the group can create an illusion of solving a problem without facing the threat it poses.

Scapegoats are not singled out at random in such situations. The unlucky individual usually displays traits or behaviors that somehow represent or symbolize a group issue that participants are seeking to avoid. For example, a weak or vulnerable member may be persecuted so that the peer group as a whole can avoid acknowledging its own helplessness to cope with a difficult problem. Hence, when a parent or teacher is abusive or negligent, the children may fight with each other rather than confront an irresponsible authority. The children, in so doing, need not acknowledge their dependency upon and paralysis before the power of the adult. Have no doubt, the youngest or smallest of the group invariably suffers the most.

There are several indicators that a group has made one of its members a scapegoat. One is that the time and energy invested in attempting to correct or fix a scapegoat's troublesome ways is excessive. That is, the group problems created by one individual's troublesome behavior is relatively minor in comparison to the effort expended to correct it.

If the troublesome member presented problems to the group that were truly proportionate to this effort, the group would exercise its only legitimate power in seeking a remedy. This power is to cast out or ostracize the person in question. The abuse heaped upon the scapegoat is not an exercise of such legitimate power.

Another indicator is that a larger group problem is embedded and can be identified in the content of the assault on the scapegoat. The usual discovery, upon examination, is that the scapegoat's behavior is somehow representative of unresolved group issues related to power and control, intimacy, or conditions of membership.

Unfortunately for the victim and the group as a whole, the destructive potential of such behavior is great. The scapegoat may emerge battered and bloody in mind, spirit, and in extreme cases, body. The group exhausts itself as it squanders energy it might better use solving the real problem. And trust is shaken as each individual member fears the possibility of being a future target at whom the anger of the group will be directed. Thus, the foundation of family surrogate opportunity may be irreparably damaged, especially for those among the peer group who most need such experience.

At another extreme, the peer group may become a rampaging mob as it seeks to vent outwardly its disappointment, anger, and frustration. In such cases, peers are swept into mindless behavior as the impulsive acts of a few appear to give legitimacy to the acts of the many who follow. As the critical mass of a rampage grows in size, so does the illusion of its legitimacy.

In acting out the passions of the moment, members of the peer group need not face the meaning of their behavior because individual judgment and control are suspended or relinquished, and consciousness of the consequences and irresponsibility of individual acts are swept aside. In this way, an avalanche may begin with a few loose pebbles, or a forest fire may ignite with a single spark, under appropriate conditions. Similarly, the peer group may explode when it is energized and made volatile by latent frustration, anger, or fear.

Similar negative potential within the peer group is inherent in trends and fads. Though not sudden and explosive like a rampage, potentially destructive actions may gradually and insidiously gain momentum as members unconsciously follow one another.

The child claims that "everyone is doing it," as he rationalizes his behavior and denies the need to maintain awareness of individual risks, consequences, and responsibility. The danger to those contemplating experimentation with drugs is clearly evident in many a child's report that drug use is far more prevalent among the peer group than is actually the case. Personal judgement may therefore be suspended as the individual accedes to peer pressure and uses drugs to comply with a mythical norm.

The destructive action that peers may suddenly or gradually exhibit is not to be confused with unity, spontaneity, or righteous indignation. The blind and sheep-like followership that characterizes the behavior described above is aided and abetted by illusions of unity and spontaneity, and is rationalized as an appropriate expression of indignation.

This rationalization parallels the one implicit within Freud's discussion of the myth of the primal horde (Freud, 1922). The horde, or mob, is swept into action by the initiating behavior of a few. It finds comfort in a myth that authority has been challenged and held accountable in an act of heroism by the initiators. In this way, the group places emotional buffers between itself and acknowledgment of its irresponsibility, destructiveness, and nihilism.

To be sure, a peer group may have just cause to protect its members against acts of betrayal, neglect, abuse, exploitation, and abandonment. However, genuine effective action demands awareness, planning, organization, skill, and discipline. These are notably absent in the dangerous behavior described above.

LEADERSHIP IN THE PEER GROUP

In the absence of parent-like authority, a group of peers may appear to be a leaderless and primal horde incapable of awareness, organization, or discipline. At times, the members of a peer group may feel this way about themselves. In such instances, they may desperately seek to have issues and problems resolved by a benevolent parental figure who appears to be possessed of superior ability or higher authority. The unconscious wish is to be protected, kept intact as a group, and to have limits conveniently provided (Sampson and Marthas, 1990).

Interestingly, the very unity and cohesiveness that develop as an aggregate of peers becomes a group, brings order out of chaos. Leadership, and control and power over member behavior in the peer group are heavily invested in a structure of norms and expectations created and agreed upon, to at least some extent, by the members.

Adherence to these norms and expectations is foundational to the trustworthiness of the group. In the interest of personal security, members attempt to instill their group with the same stability, consistency, and benevolence that engender trust in families and other social contexts. The more successful the members are in creating a trustworthy structure, the greater the potential of the group to exert control.

Not all of the structure emanates from within the group. Some parts are imposed by an authority figure who is responsible for the well-being and productivity of the group, and is accountable to the agency that sponsors it. Moreover, some parts are imposed by the surrounding community as a set of conditions under which a peer group is permitted to exist.

For instance, student clubs and school organizations operate under a tacit condition that no illegal drinking or drug use occur at their social activities and functions. Usually, peers are accountable to an adult advisor who assists the group and acts as an agent of the school in representing its interests. Peers are aware that flagrant violation of this condition jeopardizes the existence of their group.

Independent adult peer groups in the community at large are subject to similar conditions. In the spring of 1993 in Waco, Texas, members of a religious cult were besieged and perished because of violation of gun laws. This tragic event is an example of community reaction to a dangerous challenge.

As discussed above, still other aspects of structure emerge as part of unconscious processes. Though some trends and fads may be dangerous, others can be harmless or serve positive ends. Clothing, hair styles, and novel language including argot or slang, are harmless examples as "preppies," "bohemians," "beatniks," "hippies," and "punkers" use their respective peer groups to express their values and outlook. On the other hand, food fads, unhealthy sexual behavior, drug and alcohol abuse, tattoos, and other more serious forms of self-mutilation are dangerous demands made by some groups.

Though peers are equals by definition, some peers emerge as more equal than others in many groups. Status in a group may be enhanced by charisma, strength, or special abilities. In such situations, some members become dominant and exercise disproportionate control as others defer to and follow them.

This may occur even though no formal positions of authority exist within the structure of the group. For the advantaged few, the opportunity and temptation to use the group to serve one's own needs are powerful. Thus, in service to self, their conscious and unconscious motivations can influence and distort the normative structure of the group. When the narcissism of dominant members of a peer group seizes the moment, the trustworthiness of the group becomes tenuous.

On the other hand, many groups of peers have healthy opportunity to democratically control their destiny. In these groups, impor-

tant aspects of structure emerge as a product of conscious deliberation, dialogue, and consensual arrangement. Rules, regulations,
constitutions, and by-laws may formalize these agreements in some
peer groups. In less formal circumstances, such arrangements are
part of a web of unwritten rules that are conditions of membership.

Whether the structure of a group is formal or informal, participation as peers in the creation of the norms, rules, and other aspects of
the structure, by those who are subject to them, enhances their
meaning (Page and Page, 1993). By virtue of the variety of outlook
inherent even among peers, flexibility must be built into the structure of the group to accommodate the diversity of needs expressed.

In addition, under such circumstances, leadership may be distrib-
uted among peers of the group in accordance with the distribution
of abilities among them. Though in some cases, participants may
take turns being a leader, leaders will usually emerge as their particular talents and skills match well with the challenges of the moment. The less rigid the structure of the group, the greater the
fluidity with which such changes in leadership may occur.

The same holds true about the group's capacity to view itself with
a sense of humor, and to resist acting out during periods of difficulty.
Just as in the real family, such qualities are important to surrogate
family opportunity because of contribution to trust. Trust grows because of the developing consciousness that the group is reliable, has
good intentions toward its members, and can be pragmatic about
meeting the individual needs the peers have joined around.

PARENTAL AUTHORITY AND PEERS
IN THE SURROGATE FAMILY

The role of persons in authority as potential surrogate parents to
peers who are potential surrogate brothers and sisters is complex and
challenging. The peer group gathers around the educator, athletic
coach, minister, arts director, or other service provider primarily
because of interest in activity and opportunity for participation.
Though some among the peer group may be seeking emotional sustenance, consciousness of such motivation is almost never at hand.

The importance of competence, responsibility, and support of
others' self-esteem is discussed at length in Chapter 7 of this sec-

tion. However, the focus of that discussion is on the person in authority as a surrogate parent to individuals. The present discussion is about the adult in charge as a promoter of interaction, trust, and reference value among the peer group as a whole.

Surrogate parents must provide support, protection, and supervision to the total peer group, just as parents and surrogates do for individual siblings. These requirements are met by offering appropriate assistance to the group as it pursues its legitimate activities and copes with problems and unexpected difficulties. Such assistance must be offered in an even-handed way, so all members have reasonably equal opportunity to benefit.

In addition, the surrogate parent must protect vulnerable individuals from other members of the group. The group as a whole must be protected from dominance and control by aggressive self-serving members, and hazards of the environment. And finally, a surrogate parent must ensure that the entire group, and its individual members, adhere to the limits and boundaries of safe and acceptable behavior.

In performing these functions, those with parent-like authority must constantly monitor the processes of the group so the dangers of unbridled competitiveness and rivalry, rebelliousness and defiance, and unconscious acting out are minimized. Preventing scapegoating, mob-like unruliness, and potentially destructive trends and fads requires vigilance, sensitivity, and the earliest possible intervention.

Thus, the real opportunities, responsibilities, and problems confronting the peer group must be brought into focus and addressed so that the group may move ahead in achieving its goals. In this way, the frustration, anger, or fear that may drive destructive behavior are kept from building to dangerous levels.

A principal task of the adult in charge is to help the peer group become a trustworthy point of reference for its individual members. The norms and expectations that guide the group must be closely monitored as they develop. Those that contribute to stability, consistency, and benevolence among the membership must be supported and affirmed. Those that detract must be resisted.

The same is true for maintaining flexibility and calm in the face of adversity. At such times, the efficacy of norms and expectations are tested by unexpected or unusual events and circumstances. For effective adjustments to be made, the group must not be trapped in so rigid a structure that its goals and purposes are neglected. Competent surrogate parenting aids the group in placing crises in appropriate perspective, assessing changes that must be made, and assisting in the change process as needed. As discussed in Chapter 2, such times of transition are always difficult.

Performance of these tasks requires diligent attention to a myriad of small acts and behaviors as well as observations and interventions on a grand scale. Punctuality, attendance, thoughtfulness, consideration of others, attentiveness, honesty, honoring agreements, sharing, taking turns, and a multitude of other small chips of behavior form a mosaic of expectations that may promote or harm trust. From a broader perspective, the surrogate parent may ask that the entire group come to a screeching halt so that members may pause and contemplate together the group's next actions.

A second such task is to support processes of identification among members. In assisting the peer group, the surrogate parent must promote and maintain a growing awareness of personal characteristics, experience, and interests held in common among members. The foundation of attachment and bonding is sufficiently fostered and strengthened through appropriately supported interaction. Ideally, intimacy will grow as peers are helped to discover the individuality in each member of the group.

When these tasks are successfully engaged, the peer group becomes an environment and a resource. In it, members test individual points of view by comparing perceptions and experience. They may give and receive support and assistance as they achieve unity and coordination of effort, and share and combine their resources. In doing these things, members may achieve consensus that enables each to validate a positive and expansive view of self and one's world. These are the ends to which the surrogate parent must dedicate his efforts on behalf of the peer group.

REFERENCES

Alexander, C. N. (1964). "Consensus and Mutual Attraction in Natural Cliques." *American Journal of Sociology,* Vol. 69, January, pp. 395-403.

Andrews, R. and Brown, E. (1974). "Firstborns, Only Children, Sex, and Three Dependency Measures." *Perceptual and Motor Skills*, Vol. 39, No. 2, October, pp. 773-774.

Asche, S. E. (1952). *Social Psychology*. New York: Prentice Hall.

Bennis, W. G. and Shephard, H. A. (1956). "A Theory of Group Development." *Human Relations*, Vol. 9, No. 4, November, pp. 415-437.

Bowen, M. (1966). "The Use of Family Theory in Clinical Practice." *Comprehensive Psychiatry*, Vol. 7, pp. 345-374.

Cartwright, D. and Zander, A. (1962). *Group Dynamics*. Evanston, Illinois: Row, Peterson and Company, pp. 165-188.

Clark, R. E. (1972). *Reference Group Theory and Delinquency*. New York: Behavioral Publications.

Freud, S. (1959). *Group Psychology and the Analysis of the Ego*. Trans. by J. Strachey. London: International Psychoanalytical Press, 1922; New York: Liveright, p. 112.

George, R. (1990). *Counseling and the Chemically Dependent*. Englewood Cliffs, New Jersey: Prentice Hall.

Glaser, D. (1956). "Criminality Theories and Behavior Images." *American Journal of Sociology*, Vol. 61, March, pp. 433-444.

Hines, G. H. (1973). "Birth Order and Relative Effectiveness of Social and Nonsocial Reinforcers." *Perceptual and Motor Skills*, Vol. 36, No. 1, February, pp. 35-38.

Johnson, P. B. (1973). "Birth Order and Crowne-Marlowe Social Desirability Scores." *Psychological Reports*, Vol. 32, No. 2, April, p. 536.

Kemper, T. (1968). "Reference Groups, Socialization and Achievement." *American Sociological Review*, Vol. 33, February, pp. 31-45.

Kohut, H. (1971). *Analysis of the Self*. New York: International Universities Press.

Newcomb, T. M. (1956). "The Prediction of Interpersonal Attraction." *American Psychologist*, Vol. 60, pp. 575-586.

Olson, M. (1979). "Succorance and the Only Child." Unpublished M.A. research project, New York University.

Page, R. M. and Page, T. S. (1993). *Fostering Emotional Well-Being in the Classroom*. Boston: Jones and Bartlett Publishers, p. 33.

Sampson, E. E. and Marthas, M. (1990). *Group Process for Health Professionals*. Albany, New York: Delmar Publishers, Inc., pp. 68-80.

Secord, P. F. and Backman, C. W. (1964). *Social Psychology*. New York: McGraw-Hill Book Company.

Schachter, S. (1974). "Birth Order and Sociometric Choice." *Journal of Abnormal and Social Psychology*, Vol. 68, pp. 453-456.

Sullivan, H. S. (1955). *Conceptions of Modern Psychiatry*. London: Tavistock, pp. 17-18.

Thelen, H. A. (1959). "Work-emotionality Theory of the Group as Organism." In S. Koch (ed.), *Psychology: A Study of Science*. Vol. 3. New York: McGraw-Hill.

Thibaut, J. W. and Kelly, H. (1961). *The Social Psychology of Groups*. New York: John Wiley and Sons, Inc., p. 253.

Warren, J. R. (1966). "Birth Order and Social Behavior." *Psychological Bulletin*, Vol. 65, pp. 38-49.

Webster, A. M. (1973). *Webster's Seventh Collegiate Dictionary*. Springfield, Massachusetts: G. C. Merriam Company, p. 845.

Chapter 7

Persons in Authority: Influence Through Interpersonal Relationship, Didactic, and Management of Social Processes and Environment

At first glance, the educative potential of persons in authority may be thought to reside in their ability to prescribe behavior, offer instruction, information, and argument, and serve as a model for emulation. These capabilities to direct the learning of others contribute to intellectual and social growth and development, and are common to a variety of methods of helping others. They also represent classical approaches to traditional education in which persons in authority are the central and dominant element of the learning environment.

However, the educative potential of persons in authority goes far beyond the power of social position and the purely didactic. Just as is the case for parents who promote and guide the interests of their own children, such potential extends into realms of emotion and meaning that are produced by and shape interpersonal relationship. Thus, the educator or other human service professional may influence not only the individual's public displays of behavior, but also his or her private internal world of beliefs, feelings, and intentions.

DIRECTION AND ASSISTANCE: AUTHORITATIVE AVENUES OF INFLUENCE

To influence this often hidden internal world, the educator must at times be responsive to the individual's needs for stability and dependency, and at other times his or her very opposite needs for change and autonomy. Traditional directive influence addresses the former needs, but often one must approach the later in less direct fashion. In fact, providing a helpless and passive recipient with opportunities for enhancement or solutions to problems differs from assisting that same person to capably and actively create his own opportunities and solutions. However, the difference is one of degree and emphasis rather than kind.

More directive assistance places emphasis on subject matter expertise, and requires skill with various modes of communication that are appropriate to the subject matter. The educator's principal task is to transmit the content of his expertise in linear fashion (Northouse and Northouse, 1992, pp. 4-5), and the learner's responsibility is to receive and retain it.

Acceptance of the educator's message is strongly connected to the viability of that individual as a reliable and expert informational resource. Social position, status, credentials, and reputation in the community are common bases for such viability. Though the learner can respond interactively at times, such response is not necessary for directive educative process to take place.

Thus, more directive forms of education and assistance shape the educator's role into one that may very much resemble that of a broadcaster, except in the case of telephone talk shows. The educator engages in an abundance of transmitting but does little, if any, receiving.

In contrast, interpersonal skill becomes increasingly important as needs for less directive assistance become salient. At such times, the appropriately responsive educator is more the midwife to the learners' own understandings, ideas, and decisions about action, and less a transmitter of preexisting notions. Though the learner's acceptance of the educator as a subject matter expert is certainly important, interpersonal relationship becomes an increasingly prominent catalyst to discovery and growth (Watzlawick, Beavin, and Jackson, 1967, p. 54).

This is so because less directive education and assistance is transactional, and interaction and reciprocity between educator and learner are its core (Wilmot, 1979). Thus, the less directive the education and assistance, the more the educator's role resembles that of helper or collaborator.

Though more directive and less directive forms of assistance differ in these basic ways, both use words and imagery as principal tools of practice. Most educational and other human service activity incorporates a blend of directive and nondirective methods. The dominance of an approach is dependent upon the goals and aims of activity, the needs of the participant, and the conditions under which activity must be carried out.

Directive forms of authoritative assistance provide important supports at beginning stages of activity in new areas of endeavor. At such times, participants not only begin the learning process, but confront the ambiguity and ambivalence of new experience. In the case of an automobile with a dead battery, one must make sure the basic mechanisms of the charging system are in working order, and provide energy from an external source if one wants to start the motor. Then, once running, the motor can charge the battery, permitting the driver to restart without external assistance. As the above analogy implies, the learner often needs a directive "jump start" at the infantile and dependent stages of new beginnings in learning and growth.

Similarly, more directive forms of assistance support basic cognitive learning such as recognition, recall, and comprehension of practical, technical, or intellectual material. Such basic learning usually occurs early in the growth process and is foundational to more advanced development.

More directive assistance is particularly appropriate as learners engage subject matter that is neither too emotionally neutral nor too emotionally arousing. Directive approaches are less effective when such content is pointedly intrusive into the learner's private internal world. This is attributable to the anxiety, anger, or other powerful and distracting emotions that may be evoked.

Similarly, directive methods may fail with subject matter that produces emotionally flat reactions in learners. When learners view educative activities as irrelevant and nonstimulating, they may, at worst, become actively or passively resistant to participation. At best, their attentiveness, curiosity, and readiness to contemplate the material at hand will be dulled.

Consequently, the less developed the learner's capabilities and insight about rational and emotional issues with which he is engaged, the more dependent upon the directive influence of others the learner will be. However, such directive influence may falter when it runs afoul of learners' sensitivities and needs.

On the other hand, more mature activities such as analysis and creative application of concepts and ideas, and judgment and evaluation in connection with problem solving and decision making, are probably better understood through less directive approaches. This is particularly true for content that has social and emotional meaning, aesthetic and artistic implication, and/or touches deeply into the private internal world of the learner.

This suggests that as learning progresses, learners become increasingly separate from and independent of those who have taught them. This is analogous to a maturing child's separation from the directive and controlling influences of parental authority in the family. In the family or other settings in which learning and growth occurs, those in authority must then not only change their ways of helping, but also must change ways of relating, as a learner matures in his skill and understanding. Thus, movement from more directive to less directive avenues of influence is very much dependent upon the needs of the learner. This movement is also an acknowledgment and celebration of success.

THE EDUCATOR AS SURROGATE PARENT

Though one can usually determine in advance the focus and level of complexity of educational activity, the meaning of such activity to the learner is more difficult to predict. As a result, the educator's best delivered directive presentations, or most sensitive nondirective responses may seem to miss the mark. This occurs, at least in part, because the learner's experience of the moment is influenced profoundly by his or her personal history, developmental status, and immediate life situation. To the learner, the subject matter and its source often represent more than the message and the presenter.

This occurs partially because participants in various educational activities often experience persons in authority as parental figures at both conscious and unconscious levels. At times, participants attribute omnipotence to the educators' role and weave grand fantasies into exaggerated images of the person in the role. In the private hopes and dreams of some participants, the educator is a towering figure and attractive as a target for attachment and bonding.

Thus, the educator acquires secret potential as a surrogate parent at the fringes of consciousness for the needy but hopeful. For the hopeless, whose ability to trust has been too damaged, such palliative opportunity may be lost in reactive denial against the humiliation of profound need, and in rebellion against those who might ease the pain of such need.

From a practical perspective, needy participants' underlying wish is that parental figures will help to develop strategies and tactics, and provide needed resources for coping with difficult challenges. At a deeply emotional level, the desire is for such a figure to be present to root from the sidelines when life's battles are joined. And finally, the hope is that parental figures will be steadfast as a resource, regardless of performance or outcome.

Though such yearnings may be powerful in the very needy, many of the hopes and dreams they portend are impossible. Teachers and other professionals cannot adopt and take home the children with whom they work. Those serving adolescents and young adults, in the vast majority of cases, cannot wed their charges and ride off into the sunset. These and many other glorious fantasies and wishes are far afield from the appropriate limits and boundaries of professional role. Unfortunately for some young people in desperate need, anything short of these romantic but impossible extremes is yet another blow to a fragile and tenuous ability to trust.

However, persons in authority can address many of the needs that underlie such wishes in reasonable ways. From the practical perspective, educators and other human service providers in parental roles, can reliably provide instrumental assistance that is appropriate to educational purpose and setting. From a relational perspective, practitioners can behave as stable, consistent, and benevolent figures regardless of performance or outcome. And from an emotional perspective, they can cheer their charges on by means of positive expectations and hopes, acknowledgment and celebration of success, and continued optimism and enthusiasm in the face of difficulty.

Because the emotional is so central to interaction between a person in authority and those he serves, authoritative expectations, acknowledgment, and enthusiasm can create self-fulfilling prophecies (Page and Page, 1992). There is ample evidence that parental figures who expect the best of their charges usually get it (Rosenthal and Jacobson, 1968; Pope, McHale, and Craighead, 1988). Those who expect the opposite get just that (Hamachek, 1978).

This Pygmalion effect is a two-way street, because those receiving service have long histories of experience with parents' authority, and expectations and demands of their own. This history can produce expectations of neglect, abuse, exploitation, betrayal, or abandonment to a negative extreme. In other difficult cases, this history can produce demands for overindulgence, pampering, and dependency. Such expectations and demands can bring out the best or the worst in educators. Thus, for better or worse, participants' immediate expectations and perceptions of an authority figure often are linked to those established in past times with their own parents.

TRUST AND THE SURROGATE PARENT

Persons in authority symbolize much that evokes special feelings toward our parents, which presents a double-edged sword regarding trust. As described in Chapter 1 of this book, childhood illusions of parental omnipotence, knowledge, and wisdom go hand-in-hand with our dependence on parents as benevolent figures. However, for children whose parents were dangerous, negative expectations and illusions of parent-like figures may exist.

Unfortunately, the credibility and potential for salience of persons in authority are in part a consequence of such illusions. As a result, authoritative figures often must contend with unquestioning dependence associated with unreasoned trust, or knee-jerk reactivity spurred by unreasoned distrust. Therefore, an important aspect of the authority figure's educative capacity and potential as healthy parental surrogate is the ability to dispel the illusions described above. One route to this is establishment of relationships and an environment that are separate from and independent of past experience, especially negative past experience.

This means that the day-to-day, "here and now" of educational activity must acquire a life of its own. This educative here and now must offer opportunity rather than danger, and provide practical means for accomplishment rather then a potpourri of tempting yet frustrating impossibilities. And educators must create educative relationships between themselves and participants that demonstrate the same stability, consistency, and benevolence that are requirements of healthy child rearing. Such relationships must be devoid of pretense, and uncontaminated by trauma and disappointment that shatter trust.

For needy participants, such activity and relationship pass into memory, and each experience becomes part of an accumulating new personal history. As this new personal history becomes large and prominent, it may begin to reshape the mosaic of personal meanings that form individual consciousness. The memories that comprise this new history should contribute to excitement and optimism about the future. Thus, the educator's challenge, as a surrogate parent to those in need, is to create new and positive recollections of family-like experience with a parental figure.

ELEMENTS OF PARENTAL AUTHORITY: SOCIAL POWER, WISDOM, AND TRUST

An important similarity between parents and persons in authority is that people expect both to provide direction and control. Others accept this direction and control because power is ascribed to certain positions in the social structure, or because some people are seen to possess special knowledge, wisdom, and skill.

Thus, an authority figure may be "in authority," "an authority," or both. Teachers, parents, and traffic police are in authority because they occupy defined positions and have special responsibility in the schools, family, and community. Creating and implementing policy and controlling resources are at the core of these roles and responsibilities. This core contains power to support and protect, to supervise activity, and to manage the social and physical environment in which activity occurs. Corruption and coercive harassment are latent, but troublesome, possibilities when such power is misused.

In many instances, people view a parent, teacher, or police officer as "an authority" because a person occupying such a position is assumed to be a credible repository of special knowledge. Possession of special knowledge carries with it power to advise, to recommend, to inform decisions, and to perform important tasks. However, corruption and seduction are dangers that are latent to possession of esoteric knowledge and skill.

Regardless of the source of one's authority, the true measures of one's capacity to influence or educate rest in the degree to which others believe and attribute significance to one's statements, willingly follow one's directives, or imitate one's actions. Because of powers to coerce, seduce, and corrupt, trust becomes a major determinant of such a capacity.

TRUST: A FRAGILE AND IRREPLACEABLE ASSET

Abraham Lincoln's conclusion that one cannot fool all of the people all of the time is an astute observation and fair warning about violating trust. For the short term, a person of authority may usurp the power of individuals and entire communities by hiding facts, concealing choices, restricting purposeful action, and limiting participation in processes of control (Barrett, 1983).

However, the likelihood of failure is great. In some cases, "mistakes" can produce inadvertent revelations, and chance circumstances can produce purely accidental discoveries of questionable behavior by persons of authority. In other cases, informers emerge from duplicitous conspiracies because of disenchantment, other self-serving motives, or just plain guilty conscience. These "whistle blowers" may actively complain, or surreptitiously "leak" information. Thus, as Lincoln implied, misuse of authority is a tenuous strategy because many uncontrollable avenues lead to being "found out," and such duplicity arouses suspicion and reaction in all social contexts.

Unfortunately, subsequent confirmation of such suspicion not only has negative consequences for wrongdoers, but also for disappointed witnesses and victims. In addition to wasting resources and squandering opportunity, abuse of trust breeds grinding and malignant cynicism.

The terms used above are suggestive of such events in broad and sensational terms. However, lying, cheating, and stealing by political figures and corporate executives is analogous to broken promises, deceit, and disappointment in the more circumscribed interpersonal world of the individual. The scale may be less grand in the latter instance, but pain and disillusionment close to the heart cut more deeply into the core of one's willingness and ability to trust. Readiness to protest is heightened, as are despair and readiness to withdraw. Thus, in the absence of trust, authority derived from social position or special knowledge is a house of cards for a wide range of social, educational, and human service settings.

This may explain the lengthy history of failure of education-oriented drug abuse prevention efforts. In these efforts, educators, clergy, and law enforcement officials attempted to frighten, deceive, and indoctrinate people about the evils of drugs and alcohol. The information they disseminated was often invalid, exaggerated, and overgeneralized (Fields, 1992). Trust and credibility were so shaken that concern arose about prevention programs stimulating drug use rather than reducing it (Carroll, 1985). As this sad educational history vividly demonstrates, persons in authority are perched precariously atop the confidence of those who accept their influence.

COMPETENCE, RESPONSIBILITY, AND EMOTIONAL FEEDING: KEYS TO ATTACHMENT AND BONDING

Trust is a central issue to success as a surrogate parent because the means through which people form later attachments contain the same preconditions that were necessary during infancy and early childhood. A child seeks attachment and bonding with capable, reliable, and kindly adults he admires and idealizes, and who fuss over him. Similarly, more mature individuals are drawn to authority figures who are competent, responsible, and strengthen self-esteem. Therefore, a model for good parenting in a functional family may serve as a guide to behavior for educators and others who direct activity in human service settings.

For educators, competency is invested in grasp of subject matter, supervision of learning activities, and quality of management of the learning environment. For other human service providers, competency is invested similarly in the skill with which tools of service are applied. Children and more mature individuals infer responsibility from consistency and stability, and self-esteem is fed through empathic acceptance, positive expectation, and benevolent exercise of adult authority.

Hence, educators and other human service professionals become targets for family-like attachment and bonding by being good practitioners and behaving like good parents. Practitioners, in achieving such a position, become trustworthy parent-like resources and a part of a network of social-emotional support.

AUTHORITY AND MANAGEMENT
OF EMERGENT SOCIAL PROCESS

As described above, the role of authority figures in creating opportunity for surrogate family experience is centered emphatically on the interpersonal concern of trust. This trust is established not only through demonstrations of honesty and reliability, but also through observable demonstrations of knowledge and skill in the course of ongoing activity. Sincerity must be visibly linked with effectiveness, and pragmatic needs must be adequately satisfied. Thus, practical management skills are important to trust, too.

Management addresses requirements for monitoring and controlling "activities and processes." Activities and processes refer here to the flow of events that form participants' experience. As in most cases of plans produced by mice and people, some of these events are intended, some are unintended, some turn out to be positive, and some to be negative. As a result, practitioners must effectively attend to the planned and intended as well as the emergent and unintended.

Competent managers influence activity so the positive is maximized and the negative is minimized. This applies to adjusting or abandoning intended activity that has gone bad, and to embracing unexpected opportunities. To be seen as competent, practitioners must respond in timely fashion to such events and processes, and to participants' needs as needs arise.

Action-oriented skill is especially critical in assessment and intervention that can be applied immediately as events occur and processes unfold. However, these skills are fragile contributors to trust. They become robust when exercised in concert with displays of flexibility, a sense of humor, and an ability to stay calm during time of crisis. Such qualities were described in earlier chapters as foundational to basic trust.

In addition to action and crisis-oriented management problems, educators and other practitioners confront recurrent and predictable concerns, too. Fortunately, their predictability permits anticipation and planning.

Principal among these concerns are those created by the developmental nature of activities and processes. That is, activities and processes have a beginning, an ending, and a series of predictable phases that occur in between. Because the different phases impose different demands, all who are engaged in activity must adjust expectations and behavior as a phase is encountered. These adjustments address the recurrent social issues of ambivalence about new activity, control, information sharing, conditions for participation, and evaluation and termination of activity. The nature of these issues was discussed fully in Chapter 3.

In theory, competent management requires that practitioners understand this unfolding process, organize activity in concert with it, and facilitate participants' orderly passage through it. Each requirement and its concomitant tasks demand the exercise of planning, diagnostic, and intervention skills. Educators must also be sensitive to stressors associated with various aspects of the process, and be prepared to anticipate, prevent, and solve such problems.

In the most simple terms discussed above, social process may be described as containing "beginning," "middle," "end," and "transition" stages. The following outline is a description of the stages and the distinct issues each raises.

Stages of Social Process

I. Beginnings
   A. Preparation of space, facilities, supplies, and coordination with other practitioners and support personnel when appropriate
   B. Preparation of participants for engagement in learning and other growth-promoting activity

1. Resolution of ambivalence and ambiguity
2. Establishment of controls on activity
3. Establishment of channels of communication and information sharing
4. Establishment of conditions for participation

II. Middles
   A. Movement into activity
   B. Establishment of self-perpetuation of activity
   C. Monitoring and influencing self-perpetuating activity

III. Endings
   A. Completion of tasks and resolution of the as yet unresolved
   B. Restoration of the environment
   C. Evaluation
   D. Considerations of future value of present accomplishment
   E. Termination and separation from activity

IV. Transitions–reawakening of ambivalence and ambiguity
   A. A point of new beginning

Thus, persons in authority serve to improve the effectiveness, efficiency, and comfort of activities and processes through which participants receive service. And, by doing so without a lot of fuss and bother, they also strengthen bonding and attachment by confirming and reconfirming trustworthiness.

AUTHORITY AND MANAGEMENT OF ENVIRONMENT

Environment refers to the social and physical atmosphere in which activity takes place. The social and the physical may be viewed as distinct but interacting aspects of a total environment because enjoyment of one is usually dependent on conditions established by the other.

For example, a wonderfully maintained and beautifully supplied facility portends sterile and vapid experience in the absence of social conditions that promote its use and preservation. On the other hand, a social atmosphere that is ripe with enthusiasm, cooperative spirit, and creativity may founder in spaces that are poorly maintained and ill-equipped.

Social environment is a qualitative concept rather than a material one. Its quality is the product of interactions between practitioner and participant, participants as peers, and individual experience with activities. Quality is shaped to a great extent by the degree to which expectations and demands regarding social interaction serve the purposes and goals of activity, and the needs of participants. It is shaped further by the uniformity and clarity with which these demands and expectations are understood and accepted. And finally, quality is influenced by the rigidity or flexibility with which such expectations and demands are applied.

Persons in authority and the peer group each create and impose some of these expectations and demands. The culture of the sponsoring organization imposes others. Regardless of source, flexibility is important for adaptation to real-world contingencies, and for responsiveness to idiosyncratic expectations and demands of individual participants.

In contrast, the physical environment addresses material concerns. It does so because physical environment challenges individual sensitivities about comfort, safety, cleanliness, and availability of appropriate facilities, space, and equipment. Management of the physical environment generally requires that service providers act prior to participants' engagement in activity.

However, adequate preparation not only addresses the material needs of participants, but also relational concerns. A clean and ready space when needed, conveys benevolence, caring, and responsibility by those in charge, and is a first step in fostering trust. Though some participants may differentiate between the social and physical, negative experiences seem to bleed across the very permeable boundaries between the two.

Thus, an uncomfortable room may cause participants to become cranky and irritable toward one another. On the other hand, interpersonal tension may cause normal room temperatures to suddenly seem too high, or usually comfortable chairs to inexplicably feel too hard.

Because relational concerns are important to attachment and bonding, the quality of the social and physical environment merge as important issues in promoting family surrogate experience. Competent management reduces the occurrence of negative events as participants experience the total environment.

Clearly, individual participants depend upon persons in authority to provide protection and support against aversive potentials in immediate experience. Educator's must strive to create an environment that subjectively is uplifting, invigorating, and promotes enthusiasm, and to avoid conditions that leave participants drained, defeated, and relieved that the activity is finished.

MANAGEMENT OF INTERPERSONAL RELATIONSHIP

The following list includes negative events that have been discussed repeatedly in this writing. These events primarily refer to forms of dereliction of responsibility by persons in authority, but, as discussed in Chapter 6, such acts can be perpetrated by peers, too. For persons in authority, they are often a product of failures to adequately manage social and physical aspects of environment. The definitions provided here give them added specificity as destructive interpersonal issues.

1. Neglect – failure to provide appropriate support, protection, or supervision.
2. Abuse – physical and/or psychological assault.
3. Exploitation – use with or without consent, or otherwise deriving benefit from a participant's efforts or presence. And, to do so without consideration of the individual's best interest or well-being, and without equitable compensation. Seduction, corruption, and coercion are elements of exploitative behavior.
4. Betrayal – violation of agreements, breaking promises, misrepresentation, and deceit.
5. Abandonment – inappropriate disavowal of responsibility for support and protection, especially in a time of need.

Thus, control of the social and physical environment appears to address most directly a tension between the power of an authority figure and the trust of the individual. As discussed in earlier chapters, the individual, in part, bases trust on assessments of benevolence. Participants' perceptions of benevolence take the form of expectations regarding the use of power. The use of power on one's behalf or constructively integrated into one's own life is central to expectations and perceptions of benevolence.

The negative events listed above are subversions of power in which one's authority is used selfishly to control, dominate, or defeat others (May, 1972). They are also examples of dereliction of duty that readily convert to interpersonal failure. The consequences of such negative events are a repudiation of the values inherent to family surrogate experience.

AUTHORITY AND THE MANAGEMENT OF SOCIAL CONSTITUENCIES IN THE SURROGATE FAMILY

Persons in authority are in a challenging position in relation to the other social constituencies present and active in the human service environment. Principal among the many challenges that authority figures must cope with, are internal and external pressures to dominate and control. Similarly, they must contend with temptations to withdraw into indifference and inactivity.

Instead, they must seek to establish and maintain a balance of appropriate influence between themselves, the peer group, individual experience, and the culture of the organization in which they work. The importance of this balance to surrogate family experience is discussed at length in Chapter 4.

Of the four social constituencies, persons with parental authority are likely to be the sole players to consciously pursue such a balance. This is so because the natural order of things is one in which all constituencies are blindly competitive to dominate the social contexts in which they are operative. Though a healthy equilibrium may emerge without intervention, the possibility always exists that one or another of the constituencies may dominate and tyrannize.

In creating and preserving a balance of influence, the surrogate parent seeks to establish and maintain the surrogate family as a functional system. This system parallels that of the real family as described earlier in Chapter 1. The system is functional if participants have access to the resources and influences of all constituencies but are protected from engulfment and tyranny by any one of them. Thus, the surrogate parent's responsibility is to enable each individual to use and contribute to the system to enhance self.

In so doing, individual participants are helped to become integrated with the peer group so that they may have access to its support and protection in pursuit of growth and change. Independent action and individual perspectives are assisted so personal vigilance, curiosity, and contemplation are promoted and enhanced in pursuit of opportunity. Adult authority is made accessible for instrumental assistance, emotional support, and maintaining limits and boundaries of acceptable behavior. And finally, the individual is helped to comprehend and respond to the demands and opportunities of the culture that defines civilized life in his community.

LIMITS AND BOUNDARIES OF INTIMACY BETWEEN PERSONS IN AUTHORITY AND PARTICIPANTS

A troublesome dilemma often plagues persons in authority who wish to provide opportunity for attachment and bonding, and surrogate family experience. The struggle is one of establishing and maintaining appropriate separation between authoritative role and interpersonal relationship with recipients of service. The idea of parental figures becoming friends or even pals with those they serve is seductive but problematic.

The blurring of boundaries, as would be the case in such instances, is seductive in its potential to create illusions of intimacy and closeness. In real families, naive members often view inadequate boundaries and enmeshed relationships, particularly between parents and children, as ongoing exchanges of love. Unfortunately, such family arrangements may emerge out of a parent's narcissistic needs and are particularly destructive to children. Even the most innocent exchanges that violate the needed separation between authoritative role and the participant have numerous risks associated with them.

Primary among these risks is the service provider's exploitation of professional relationship to meet personal needs better met elsewhere. In such instances, a parental figure may have difficulty subordinating personal needs to the best interests of those to whom he provides service. To make wise but unpopular decisions may become an ordeal if a source of love is to be jeopardized.

Also, persons in authority often must contend with work-related issues and problems that are clearly of no concern to those receiving service. Unfortunately, knowledge of power struggles, conflicts, and problems between "adults" in a school or other setting is loaded with potential for difficulty for children. Just as life for children in conflict-ridden families is even more harmful than parental divorce, exposure to adult conflict to which children may be exposed in surrogate families can needlessly destroy opportunity (Cooper, Holman, and Braithwaite, 1983).

Similarly, some issues and behavior in the peer group are better kept from view of authority. Some of the private goings on of individual participants, and the group as a whole, are clearly their own business. In fact, adult knowledge of some activities places both the adult and children in a difficult bind.

In some such instances, even the most well-intentioned adults may be precluded from helping children involved in questionable, prohibited, or illegal activity. In most settings, administrative policies usually require responsible adults to report problematic events to designated authorities. Unfortunately, control rather than management becomes the priority once such a report has been made.

For example, most schools and other human service organizations have policies that declare abstinence to be the only acceptable behavior with regard to drug or alcohol use among adolescents. Though some adults may discover behavior to the contrary, they cannot, without jeopardy to their position, intervene in ways that support responsible use or attempt to reduce harm. This is so even though drug or alcohol use may be thought to continue despite admonition and/or punishment by persons in authority.

Unfortunately, a blurring of boundaries in such cases risks creation of troubling illusions and expectations among children or others receiving service. One illusion requires an omnipotent adult to keep such matters undisclosed in an act of unshakable loyalty, and regardless of potential personal cost. Another is that he will use his adult power to shelter those who have confided in him in order to pursue a transcendent goal of heroic rescue. The fantasy is that this transcendent goal justifies a benevolent conspiracy between parental authority and the served. In the end, the dream becomes a rationalization for violation of rules or policies, and the adult begins to blend with the peer group as a powerful, but nevertheless, over-aged member.

Consequently, as discussed above, many troublesome behaviors and arrangements inevitably come to light, and misguided adults will be forced to take action to protect themselves. The conspiracy will collapse, and the facts of troublesome behavior will be revealed. Those children involved will not only face the consequences of their actions, but will feel betrayed and abandoned by yet another untrustworthy adult.

Therefore, persons in authority must subordinate personal needs to the best interests of those they serve, and those best interests at times require unpopular decisions and actions. These realities highlight the need for appropriate boundaries. In the absence of stable, consistent, and benevolent maintenance of such boundaries, authority figures lose their efficacy as surrogate parental figures. They become untrustworthy because persons in positions of authority have needs of their own and eventually must withdraw from overly personal involvements.

UNCONSCIOUS ISSUES AND THE EXERCISE OF ADULT AUTHORITY

The fact that positions of authority contain living, breathing human beings beneath their mantle is loaded with potential for difficulty as well as benefit. These human beings possess a wide range of attitudes, values, beliefs, expectations, and personal needs. Unfortunately, certain behavioral predispositions can create serious problems in the provision of educational service to others.

This is especially so for those practitioners who might fall victim to what they are unaware of in themselves. The Pygmalion effect and the boundary issues discussed above are but two examples of problems persons in authority can create by acting on unconscious motivations. Unfortunately, many other unconscious impulses and reactions, with equally damaging consequences, can also find their way into the behavior of authority figures.

For example, repressed anger and hostility about past events and people can intrude into the present in dangerous ways. Sarcastic responses, hostile humor, and passive-aggressive behavior are subtle and insidious forms in which such latent negative feeling can shape immediate reaction. Undoubtedly, such expressions are abusive, leave their targets confused and angry, and destroy perceptions of benevolence. Obviously, they are a serious threat to trust.

Unconscious statements of another kind include tardiness, absenteeism, and disorganization. Narcissistic irresponsibility, job dissatisfaction, drug or alcohol addiction, depression, burnout, and unhappiness about institutional politics are among the wide range of forces that may drive such troublesome behavior. Regardless of source, persons in authority displaying such behavior do not inspire confidence and trust. At best, professional peers and those to whom they provide service see them as unstable and inconsistent. At worst, they see them as incompetent and dangerous.

Fortunately, the practicing educator or other human service professional does not work in isolation and has usable resources to resist such troublesome potential. These resources are the same social constituencies that serve all people in all social contexts. The authority of supervisory personnel, the peer group of professional colleagues, the cultural dictates and ethical standards of one's profession, and one's capacities for vigilance, curiosity, and contemplation all have potential to bring to consciousness what one is unaware of in self.

Individuals access these resources through consultation with trusted supervisors, case conferences with colleagues, active participation in professional organizations, and introspective self-monitoring. In this way, the professional can enhance self-awareness and promote personal growth by joining other professionals to create a family-like work environment, and by forming meaningful links with the larger professional community. In so doing, one may not only avoid some of the dangers described above, but will live the values and ideals one seeks to promote among those one serves.

REFERENCES

Barrett, E. (1983). *An Empirical Investigation of Martha E. Rogers' Principle of Helicy: The Relationship Between Human Field Motion and Power.* Unpublished doctoral dissertation, New York: New York University.

Caroll, C. (1985). *Drugs in Modern Society*. Dubuque, Iowa: W. C. Brown Publishers.

Cooper, J., Holman, J., and Braithwaite, V. (1983). "Self-Esteem and Family Cohesion: The Child's Perspective and Adjustment." *Journal of Marriage and the Family*, Vol. 45, pp. 153-159.

Fields, R. (1992). *Drugs and Alcohol in Perspective*. Bellvue, Washington: W. C. Brown Publishers.

Hamachek, D. (1978). *Encounters with the Self*. New York: Holt, Rinehart, and Winston.

May, R. (1972). *Power and Innocence*. New York: Dell.

Northouse, P. J. and Northouse, L. L. (1992). *Health Communication: Strategies for Health Professionals*. 2nd ed. Norwalk, Connecticut: Appleton and Lange.

Page, R. and Page, T. (1992). *Fostering Emotional Well-Being in the Classroom*. Boston: Jones and Bartlett Publishers.

Pope, A., McHale, S., and Craighead, W. (1988). *Self-Esteem Enhancement with Children and Adolescents*. Elmsford, New York: Pergamon Press.

Rosenthal, R. and Jacobson, L. (1968). *Pygmalion in the Classroom*. New York: Holt, Rinehart and Winston.

Watzlawick, P., Beavin, J., and Jackson, D. D. (1967). *Pragmatics of Human Communication*. New York: W.W. Norton and Company.

Wilmot, W. W. (1979). *Dyadic Communication: A Transactional Perspective*. 2nd ed. Reading, Massachusetts: Addison-Wesley Publishing Company.

Chapter 8

Custom and Tradition: Influence Through Culture, Precedent, and Social Precept

All living organisms wrest supplies from the environment to survive, but we, as human beings, have learned to create processes, procedures, and implements that lend stability and consistency to such efforts and resultant gratifications. These devices invariably capitalize on our realization that we are more effective at solving problems of individual survival and comfort by joining with others than by struggling alone (Roberts and Kloss, 1974).

As a result, many of our creations are not merely tools for dealing with the environment. They have important social meaning as traditional or customary practices and beliefs around which we organize cooperative activity. One may think of customs and traditions as habitual ways that we, as members of families, groups, organizations, and communities, behave in order to meet our individual needs (Malinowski, 1960).

Yet, a further perspective considers that custom and tradition serve as recipes for survival, and also as devices for imposing trustworthy secondary environments upon that provided by nature. Just as buildings, furnishings, heating, and air conditioning offer a physically stable secondary environment, parliamentary procedure (Robert, 1981; Sturgis, 1966), and rules of etiquette provide a socially stable secondary environment.

Hence, people construct many physical environments, and also develop customs and traditions to guide social behavior within them. These include diplomatic and official protocol for the halls of business, industry, and government (McCaffrey and Innis, 1985), and vehicular traffic laws and regulations for sharing the roadways. They also include everyday manners for behavior at the dinner table, in restaurants, theaters, religious settings, and a variety of transitional life events such as weddings, births, and deaths (Post, 1985).

When these secondary environments are established, variation in weather and season, the content of issues, levels of consensus, and tastes and preferences need not interfere with activity at formal meetings, informal social gatherings, and at traffic intersections. None of these creative innovations are available in the natural environment, but elaborate secondary environments have become the rule rather than the exception among peoples across the world.

In these ways, people not only use custom and tradition to solve practical problems of everyday life, but also to instill the community with social predictability. The latter links with the former because many solutions to practical problems of living require alteration of existing, or creation of new social arrangements. As a result, social aspects of such solutions are often integrated into the fabric of the community as mandated ways of behaving.

Thus, custom and tradition lend stability and consistency to participating in and deriving benefits from community life. Custom and tradition make trustworthy one's entry into community activity, the exercise of authority and power in the community, communication and intimacy among members, and conditions of membership within the community. Just as children who join one another must address the very basic issues of cooperation and sharing when building castles of sand, so must adults, as they join together to feed, shelter, and clothe themselves and their families.

CULTURE: AN INTEGRATION OF MEANING, SOCIAL PRECEPT, AND ACTION

Because the natural environment is complex and often unreliable and human needs extend beyond the basics of physical survival, we create almost uncounted numbers of customs and traditions to cope with a wide range of contingencies. People, in explaining their vast array of customs and traditions, refer to the intricate pattern of their beliefs and practices as their culture.

Even the most basic activity, such as a child learning to walk, is a product of teaching and learning, or culture, rather than an inborn reflex (Devine, 1985). The great variation between cultures in postural habits, footwear, walking "single file" versus abreast, and locomotor style and gait strongly indicate that basic bipedal movement is best described as a biologically based cultural trait (Devine, 1985). People express, even in apparently simple acts of moving about, their adherence to a variety of culturally determined beliefs and precepts about themselves and their world.

The family is profoundly influenced in similar ways. The cultural variation in customs and traditions surrounding courtship, marriage, childbirth, and child rearing are reflective of a great diversity of interpretation. In each human community, practices in every aspect of family life are part of a larger integrated system of culturally derived beliefs about gender, family, community, nature, religion, and the supernatural (Lefkarites, 1992). Adherence to such beliefs and practices in the community to which they are relevant gives family life the trustworthiness needed for child rearing in that community.

Subsequently, culture is the glue of community life. Through members' adherence to its customs and traditions, the community provides a sense of belonging, a shared vision of the world, and a variety of feelings and attitudes about the challenges of existence (Allen and Allen, 1990). Unfortunately, just as glue can become hardened, brittle, and fail catastrophically, the cultural bonds that hold together a community are neither automatic nor without their negative potential.

STABILITY AND UNIVERSALITY: SAFEGUARDS FOR THE COMMUNITY

Sociologists and anthropologists have an abiding interest in the processes and mechanisms through which customs and traditions come into being and are adopted by communities and groups. Debates about the efficacy of cultural innovation versus cultural diffusion notwithstanding, the most simple explanation is that some person or group invents a social or technical idea that other people find out about and try for themselves. The idea can emerge from the collaboration of members of a peer group, the ingenuity of one individual, or from persons in authority.

If the initial spark of an idea ignites enough interest in growing numbers of people, then it becomes identifiable as a "social trend" (Roberts and Kloss, 1974). Because social trends are usually an aggregate effect of the individual actions of many people, they are often unplanned and represent the self-interest of individuals rather than the common good of the broader community (Heberle, 1951).

For social trends to achieve stability as a customary or traditional way of doing things, people must test relevant practices and beliefs. Tradition may be established when enough people in a group or community find these practices and beliefs to reliably solve some problem or serve a needed function. The practices and beliefs must be found to work in trial after trial, and across the circumstances for which they are needed. One major test of any trend, then, is the test of time.

Many social trends are transient or faddish and do not pass this test. They fail because they are either ineffective, too costly, create problems equal to or worse than the ones they solve, or conflict too much with other strongly held values. Communism, fascism, hula hoops, slavery, racial segregation, thalidomide, the turkey trot, and the musical compositions of Salieri are all examples of cultural innovation that have been discarded over time.

In contrast, colleges and universities, separate public bathrooms for men and women, Judaism and Christianity, capitalism, literacy and the printing press, and the works of Mozart are constructs that have been sustained. However, the test of time is ongoing. Some of these, too, may go the way of the dinosaur as they lose efficacy or are superseded by new problems and new solutions to old ones.

In some cases, ideas and trends simply fade because of the failures just cited. In others, active opposition to them forces the issue as people organize social movements to resist trends they think to be troublesome for themselves and their community (Roberts and Kloss, 1974).

From a broad social perspective, such movements appear to be most prominently associated with struggles about social class, race, sex, and community priorities. Still, beneath the surface of these struggles, one can readily identify very basic concerns about community life. All such movements are reactions to established custom and tradition, or new trends that various segments of the community perceive to produce inequities in cooperation and sharing.

Some struggles are about membership status as it relates to power and influence. Others are about benefits to be derived from various community goals, methods, and values. The true challenge of these struggles is about the degree to which various segments of a community can subordinate their narcissism, acquisitiveness, and tribalism to the best interests of the larger community.

Though the test of time is a powerful safeguard, we are fortunate that time is not the only test. While many people confronting problems inherent to their territories develop admirable and creative innovations, others within their own community or in surrounding communities do not adopt them as custom or tradition. Thus, good ideas may vanish simply because they do not attract enough attention to be tested as a trend. To those who might adopt them, such ideas may seem too complicated, or the potential irreversibility of their impact too frightening.

On the other hand, some innovations stimulate so much attention that people within the inventor's own community begin to copy, modify, and adapt the ideas. These ideas then spread until many communities in an area where they are applicable also incorporate them into their culture. In this way, diffusion or universality is yet a second test through which the value of traditions and customs is confirmed.

Thus, for new ideas and subsequent trends to become truly integrated as customary or traditional ways of doing things, they must establish longevity and be adopted by more than a small minority of people in the community. Both of these tests are important because culture not only embodies activity, but also imposes rules for participation, explanation, meaning, and standards against which the individual may evaluate self and others. In these ways, culture pushes and pulls at behavior, feelings, and thought regarding self and one's world.

Therefore, the community uses these tests to protect itself against customs and traditions that are capricious, arbitrary, dangerous, and create unmerited social advantage for some and disadvantage for others. Unfortunately, these tests are not foolproof, and history is replete with tragic instances of their failure. History, particularly that which has been ignored, repeatedly reveals that the consequences of these failures create pain and misery for large numbers of individual people.

HISTORICAL CONSCIOUSNESS AND CULTURAL NARCISSISM

Since few groups and communities exist in total isolation from others, the cultural fabric of most might best be described as an intricate weave of invention and imitation. Unfortunately, the source of the threads that form the weave are often undifferentiated because many people live the ethos of their community with little or no consciousness of its history. Even among those with heightened historical consciousness, many may subscribe to grand reconstructions that have little resemblance to fact. As British aristocrat Thomas Macaulay observed in 1835, history abounds with kings thirty feet high, reigns thirty-thousand years long, and geography made up of seas of molasses and butter.

Thus, just as individuals unconsciously internalize the attitudes, values, and norms of family or peer groups, communities can live their culture in a manner that is oblivious to the profound internal and external forces that may have shaped it. In part, this occurs because the source of many traditions and social inventions is difficult to discern, even though the originators of some are well known.

The passage of time and generations causes this difficulty to become increasingly challenging. The time that tests the value of customs and traditions often lends obscurity to their origins and provides opportunity to fabricate distorted and glorious histories about them. Therefore, time serves to confirm customs and traditions as cultural icons, while it also permits adherents to indulge in narcissistic elaboration of their meaning and importance (Schlesinger, 1992).

Consequently, with antiquity, accountings of simple and expedient solutions, or even avaricious and banal ones, to practical problems of living often acquire a fantastic mythology. No doubt, modern myths about the behavior of Jesse James and Billy the Kid have transformed these villains of the Old West into heroic figures. In the folklore, art forms, and oral and written histories through which such mythology is transmitted, these and many other questionable notions may be portrayed to be timeless, culturally absolute, and sacred.

Resultantly, in the absence of historical awareness, the power of custom and tradition to influence the individual is amplified and exaggerated in dangerous ways. Just as the unconscious may trap individuals by depriving them of choice and causing personally injurious behavior to be repeated again and again, historical obscurity may force communities to relive the mistakes of the past, again and again.

CULTURE AND INDIVIDUAL EXPERIENCE

The manner in which culture organizes interaction with the social and physical environment may be seen to parallel that of personality in defining and organizing individual behavior and outlook (Marcus, 1993). The habits, traits, attitudes, perceptions, and values that organize and protect one's personality are analogues to the customs and traditions that organize and protect a community.

Of particular relevance to this discussion is the fact that culture does more than shape one's behavior. It also alters one's experience and consciousness because customs and traditions contain within them implicit and explicit explanation and inference about the issues and problems they attempt to solve. In consequence, culture confronts the individual with a myriad of claims about self and the nature of one's world.

As with most human constructions, such claims usually address a combination of rational and emotional issues. To be worthy of consideration, claims must work to satisfy practical needs and serve to maintain psychological comfort. It follows that the physical problems of food and shelter are paralleled by emotional struggles for self-esteem and identity.

To meet these diverse and, at times, conflicting needs, communities may embrace myth and mysticism to explain and justify their customs and traditions. As a result, cultures often contain a variety of rites and rituals that their respective community members piggyback onto practical behaviors. These rites and rituals are outward expressions of the struggle to maintain a balance between acceptance of harsh and unflattering realities, and the need to find inner peace.

For example, rites of passage such as weddings, baby showers, christening, bar mitzvahs, confirmations, graduations, and funerals bring families and communities together to share the joys of success and ease the pain of loss. The transitions these events mark confront us with the reality that our children will eventually grow up and leave us, and that we are all mortal. Such events permit us to mobilize spiritual and social resources so we are not overwhelmed by these joys and adversities. Though they acknowledge the reality of stress in transitions, most rites, rituals, and ceremonies are predicated on faith in unconfirmable claims and beliefs about the supernatural.

However, the expression "different strokes for different folks" implies that what is "good for the goose" is not always "good for the gander." Though the history of the first of these cliches suggests that it originally referred to sexual tastes and preferences, its usage has gradually come to refer to the very diverse ways people meet their needs. According to the derivation of the second cliche, those claims that offer practical solutions and inner comfort to some people do not do so for others.

As discussed in earlier sections of this chapter, many claims may cause problems and create discomfort for some segments of a community. For this reason, customs, traditions and, indeed, a culture cannot exist if they are ignored or resisted by large numbers of individuals who are depended upon for continuance of such social creations.

Therefore, proponents, advocates, and adherents emerge as conservators of customs and traditions in every community. Conservators will seek to maintain or even strengthen social support for those traditions they hold dear. They demand adherence by attempting to persuade, coerce, seduce, or corrupt other individuals to conform to behavioral proscriptions, and to accept relevant claims as truth. When conservators are active, determined, and organized, custom and tradition become political issues. When they are successful, custom and tradition find their way into public policy and law.

In these ways, custom and tradition become powerful behavioral mandates, and definitions of reality are then imposed. In well-developed communities, custom and tradition are codified into written documents such as a national constitution, religious scripture, or laws and regulations. The community may then identify those who resist as criminals, deviants, perverts, heretics, and reactionaries. And those in authority may attack them.

When tradition becomes truly time-honored, its written form assures its continuance for generations to come. This is particularly important because most people are born into families and communities, and often join groups and organizations, whose existence predates their birth by many years and generations. Because custom and tradition are associated with god-like illusions children hold about parents, children experience culture, family, and community as eternal and infinite.

Thus, custom and tradition acquire an aura of permanence, incorruptibility, and clarity that appeals strongly to individual needs for trustworthy rules, standards, precedents, and guidelines. When these needs are met, the individual person has a set of stable values, precepts, and explanations against which to weigh behavior, performance, and perception. This encourages the individual to be dependent upon and trusting of his or her culture.

Because of this, tradition and custom offer many benefits but also contain considerable potential for harm. They are another social constituency to which the individual must be carefully responsive. As described here and in Chapter 4, the standards of the community are a powerful force, and at times they are in contention with the dictates of authority, the pressures of the peer group, and the needs felt by the individual.

CULTURE AND SUBCULTURE: LAYERS OF COMMUNITY LIFE

Most people think about culture in terms of monolithic community. That is, they think of culture in its broadest sense as exemplified by nationality, ethnicity, race, religion, or the membership of a primitive tribe. Yet, where populations are large enough, communities contain many discernable sub-communities.

For example, in the United States we have no single homogeneous black, white, Asian, or Middle Eastern racial community, though people often speak as though we do. The black population is diverse because its members are either American descendants of enslaved Africans, or more recent emigrants who represent a wide range of African and Caribbean ethnic diversity. Similarly, whites represent the ethnic diversity of eastern, western, northern, and mediterranean Europe, and Asians and Middle Eastern peoples represent the diversity of their respective regions.

The subgroups of these larger racial populations each have a culture of their own that may radically differ from others of their own racial grouping. Further, each subculture extends, stretches, and bends larger American culture that surrounds it. Such smaller cultures are generally consistent with the culture of the larger surrounding community but also include customs and traditions that address their own special needs and beliefs. To meet these special needs, each smaller culture imposes its own customary and traditional beliefs and practices on its members. Evidently, in each smaller culture, every child emerges from the culture of the family into an ethnic and/or religious subculture, the culture of the immediate neighborhood, church, school, particular classroom and peer group, and the larger community.

When one considers culture from this perspective, the individual may be seen to contend simultaneously with numerous subcultures. Each group, organization, and sub-community in which one holds membership exists under the cultural umbrella of the larger community. Each, in turn, creates its own customs and traditions, with its various units and subdivisions doing the same.

Hence, true to the concept of America as a melting pot, the Constitution is a body of custom and tradition that dominates civic and political life in the U.S. Beneath the umbrella of the U.S. Constitution, one will find a vast array of federal, state, and local legal customs and traditions, many of which reflect the cultural beliefs, precepts, and values of various subcommunities. The U.S. Constitution is the cultural standard which measures the acceptability of these other mandated customs and traditions and every person must contend with all rules that pass the Constitutional test in every American community.

CULTURAL TYRANNY:
CHAOS AND DISORGANIZATION, REACTIVENESS AND INTOLERANCE, AND RIGIDITY AND INDIFFERENCE

As described above, an individual functions within a nesting of subcultures, each of which is subordinate to those that are larger and more dominant in a hierarchy of size and social power. As a result, people face many layers of custom and tradition. As these layers increase in weight and complexity, they also increase in inertia. That is, community response to new crisis and need is slowed and becomes cumbersome. Also, adjustment or elimination of anything established but no longer helpful becomes increasingly difficult, and requires more and more effort.

Under such circumstances, the beneficial opportunities and demands offered by custom and tradition are balanced precariously against considerable potential for tyranny and harm. In a troubled community, the individual may experience the cultural status quo as either chaotic and disorganized, reactive in negative ways, or rigid to a point of absolute and overwhelming indifference. When the balance is swung too far in any of these directions, the community loses its viability as a trustworthy resource to its members. It becomes unstable, and inconsistent, and members lose perspective about the place of community in their individual lives.

Interpersonal and intergroup relationships then become adversarial and antagonistic rather than cooperative and benevolent. Crises bring out the worst rather than the best in community members (Farney, 1992; Rose and Kotlowitz, 1992). In certain cases, warring factions may force truth to be subordinated to narcissistic and political ambition. As in the current era of "political correctness," contentious community members may be quick to bury reality beneath dogma and ideology in the conduct of organized social activity (Farney, 1992).

Unfortunately, such responses distract attention from the real issue that confronts all community members. This issue is either that people no longer trust each other to adhere to the customs and traditions that make cooperative living possible, or that existing traditions create distrust and divisiveness. This produces the instability and inconsistency of chaos and disorganization, the punitive defensiveness of overreaction and intolerance, and the nonresponsiveness of rigidity and indifference. The net result of these difficulties is that community members are deprived of positive, universally accepted, and time-honored custom and tradition that anchor stable values and standards. Concepts such as anomie describe the normlessness of such troubled communities (Durkheim, 1951).

Alienation describes the psychosocial reactions of people who struggle to sustain themselves in a troubled community (Robinson and Shaver, 1973). Prominent among the subjective experiences of alienated community members are feelings of powerlessness, discontentment, normlessness, anxiety, meaninglessness, cultural estrangement, and social malintegration (Middleton, 1963; Dean, 1961). The pain of these gnawing feelings is compounded by attitudes of distrust, pessimism, and resentment (Davids, 1955).

CUSTOM, TRADITION, AND CULTURE AND THE FAMILY

Preparation for life in the community begins in the family and is generally referred to as socialization. To become socialized, an individual must be taught by others the traditions and customs of the community's culture and the skills and beliefs needed to adhere to them. These customs and traditions, and their requisite beliefs and skills, boil down to cooperation, sharing, and attention to the impact of one's own behavior on other people.

Though children are socially dependent, they are not born socialized, in the least. For example, the normal two-year-old is destructive of property, insistent and demanding, unwilling to share toys, impatient, helpless and needy, has kicking and screaming tantrums, and can be quite violent in expressing feelings. An older, larger, and stronger version of such a child would be regarded as a monster, and could not be unleashed upon the community without serious consequences (Allport, 1955, p. 28). In this vein, the notion that "a wicked man is but a child grown strong," or to be more contemporary, "a child with a gun" suggests that child rearing is a race between socialization, and the development of physical and mental capacities to be truly evil and destructive.

Because they are the first to feel the bite of unsocialized behavior, parents, other adult family members, and older siblings begin the process of socialization. They levy demands that the child accept beliefs and master necessary skills to conform to the family's customs and traditions as the onrush of physical maturity permits. In this way, the family, to the degree that its own needs must be met, is a microcosm of the community, and a flight simulator for life in the community. Not only does socialization into family life provide tools for community life, but family members also demand that a child behaves in ways that reflect well on the family when he or she ventures out into the community.

As described in the first section of this book, the family, as a microcosm of the larger community, can have a culture of its own that spans many generations, and that culture can be troublesome (Schulman, 1973). The family can be chaotic and disorganized, punitive and controlling, or rigid and unresponsive in ways that resemble a troubled community. This is problematic because the family, in rearing its children, provides support, protection, and supervision to persons who are in the process of "becoming" (Allport, 1954). In part, this refers to the fact that neither the person "to be" in each child, nor the strength and resilience to emerge reasonably unaltered and intact from trauma and disappointment, are complete. Because young children are vulnerable and dependent in just these ways, the culture of the family provides the social resources and an atmosphere necessary for the embryonic adult to hatch into personhood.

Inadequacies in resources and a poisonous atmosphere can stunt growth and twist people before they can take truly effective action on their own behalf. As a result, a troubled family can be even more destructive than a troubled community.

No doubt, parents who become alcoholic, drug addicted, mentally ill, or lost in marital conflict can subvert a family's culture in ways that are terribly damaging. Certainly, some children of desperately troubled families are subject to extremes of mistreatment. Fortunately, these cases are the exception rather than the rule, even for troubled families. More commonly, troubled parents exhibit customary ways of dealing with their children that are less obviously negative, but may be grinding and destructive, nevertheless.

For example, some parents are so overwhelmed with responsibility and/or personal need that they have few emotional reserves to share with their children. Other parents may unwittingly pass on to the next generation a tradition of troubled parenting they received themselves. Thus, most children in troubled families are victims of a steady rain of subtle and insidious events. Customary practices in such families may include leaving children alone too often, not helping with homework, and showing no interest in other school activities. As a result, some children may repeatedly find their way to school with inadequate clothing and no breakfast. Additionally, some may be deprived of opportunities to participate in important community activities because of a lack of necessary and appropriate assistance from family members.

For others, the mess of a chaotic and disorganized home or the slovenly precariousness of a frequently inebriated parent may be too embarrassing to risk inviting friends to visit. In some cases, family members may lie or break promises, and even cheat their children and steal from them. Some children may repeatedly witness violent encounters in the home as adults act out the family's customary means of conflict resolution. For these reasons, in a family culture of neglect, predation, and/or chronic isolation, the child is forced prematurely to accept a tradition of responsibility for his own care.

At the opposite extreme, some troubled families may be so controlling and narcissistically involved in a child's life that the child is at risk of drowning in a morass of personalities. Developmental imperatives of establishing individuality and personal separateness are frustrated and distorted by a tradition of exaggerated togetherness and symbiosis.

THE SOCIAL MEANING OF A CHILD'S NEGATIVE FAMILY EXPERIENCES

A child's immediate experience of assaults, disappointments, and deprivations by family members is basic and direct. Not surprisingly, he feels pain, fear, sadness, and anger. Because human beings have evolved to be tough and resilient survivors of adversity, the meaning of occasional negative experience usually does not extend beyond the moment of occurrence. For this reason, family culture need not be perfect, but only good enough.

Still, if a child's negative experiences are extreme and frequent, the repeated behavior that causes the child's pain may be part of family tradition. When this occurs, the feelings associated with the child's negative experiences cease to be singular or closed-ended events. This is so even though the sensations that define these events may pass relatively quickly.

In such a family culture, a child's vigilance and sensitivity to threat are heightened to hair-trigger levels, but curiosity is dampened because the unknown portends too much danger. The child attemps to conform to a most honored family tradition, which is to maintain an idealized illusion of one's parents. Simultaneously, in an effort to understand what has happened, the child pushes anger inward and blames self for the pain of family experience. Because of this, the child becomes unlovable and unworthy in his own eyes, and begins a process of destroying self. Denying his outrage and energized by inexpressible anger, the child strives mightily for his parents' love by attempting to grant them what he believes they want most–to be rid of him! (Farberow, 1980).

The child's innocence, naivete, and desperate need for the love of an admired parent blind him to the truth of what is happening. The truth is that the child's parents, if not purposely victimizing the child, are, in some cases, unaware of the pattern of their behavior or its consequences for the child. They are, therefore, dangerously incompetent. In other cases, parents are aware of what they are doing, but are coldly indifferent to the consequences they inflict upon their children. These parents are dangerously irresponsible. Hence, custom, tradition, the law, and need for love trap the hapless child in a noxious family culture to which he is oblivious. Parents are unaware or uncaring and the child blames self for the pain of parental incompetence and irresponsibility.

Unfortunately, many cultures provide abundant opportunities and means for children to act out their self-blame. Though adolescent suicide is an all too common occurrence in our own society, a child ending it all in a single tragic act is relatively rare among even the most troubled of children. More commonly, such children engage in behavior that is indirectly suicidal and risk possible self-destruction in the longer term rather than certain and immediate death. Tobacco, alcohol, drugs, and delinquency are certainly available to those children determined to pursue them. However, even these culturally provided, though disapproved, avenues of risk are followed by a small minority of troubled children.

Usually, self-destructive children do things that may ruin their lives rather than end them. Tendencies to repeatedly defeat oneself in the innumerable competitions that are part of growing up, or to avoid the risks of failure by quitting before one even begins, are common, subtle, and insidious paths. Irresponsible behavior such as absenteeism, tardiness, carelessness, and culturally inappropriate dress and behavior are still other paths to ruined lives. In these ways, the child whose ability to trust has been damaged becomes marginal and untrustworthy himself, and is left to survive at the fringe of the community.

Healthy adults are not as inclined to be self-blaming and defeating as vulnerable children. In the adult world, maturity provides many tools for coping with others' hostility, incompetence, and irresponsibility. The victim does not blame self so readily, and the finger of culpability is more readily pointed at guilty parties. Very negative labels are applied to the manner in which these parties violate the person and domain of others. Unfortunately, these labels have powerful social meaning and are difficult and painful for children to apply to even the worst misconduct of family members.

An adult victim of violations which children may regularly suffer readily labels assailants as "brutes, bullies, and cowards." An adult refers to those who would abandon him at a time of need as "rats," and an adult victim's contempt is clearly evident in branding perpetrators as "users and leeches" for their exploitative ways. Adults disdain guilty parties as "traitors" for broken promises and violated commitments. And finally, an adult will revile irresponsible persons as "screw-ups" and "goof-offs" for their negligence.

These labels, and their extremely negative meanings, are very bitter pills for any child to swallow when connected with attitudes and perceptions about one's own parents or other family members. This is so, in part, because of the intimate connection between a child's sense of self and parental love, and the painful dilemma of risking rejection, and/or other vengeful acts, by those one needs so much. So, guilt, shame, and anxiety become powerful emotional levers many children are powerless to resist.

Unfortunately, the child's dilemma is compounded within the culture of most families and the surrounding community. These cultures place great premium on family loyalty. They demand that children honor and respect their parents, and that family members always present the family to the outside world in glowing terms.

Nevertheless, the objective facts and social meanings that define the victimization of children by their caretakers are terribly negative. As indicated repeatedly in this writing, one may define some children as victims because they are repeatedly abused. That is, they are assaulted physically, verbally, and/or psychologically. One may define others as victims because they are consistently exploited or used with no regard for the consequences of such exploitation. One may define still others as victims because they are neglected and left to do without necessities they cannot provide for themselves. Some children suffer repeated betrayal in a deluge of broken promises, confidences, allegiances, and agreements, and are also victims. And finally, some are abandoned to fend for themselves at times when parental support and protection are needed most.

To be sure, these destructive acts can represent the intermittently idiosyncratic behavior of a troubled parental adult, or siblings who are occasionally prone to scapegoating each other. However, such behavior can also become integrated into the culture of the family so that family members repeatedly and systematically respond to each other in destructive ways. When such families begin to damage a family member, they have become dysfunctional.

CUSTOM, TRADITION, AND CULTURE IN THE SURROGATE FAMILY

Though the process of socialization begins in the family, other entities begin to contribute as the child matures and begins to participate in community activity outside of the home. Churches, schools, recreation centers, civic and other organizations representing the range of community activity for children each influence the process. These organs of the community not only contribute resources and experience that are beyond the abilities of the family, but they also provide children with opportunities for healing and growth in areas where the family has failed. Needy children are exposed in this way to adults and children, and organizational cultures that may be alternatives to those available in a troubled home.

Fortunately, educators and others who provide service to children can create surrogate family opportunity at little risk and small cost. They can minimize these risks and costs by creating a working atmosphere of customs and traditions that benefit all children with whom they work, not just those with special needs. Except for suspicion of injurious physical abuse or neglect, one need not even identify children who live in troubled families. Many adults contribute to the most miraculous rescues and much of the greatest emotional healing for children on the brink while unaware of the facts of their heroism.

They do this by creating a culture of trustworthy customs and traditions around which children can participate in activities, talk with adults and other children, and establish personally meaningful relationships. Such a culture for children is analogous to a garden in which good soil, water, sunlight, and protection from predators and pests are abundantly available. These are the basic requirements for plants and children to grow to healthy maturity as comes naturally. Custom and tradition are the soil, water, and sunlight from which children may grow themselves into adults. Unusual individual attention to children or plants may be the exception in a well-managed environment.

Obviously, the cultural medium in which children can grow must be appropriate to their needs. Since children are dependent upon adults for the material necessities of survival and growth, this medium is largely social. Children's specific needs to which culture must respond are discussed below, and revolve around the theme of trust. Adequate response creates a social medium that is controlled and predictable instead of chaotic and disorganized. Such a culture is responsive and accepting as opposed to reactive and intolerant, and is flexible and caring rather than rigid and indifferent.

First, surrogate family culture must be responsive to a child's need for stability. As stable entities, custom and tradition must instill constancy into ways of relating, ways of doing things, and the limits and boundaries of behavior. Rules, routines, and important expectations are not changed on impulse or whim. Ambiguity and painful surprises are kept at a minimum so both adults and children can exercise such control.

Because the real world is constantly changing, and therefore unstable, surrogate family culture must work to maintain stability in the face of transition. Whether a new child has joined the group, another has moved away, a recreation leader has transferred to another community center, or a turtle in the class science project has died, participants should have reasonable and systematic access to resources beyond self in order to cope. Importantly, rites, rituals, and ceremonies must be developed to mark comings and goings that are endemic to classroom membership and other community settings.

Second, surrogate family culture must be responsive to a child's need for consistency. Consistency refers to a group's regular adherence to its customs and traditions. Do participants follow a rule or routine one day and ignore it the next? Do adults or a peer group punish or reward Johnny for certain behavior while they do not respond to Billy for the same acts? To feel safe and trusting, children need to observe consistency between behavior and consequence regardless of who displays the behavior or when it occurs. Thus, a tradition of consistency is an important element of a growth-promoting culture.

Similarly, children need to witness consistency between word and deed. Custom fosters trust when it embodies a tradition of basic honesty to share truth with children. Though the notion of truth seems to be such a simple thing, sharing it is not. This is especially so when one must share negative truths. From time-to-time, the surrogate parent and members of the surrogate family may face hard choices about what to say to one of its members (Northouse and Northouse, 1992, p. 261).

In some instances, paternalistic lying in an effort to shelter a vulnerable participant from painful truth may be a tempting option. In other instances, benevolent deception, which requires the use of distortion and half-truths, may serve this same purpose. On the other hand, unmitigated honesty may subject its recipient to unnecessary suffering. Unfortunately, revelation after-the-fact of even the whitest of white lies can shake trust very dramatically.

Clearly, trust is supported by a tradition of honesty in which surrogate families share truths that are important to a member's choices and decisions, and truths that an individual requests. For those issues that are personally relevant, a child needs to know that the people in his or her life say what they mean and mean what they say. As illustrated, honesty is a complex but important cultural imperative for children.

Third, surrogate family culture must follow a tradition of benevolence toward children. Children will feel safe and trusting once they recognize that customs to which they are subject are organized to promote their own well-being. A child must observe culture to bestow rewards enthusiastically and withhold gratifications reluctantly. The child must also recognize that custom and tradition have staying power in the face of anger, and will force unpopular decisions in the child's best interest.

Fourth, surrogate family culture must be responsive to a child's need for flexibility. In order for children to feel safe and trusting, they need to observe adaptive and pragmatically effective cultural responses to novel occurrences and unexpected events. Children become suspicious when custom and tradition appear to be rigid and arbitrary in adherence to established, but no longer effective, ways of doing things.

This applies to environmental contingencies as well as to the idiosyncratic and developing needs and inclinations of the child. It includes responsiveness to the cultural imperatives children bring to the human service setting from the outside. Language, moral beliefs, and religious practices may be immutable elements of survival in the family and subcommunity of a child outside of the school's or church's doors. To force a child to violate important customs and traditions of the outside world may destroy opportunity on the inside. Therefore, a readiness to make reasonable adaptations and exceptions is important to such children.

Moreover, healthy flexibility permits children to participate in the evolution and change of culture as it occurs. There is no reason why good ideas and innovations cannot emerge from individual children, smaller coalitions of the peer group, or the peer group as a whole. Regardless of outcome, when childrens' ideas are put to the same tests of time and universality as adult ideas, trust is reinforced in the surrogate family.

Fifth, children need surrogate family culture to provide a realistic and appropriate perspective about the purpose and importance of activities in which they are engaged. This includes setting healthy priorities, and establishing a workable balance between present- and future-oriented concerns.

For example, in instances where health and safety are at risk, custom and tradition may be strict and harsh to maintain order and discipline. In others, where there is much more freedom to make mistakes, to fail, or to laugh and play, the future benefits of present activity may be balanced against needs for relief from the pressures of the moment. The idea that all work and no play makes Jack a dull boy refers not only to dulled enthusiasm, but also to Jack's inclination to see his immediate social environment as rigid and uncaring. The culture of the surrogate family must acknowledge that work and fun are both important to children.

Trust is shaken when customary responses are over-reactive, attribute exaggerated meaning to relatively minor events, or when tradition minimizes what is serious to a child. Taking seriously a child's self-recrimination about his error costing his team a ball game, and keeping the outcome of the ball game in proper perspective are both important to trust.

The narcissistic, overly demanding, and destructive antics of "stage mothers" and some little league baseball coaches shake the child's confidence in the cultural meaning of participation in community activity (Weinstein, 1991). In the end, custom and tradition must reinforce trust by enabling people to step back from the heat of the moment to laugh at self and smile about the absurdity of events that seemed so important only a moment before.

Sixth, and finally, children need to know that the surrogate family follows a tradition of calmness, objectivity, and focus during crisis. At such times, when things seem to be getting out of control, children depend on custom as an anchor to ease their fears. They will be shocked and disappointed to find the traditions they heavily rely on to be mythical and illusory. This will occur when they are witness to the abandonment of custom and tradition, anarchic and wildly impulsive action, and the collapse of organized activity.

ADULT AUTHORITY AND CULTURE
IN THE SURROGATE FAMILY

To accept a position as surrogate parent to someone else's child is a troublesome proposition to sensible adults. Cultural prohibitions about intrusion into the private family life of other people, and personal concerns about becoming engulfed in the difficulties of a troubled child, are painful issues. For more personally needy adults, the wish to achieve glory in an heroic rescue, or even adopt and take home a needy but loveable child, are impossible dreams. Nevertheless, these are just a few of the fantastic and realistic extremes which concern adults about lending a helping hand to children in need. Fortunately, those on the front lines of the community do not need to fall victim to such extremes.

Though the needs described in the section immediately above are at issue whenever a family, group, organization, or community neglects, abuses, exploits, betrays, or abandons a child, surrogate parents need not extend themselves in unreasonable ways to address these needs. In many ways, consciousness of these needs may serve as principles and guidelines for the emotional care of children.

As the principles imply, a tradition of others "being there" for each other in ways that children can count on and that are appropriate to role is "good enough." In this way, culture, custom, and tradition provide children with the emotional resources to rescue and heal themselves. The process of rescue and healing is the same whether it occurs in the classroom, the school concert band, a local chess club, a Bible study group, the ball field, or any of the numerous settings where children and adults come together in the community.

Unfortunately, no guarantee of success comes from the best care the adult administers in the social medium of one's work with children. Therefore, the adult's primary concern should be about the process rather than the outcome. In essence, the adult's role is to create as many social and cultural lifelines as one can for the child to seize in his struggle to reach healthy maturity.

In the end, adults marshall cultural and social raw materials that enable children to construct a realistic internal image of themselves and their world as trustworthy entities. When successful, the children begin to take control of important aspects of their lives and to join peers and the larger community. They become optimistic and flexible in deriving meaning from the events of their lives, and begin to trust their feelings as a gauge of the impact of those events upon them. And most important of all, the children begin to regard themselves as precious and worthy. Thus, the true heros are the adults who serve the children in a responsible, competent and caring manner, the peers who join together to share their voyage to maturity, and the child who uses these adult and peer contributions to transcend the adversity of life circumstances.

REFERENCES

Allen, J. and Allen, R. F. (1990). "A Sense of Community, A Shared Vision, and a Positive Culture: Core Enabling Factors in Successful Culture-Based Change." In R. D. Patton and W. B. Cissell (eds.), *Community Organization: Traditional Principles and Modern Applications*. Johnson City, Tennessee: Latchpins Press, pp. 5-19.

Allport, G. W. (1955). *Becoming: Basic Considerations for a Psychology of Personality*. New Haven, Connecticut: Yale University Press.

Davids, A. (1955). "Alienation, Social Apperception, and Ego Structure." *Journal of Consulting Psychology*, Vol. 19, pp. 21-27.

Dean, D. (1961). "Alienation: Its Meaning and Measurement." *American Sociological Review*, Vol. 25, pp. 753-758.

Devine, J. (1985). "The Versatility of Human Locomotion." *American Anthropologist*, Vol. 87, No. 3, September, pp. 550-570.

Durkheim, E. (1951). *Suicide*. Glenco, Illinois: Free Press.

Farberow, N. (ed.). (1980). *The Many Faces of Suicide*. New York: McGraw-Hill Book Company.

Farney, D. (1992). "Ethnic Identities Clash with Student Idealism at a California College." *The Wall Street Journal*, December 2, pp. a1 & a4.

Heberle, R. (1951). *Social Movements: An Introduction to Political Sociology*. New York: Appleton-Century-Crofts.

Lefkarites, M. P. (1992). "The Sociocultural Implications of Modernizing Childbirth Among Greek Women on the Island of Rhodes." *Medical Anthropology*, Vol. 13, pp. 385-412.

Malinowski, B. (1960). *A Scientific Theory of Culture*. New York: Oxford University Press, pp. 36-42.

Marcus, A. (1993). "Remarks to the Faculty." Faculty meeting of the School of Education, New York University, September 13.

McCaffrey, M. and Innis, P. (1985). *Protocol: The Complete Handbook of Diplomatic, Official and Social Usage*. Washington, DC: Devon Publishing Company.

Middleton, R. (1963). "Alienation, Race, and Education." *American Sociological Review*, Vol. 28, pp. 973-977.

Northouse, P. G. and Northouse, L. L. (1992). *Health Communication: Strategies for Health Professionals*. Norwalk, Connecticut: Appleton and Lange.

Post, E. L. (1985). *Emily Post's Etiquette* 14th ed. New York: Harper and Row, pp. 77-216.

Robert, H. M. (1981). *Robert's Rules of Order Newly Revised*. Glenview, Illinois: Scott, Foresman and Company.

Roberts, R. E. and Kloss, R. M. (1974). *Social Movements: Between the Balcony and the Barricade*. St. Louis, Missouri: C. V. Mosby Company.

Robinson, J. P. and Shaver, P. R. (1973). *Measures of Social Psychological Attitudes*. Ann Arbor, Michigan: Survey Research Center, Institute for Social Research, University of Michigan, pp. 245-251.

Rose, R. and Kotlowitz, A. (1992). "Strife Between UAW and Caterpillar Blights Promising Labor Idea." *The Wall Street Journal*, November 23, pp. a1 & a8.

Schlesinger, A. M. (1992). *The Disuniting of America: Reflections on a Multicultural Society*. New York: W. W. Norton, pp. 45-72.

Schulman, G. (1973). "Treatment of Intergenerational Pathology." *Social Casework*, October, pp. 462-472.

Sturgis, A. (1966). *Sturgis Standard Code of Parliamentary Procedure,* 2nd ed. New York: McGraw-Hill Book Company.

Weinstein, S. (1991). "Prevention of Emotional Distress, and Drug and Alcohol Abuse Among Musicians and Other Arts Performers and Students." *Canadian Band Journal*, Vol. 15, No. 4, Summer, pp. 39-40.

PART III.
THE SURROGATE PARENT
IN THE REAL WORLD:
SPECIAL CONSIDERATIONS
AND IMPORTANT CONCERNS
ABOUT SURVIVAL

Introduction

The chapters in Part II present important understandings about the place of one's own experience, the peer group, adult authority, and customs and traditions in the psychological development, socialization, and education of the individual. An individual's need for environmental stimulation drives sensation-seeking behavior that produces individual experience. Individual need for affirmation of such experience leads one to join with peers to find consensual validation. One also seeks affirmation through support, protection, and supervision in relationships with persons who hold special knowledge and responsibility. And finally, the need for reliable standards to use to assess experience of self, others, and the world draws the individual to the customs and traditions of one's own culture.

Early in life, the individual is totally unprepared to draw upon any of these personal and social resources. Individual experience characterized by raw and chaotic sensation provides little instrumental utility and no lasting gratification in the absence of meaning. No peer group exists, and adult authority is experienced as a nurturing extension of self. The infant has no notion of custom and tradition, even though the culture into which one is born has profound impact on the way an individual will be raised.

The child finds meaning as internal means develop to organize the chaotic stream of consciousness. When these means are in place, individuals may harness vigilance, curiosity, and introspectiveness to comprehend one's experience. Until this occurs, one is totally dependent upon the family for survival and growth toward maturity. The family not only meets the child's material needs, but also prepares the child to be self-sufficient, to respond to the social obligations of life, and to enjoy existence. Unfortunately, disrupted family circumstances may subvert and impair such preparation.

In instances where the child is not irreparably damaged, the surrogate family may serve as a supplementary or alternative source of support, protection, and supervision. As an alternate resource, the surrogate family assists the individual to enhance the scope and meaning of personal consciousness, to join the peer group, to relate to authority, and to understand the customs and traditions of one's culture. In so doing, the surrogate family becomes a trustworthy environment in which one may consider one's own subjective world from the perspective of one's peers, adults with authoritative views, and the cultural precepts of one's community.

Because the preceding sections of this book focus heavily on issues relevant to life within the surrogate family, the present section addresses some important concerns that are external to the surrogate family. These concerns confront educators and other human service providers with both opportunity and danger.

Since families and surrogate families alike exist within the culture of the larger community, educators and other human service providers must be alert to the social meanings and risks of their work. Because we live in a violent and highly litigious society, these meanings and risks have serious implications. There is no reason to think that families who are harsh and abusive toward their own members will be any less so if threatened or offended by outsiders.

In addition, upheaval about broad social issues of rights, privileges, and protections linked to membership and status in our society has raised sensitivity to very high levels. This is particularly true among minority groups, the disabled, women, and, most recently, among childrens' advocates. All of these groups are seeking redress for real and imagined abuses and social inequities of the past.

The recent spate of legal prosecutions for sexual harassment, spouse abuse, and sexual molestation of children are disturbing evidence that our society is in crisis over issues of authority and intimacy. Parents, grandparents, teachers, day care workers, clergy, lawyers, doctors, dentists, university professors, politicians, entertainers, and professional athletes are among those charged with a range of abuses including sexual exploitation of students, children, patients, clients, and admirers.

Some investigations smack of witch-hunts and hysteria, and others suggest that those who exploit this hysteria to gain recognition as victims stand to accrue many benefits in their quest for redress. Unfortunately, some who gain protection may use their protection in ways that create new victims. These new victims may unjustly lose hard-won positions, financial assets, reputations, and, in the worst cases, their freedom.

Chapter 9 focuses on these dangers and what they mean for human service practitioners who may jeopardize self in the act of giving to others. There is possibly no more sensitive area into which to venture than the private matters of someone else's family. The surrogate family is one that may easily alarm fragile parents, themselves distrustful of authority, and fearful about their children's affections. Tactics and strategies for service and survival under such potentially dangerous circumstances are the emphasis in the final section of this book.

In addition, Chapter 10 discusses ethical issues and concerns particularly relevant to the surrogate parent. The surrogate parent is in a powerful position to influence children and others to whom he or she has become significant. The surrogate parent also has unusual access to personal and private realms of young people's lives. Chapter 10 addresses important questions about the responsibilities of such powers.

Chapter 9

Violent Children, Abusive Families, and Dangerous Communities: A Survival Guide for the Surrogate Parent

Because American communities and families of the 1990s are in the midst of an alarming epidemic of violence and abusive behavior, education and other human service fields have become hazardous professions. Not long ago, chewing a stick of gum in class was nearly a capital offense for students caught by strict teachers. This benign disciplinary issue of the past stands in stark contrast to the frightening behavior of the present.

Violence and abuse have become terrifying problems in our schools, hospitals, courthouses, transportation systems, and human service facilities, providing chilling evidence of the danger and momentum of current social trends. Today, pupils entering our schools are frisked and checked with metal detectors to catch those who might be carrying illegal drugs and semi-automatic firearms. The halls of these same schools are now under the surveillance of police patrols rather than the scrutiny of student monitors.

These measures are now necessary because children who come to schools and other centers of community activity are victims, as well as perpetrators in our increasingly lethal epidemic. As a result, fear, emotional trauma, injury, and even death threaten both those who receive service and those who provide it in community centers.

On the other hand, irresponsible acts by some human service professionals and others in positions of authority have damaged the public trust. Sensational stories appear constantly in the media about this politician or clergyman or that entertainer or sports figure who abused his power or status to extract forbidden material or sexual favors. The public's image of physicians (Toner, 1994) and lawyers is now tainted by greed and arrogance. As a result, some individuals in the best position to organize and lead social movements in opposition to current trends have lost credibility, and are viewed with contempt by frustrated communities.

This has produced a parallel epidemic of civil and criminal litigation as communities and those claiming status as victims seek redress for real and imagined violations. The cost of defending against a lawsuit is often very high, and pretrial settlements may reward plaintiffs who are encouraged by opportunistic attorneys to bring frivolous civil charges. Considering the United States has less than 5 percent of the world's population, but 40 percent of the world's lawyers, this may not be surprising. Thus, educators and others who provide human service in our violent and litigious society face not only physical dangers but also legal hazards, too.

For these reasons, this chapter focuses on problems and personal risks of those who offer surrogate family opportunity under the difficult circumstances described above. Because competent and responsible teachers, clergy, social workers, recreation leaders, and others providing socially oriented services are on the front lines, they must take care not to become casualties in the struggle to repair and strengthen the fabric of our troubled society.

To be productive and safe, service providers should understand the nature of the risks they face, and develop appropriate strategies and tactics to neutralize them. In the absence of caution, the most capable educators and human service practitioners will have nothing to offer if they lose their jobs and professional reputations, if grinding negative experience burns them out, or they suffer serious legal difficulties. The narrative that follows describes some of the problems and proposes practical solutions to them.

THE DOUBLE-EDGED PROBLEM OF CHILD ABUSE

Increasingly, very young children have become targets in the current epidemic of violence and abuse. As a result, American communities have been forced to at last confront a genuine problem long ignored (Weinbach, 1994), hidden (Gardner, 1993), and even accepted as a cultural variant in some segments of our society

(Hegar, 1994; Price, 1986). Practices such as infanticide, flogging of children, and selling children into slave labor are an abhorrent part of our history.

The hesitancy to intervene on behalf of children stemmed from long-standing conflict between powerful and opposing values. On the one hand, the individual's rights to choose whom to wed, whether to have children, and how to educate them are cherished protections of family privacy. They guarantee parents' freedom to bring up their own children, and childrens' entitlement to associate with and be reared within their own families (Hegar, 1994, p. 213). Implicit within these protections is an acknowledgment that the family is an irreducible and basic element of society.

On the other hand, safety and security are important values to the community. Because children are vulnerable to abuse and neglect, and poorly socialized children may eventually become threats to social order, society confronts an opposing set of concerns about the actions of caretakers (Sullivan, 1994, p. 217). These concerns acknowledge that when a parent fails to help children develop internal control over their behavior, society must create and impose very expensive external controls. These concerns also acknowledge that child rearing is inextricably linked with the destiny of the community.

Unfortunately, this broader concern of the community created even greater problems regarding child protection instead of helping to clarify the responsibilities of caretakers. Control of children, rather than protection of them, became the important priority. Parents in charge of providing food, shelter, and other care for their children were also expected to channel their children's energies and behavior in socially acceptable directions. Further, they were expected to use whatever means were required.

This problem was amplified by attitudes toward and perceptions of children. Parental caretakers often viewed the child as an untamed beast, incapable of reasoning, who needed fear, threat, and punishment as preparation for entry into polite society. Biblical proverbs and social comments such as, "He who spares the rod hates his son," or to "Spare the rod is to spoil the child!" and "Children should be seen but not heard!" convey these attitudes with painful clarity. Similarly, the image of children's peer groups dictated that, without forceful and coercive control by teachers, police, and parents, such groups would rapidly deteriorate into roving bands of vandals and scalawags.

Consequently, the individual child was alone with, dependent upon, vulnerable to, and helpless against omnipotent caretakers, and recognized those truths. Given the limited understandings of child development in earlier times, and the negative attitudes about children most communities wanted things exactly that way.

Therein lies the dilemma of child protection. In order to intervene on behalf of children and its own future interests, a community must address the unpleasant prospect of disrupting family autonomy. In so doing, society must ultimately choose between the integrity of the family or the welfare of children. Communities have chosen to avoid the issue of child abuse throughout most of our history because it forces society to choose between the evils of permitting abuse to continue or taking children from their parents.

Our historic indecisiveness and ambivalence about the issues raised by child abuse are dramatically illustrated in the 1866 case of Mary Ellen (Price, 1986, p. 285). This young girl was beaten, starved, and chained to her bed. The incident drew attention to the fact that customs and traditions of our society gave priority to child control rather than child protection. Society made strong demands on parents and gave them free reign to control their children, but had not created an agency to protect children.

Astonishingly, the American Society for the Prevention of Cruelty to Animals was the one organized group to finally take up Mary Ellen's cause. Only later did some concerned citizens form the Society for Prevention of Cruelty to Children. Despite the tragic circumstances of Mary Ellen, and those of numerous other children, child abuse remained largely ignored throughout the first half of the twentieth century.

Without realizing it, educators contributed to the social invisibility of child abuse. According to one estimate, as many as 90 percent of teachers see abused and neglected children in their classrooms (Carnegie Foundation for the Advancement of Teaching, 1988). Sadly, many of these teachers are hesitant to report their suspicions because of fears that are probably common to most people who harbor similar suspicions. Among their concerns are fears about personal involvement, violating the privacy of a family, alienation of and retaliation by family members, and doubts about personal competence to accurately identify and appropriately report instances of abuse (Berrick and Barth, 1991).

Despite such long-standing and deep-rooted reservations, awareness and concern about child abuse have increased dramatically since the late 1960s. This mounting concern culminated in passage of the National Child Abuse Prevention and Treatment Act of 1974. In part, this sudden awakening occurred because the number of victims of maltreatment had increased to approximately between 900,000 and 1,000,000 children annually (American Humane Association, 1989; Daro and Mitchel, 1990; National Center on Child Abuse and Neglect, 1992). These figures included 25 percent of all female children who had possibly been victims of sexual molestation prior to age 18 (Hendricks-Mathews, 1991). Clearly, even though the community is obliged to protect its vulnerable members, it neglected to address child welfare issues until the dangers and social costs posed by damaged children grew too large to ignore.

TROUBLING CHANGES IN CHILD PROTECTION

Unfortunately, society overreacted to this realization by over-broadening new legal definitions of child abuse and by producing laws that may be too stringent (Hegar, 1994; Weinbach, 1994). As a result, the well-intended federal legislation to fight the problem may have been subverted in unanticipated ways.

This overreaction appears to have ignited a new wave of hysteria. Not unlike the Salem Witch Trials of 1692 in which 19 innocent people were hanged, or Senator Joseph McCarthy's 1950s hunt for communists that ruined careers and reputations, a modern witch-hunt targets the "child abusers among us" (Gardner, 1993).

As a result, frivolous and absurd child sex-abuse charges burgeon among those that are probably valid. The motives behind some highly questionable charges are apparent in child custody suits in which vengeance and opportunism are clearly visible. In other cases, the absurdity of some charges is evident because they concern abuse in settings where surreptitious behavior with children is almost impossible.

Sadly, this hysteria is fanned by media dramatizations that convey a message that there is no such thing as a false accusation of child molestation (Rabinowitz, 1993). Worse, the federal funding provided by the 1974 Child Abuse Prevention Act has strengthened the "child protection establishment" and provided its personnel with financial incentives to encourage even the most preposterous charges of child abuse (Gardner, 1993). This conflict of interest is only one element of a child protection system that has become biased toward validating charges of child abuse rather than seeking truth.

An important provision of this act is that all human service professionals are now legally mandated to report suspicions of child abuse. Legal requirements such as mandated reporting and immunity from prosecution have most certainly brought authentic cases of child abuse to the attention of those responsible for protecting children. However, to pressure or create opportunity for people to make unfounded or even fabricated reports, and then provide protection from accountability for such reports, creates a powerful potential for abuse of the child protection system. No doubt, some mandated reporters make ludicrous charges to protect themselves rather than children, and some individuals use the system in malicious and opportunistic ways.

Unfortunately, the ravages of this hysteria only begin at the point of a report of suspected child abuse. Children, their families, and their friends may then become the targets of overzealous and coercive investigators who ask leading questions and, at best, selectively attend to the answers they receive (Gardner, 1993). Often, examiners' tactics create conditions that heighten suggestibility and may distort the responses of children from whom they are gathering information (Ceci and Bruck, 1993 a,b). Therefore, some investigations more closely resemble inquisitions than attempts to uncover the truth. Constitutional protections of the accused are often ignored and their rights to due process denied.

Even after an investigation is completed, the hysteria may be compounded in court. This occurs because, since the 1980s, U.S. criminal courts are admitting increasing numbers of children as witnesses in child sex-abuse trials, and almost all state legal systems have dropped requirements for corroboration of children's testimony in such cases (Ceci and Bruck, 1993a, p. 408). These realities present grave dangers to the prosecution of child abuse cases. Despite claims to the contrary by some child protection advocates, younger children are more vulnerable to suggestive influence than older children and adults and will lie when motivated to do so, (Ceci and Bruck, 1993a, p. 433). In addition, younger children can distort and fabricate in powerfully convincing fashion (Ceci and Bruck, 1993b, p. 11).

These dangers are compounded by the fact that even though young children are very capable of recalling events of their lives and reporting them accurately, the conditions under which their reports are obtained in child abuse investigations can defeat efforts to find truth. Despite the likelihood that child testimony may be tainted by examiners, and that child abuse experts to whom children report their victimization can be easily deceived, juries have convicted individuals accused of child abuse solely on the basis of the testimony of two- and three-year-old children. They have done so in the absence of any other evidence that abuse had actually occurred. It follows that the innocent who are accused of sexually abusing children are in great danger of undeserved penalty, and the community is in danger of falsely exonerating and setting free the guilty.

Because of the current atmosphere of suspicion and paranoia, false accusations in connection with child abuse and neglect are a serious concern for even the most responsible, trustworthy, and ethical workers involved in the care of children. This is particularly true for charges of sexual abuse. Thus, dangers that amplify the need for action against our society's onslaught of destructive and murderous behavior provide both opportunity and risks to those with the courage and dedication to step forward.

Undoubtedly, educators willing to work with the potentially violent children of seriously disrupted families, and who do so in hysterically fearful communities, are desperately needed. It is reasonable and appropriate to require educators and other human service providers to report suspicions of child abuse. Yet the fact that they may, in turn, be the target of false accusations is a frightening possibility.

Fortunately, the chances of this occurring are remote when reasonable care is exercised. Nevertheless, those who wish to provide surrogate family opportunity must be constantly alert to the physical, social, and legal dangers of helping troubled people from troubled families in troubled communities.

FAMILIES AND VIOLENCE

Apparently, an important source of violence in the community is violence in the family. Violent children usually come from violent parents who teach violence as a means for settling differences (Wodarsky and Hedrick, 1987). In these families, parents not only model violent behavior, but also fail to provide their children with the training and skills needed for other more constructive methods of resolving conflict and managing interpersonal tensions.

To be effective, such training cannot be provided in a haphazard manner or as an offhanded aside to child rearing. The strategies and tactics of negotiation, compromise, and consensual resolution (Gordon, 1970) demand important cognitive, interpersonal problem-solving, and communication skills (Spivack, Platt, and Shure, 1976). These tools of mediation can be taught, and attitudes encouraging their use can be promoted in schools (Rotheram, 1980; Cox and Gunn, 1980; Schrumpf, Crawford, and Usadel, 1991; Schrumpf, Freiburg, and Skadden, 1993). They can also be reinforced in other human service settings (Rathjen, 1980). Still, they are best transmitted to children as a stable and consistent part of family life, where the value of peaceful resolution to rational and emotional issues develops in parallel with developmental needs (Camp and Bash, 1980; Robin, 1980).

Some parents, themselves reared in a violent family atmosphere, do not have these skills and understandings, nor the personal and emotional resources to offer them in a thoughtful and systematic way to their children. In addition, the more general behavior of these parents toward their children is apt to lack the stability, consistency, and benevolence important to healthy child rearing. In such cases, extremes of abuse, neglect, betrayal, exploitation, and abandonment may be common experiences for children who pass their violent and painful legacy on to others.

Sadly, this legacy starts to develop at a time when its destructive potential is greatest (Zuravin, 1994). It begins during the formative early years of childhood when, as described in Chapter 1, one is most dependent, vulnerable, and impressionable (Price, 1986). As the child struggles toward maturity, a major challenge may be survival, to a point where one can begin to fend for oneself, or escape violence and adversity.

Fortunately many do emerge, reasonably intact, despite such a legacy (Zuravin, 1994; Weinbach, 1994). At that point, entering a sensitive and responsive community may be purely a matter of luck (Crouch, 1994, p. 47). Despite the best of intentions, the community may exacerbate problems of violence and abuse that began in the family. The availability of alcohol and drugs, dramatic portrayals in the media, like-minded peers, and weapons that support violent acting out are often beyond community control (Paige and Paige, 1993). Inadequate resources and passivity on the part of agents of the community may communicate indifference that further frustrates such children. In this way, forces within and outside of the family produce abused and neglected children. These children, in turn, are more likely to be abusive and negligent toward self and peer groups (Crouch, 1994 p. 30), adult authority and the larger community (Rivara and Widom, 1992), and, eventually, their own children (Kaufman and Zigler, 1987).

THE ENIGMATIC CHILDREN OF VIOLENT FAMILIES

Many abused children of violent families respond to their aversive home environment in ways that are as enigmatic as their lives. Some grow up to be reasonably happy and functional adults, even though the ranks of the abused are overrepresented on many negative indicators of quality of life. Obviously, violence and abuse in the family is an important risk factor in problems such as drug and alcohol abuse, delinquency, depression, school failure, mental illness, poverty, and a variety of other miseries. But abuse during childhood does not guarantee irreparable damage to all children who are victimized.

As discussed at the very beginning of this book, it is unclear why some children thrive despite the adversity of their lives. Constitutional factors such as temperament, physical toughness, and physiological adaptability may be important. Historical factors such as the age of onset and severity of abuse seem important, too. Moreover, social factors such as availability of helpful adults and other community resources are potential influences on outcome, as well. In fact, one factor that seems to be consistently associated with success in the face of adversity is the availability of alternative adults who may serve as parental surrogates. Sadly for some children, this may not be enough to salvage their lives, either.

Unfortunately for those who do not thrive, there are many ways to fail. For example, some abused children's behavior is situationally adaptive but is developmentally and socially maladjustive (Crouch, 1994, p. 31). In some instances, they survive violent family circumstances by fading into the woodwork. Their passive and withdrawn way of operating permits these children to avoid being noticed by those whom they fear. While this tactic provides such children with a modicum of safety at home, it does not serve their best interests in other circumstances of opportunity.

No doubt, countless numbers of such children have fallen through holes in community safety nets because educators and other human service providers simply have not noticed them. Harried and overextended adults often are alert to, and have their strength drained by children whose behavior creates problems. These adults have little remaining energy for noticing and attending to those children whose passivity makes them a seemingly benign presence.

On the other hand, some abused children do not respond in such a passive manner. Their behavior runs to the opposite extreme as they actively, and often violently, express their frustration and rage. Though passive children survive by hiding, this later group survives by seeking attention in negative ways, exhibiting excessive aggression, and attempting to create untenable problems for those they wish to keep at bay.

Children who use either strategy commonly face the problem of seriously impaired capacities to trust. These impaired capacities are expressed in the variety of ways described above when the children enter educational and other human service settings. The net result is that these children either miss opportunity that is available to them, or destroy opportunity before they can seize it.

Thus, the self-defeating behavior that underlies such losses is the acting out of this profound distrust. These children may be suspicious to the point of paranoia about the motives and intentions of others, and pessimistic and cynical about the outcome of situations and challenges they must face. Their self-protective vigilance often leads to distortions and negative misinterpretations of harmless events and innocent exchanges, and evokes extreme reactions to these events and exchanges. Sadly, the child who ducks and flinches when others close by use their hands to animate their speech, provides a simple and tragic portrait of this profound distrust.

Because of such difficulties, if the problem of trust is an important issue for these children and adolescents, they are often untrustworthy, themselves. The chaos, disorganization, and unpredictability of their behavior brings instability to their relationships with others. Their impulsiveness and reactivity instill their social relations with perplexing inconsistency. Their lack of empathy and abundance of angry and sadistic feelings make benevolence difficult and vengeance all too easy for them. Their rigid ego defenses and limited repertoire of social competencies rob them of flexibility. The seriousness of consequences from earlier errors and transgressions deprives them of perspective, and seriously limits their ability to laugh at absurdity and self. And finally, crisis and stress in concert with isolation and suppressed frustrations produce either paralyzing retreat or explosive irrationality in these children, rather than calm deliberation and constructive resolution.

In consequence, the adult who attempts to rekindle trust faces children who strive mightily to defeat just what they need most. Such safety and freedom children yearn for, but also struggle against, creating a difficult dilemma for themselves and those who might be of assistance. On the one hand, passive children may be inert and helpless as one opportunity after another appears for the taking. Assisting these children to seize these opportunities may take herculean effort. On the other hand, hostile and vindictive children, who have no notion of the ramifications of their destructive behavior, may lash out with any means at their disposal. For the latter group, physical assault and false accusation are among the dangerous possibilities in this era of violence and hysteria.

The enigma for potential surrogate parents is that, on the one hand, these children truly need helpful adults, but on the other, such adults must take great care not to become dangerously embroiled in the chaos of these children's lives. No doubt, the circumstances that produce poorly socialized, violent children make these children a threat to those who would come close in an effort to help them (Sullivan, 1994, p. 218).

ISSUES OF SELF-PRESERVATION
FOR THE SURROGATE PARENT

As the narrative above indicates, some risks exist when creating surrogate family opportunities for the children who need them most. Fortunately, in schools, day care facilities, and other settings, these risks can be reduced or eliminated through good policies regarding relations with children, and by adults exercising care to avoid creating suspicions of impropriety (Aronson, 1991, p. 186).

This means that the hazards of surrogate parenthood need not be viewed as analogous to risks of the battlefield medic. The medic shares dangers with combatants in an almost random way. A more reasonable analogy would be to the physician who reduces danger to himself by following stringent hygiene. The physician wants to avoid contracting the infectious diseases he treats. Therefore, clean hands, appropriate dress, and carefully limited physical contact are primary elements of prevention for both the physician and the surrogate parent.

Sexual abuse is a particularly sensitive area of concern. Young children, ages three to four, appear to be most vulnerable, but rates of incidence of such abuse in child care facilities is estimated to be relatively low, at 5.5 per 10,000 children (Aronson, 1991, p.185). With young children, abuse is most likely to occur during toileting, nap time, early morning, or late evening. However, school-aged children (Gil, 1979), and adolescent girls have been found to be at risk, too (Finkelhor, 1979). Educators and others providing service to these populations must be appropriately cautious.

For the surrogate parent, this recommendation of caution is particularly important. For one thing, family-like relationships have implicit connotations of intimacy that are beyond the usual. Further, trust is an important element of surrogate family experiences; any adult behavior that children construe to violate their trust may draw unusually extreme reactions. Powerful feelings of betrayal, neglect, abuse, abandonment, or exploitation can produce a torrent of retaliation and vengeance regardless of whether or not violations of trust actually occurred.

The stability, consistency, benevolence, flexibility, maintenance of perspective, and calmness during crisis that draw children to a potential surrogate parent may serve to protect the adult. However, they are not enough when that adult encounters the position of imposing reasonable demands or limits on an unreasonable and potentially vindictive child. In addition to their own capacities for nastiness, such children may also influence and mobilize the peer group in dangerous ways.

This can be especially problematic in the current social atmosphere if the peer group goes on a rampage of accusation. The surrogate parent must not forget that the "witches" of Salem were hanged largely on the basis of statements by children which these children later recanted. Accusations of sexual molestation by younger children, and sexual harassment and statutory rape by older ones, are modern equivalents to the dangers of life in Salem, Massachusetts in 1692.

POLICY AND SELF-PROTECTION
FOR SURROGATE PARENTS

Obviously, one cannot be completely immunized against all of the various hazards of providing service to people. Still, establishing and implementing sound policies, exercising good judgment, creating an open environment in which one's actions are in view of colleagues and other adults, and additional safeguards will go a long way to protect the surrogate parent. Aronson (1991) provides a list of potentially problematic issues which are important guides to the policies and procedures of professional practice. Though Aronson addresses caretakers of very young children, most of her ideas are applicable to all settings and for work with children and adolescents of all ages.

One issue is the imposition of discipline and restraint upon children. The school or other facility that provides care and activities for children must spell out acceptable methods and procedures for managing disruptive behavior. The surrogate parent must take great care to operate within the limits and boundaries of these policies in those unhappy instances where discipline or restraint of a child is necessary. The surrogate parent must also remember that coercive, corruptive, or seductive tactics may work to control some behavior problems, but each has its liabilities and risks.

Therefore, as a general policy, the individual practitioner should avoid physical intervention that a child might construe to be corporal punishment, or genuine corporal punishment. Discipline and restraint should first be aimed at defusing the explosive feeling that is behind unacceptable acting out. Separating children from the source of their frustration is an important and useful tactic for surrogate parents. "Time-outs" for younger children, or taking a break from troublesome situations for older ones, is often enough.

If this tactic fails to restore order, admonition and negotiations about rights and privileges can be a next step. When no procedure seems to work, the adult in charge should send for other adult assistance. Further, the adults must remember that preventing children from injuring self or others is a major responsibility under such difficult circumstances.

A second issue concerns screening prospective staff and volunteers. Maintaining sufficient numbers of competent staff is important to the safety of all, but the urgency of staffing needs must not place expediency before caution. The people who commit acts of sex abuse in human service facilities are not usually known sex offenders and have all the trappings of normalcy, such as being married and having children of their own (Aronson, 1991, p. 185). Therefore, policies and procedures for personnel selection and hiring should make screening for child abuse difficulties an important priority. Those who arouse suspicion should not be hired.

Where possible, those concerned with surrogate parenting should be active on personnel committees, and participate in reviewing credentials, interviewing candidates, checking references and background, and observing the new staff member during the initial probationary employment period. Without a doubt, one's own safety and security can be enhanced or diminished by the conduct of colleagues and other adults to whom children are exposed.

A third issue is isolation of adults with children. The surrogate parent should avoid this situation and create activity areas that provide for visibility and supervision at all times. Trustworthy cooperating adults should serve as observers of each other whenever possible, and all should exercise care about supervising parents and other family members who may visit. In addition, open doors and open spaces should be standard practice when possible and where appropriate. Policies regarding this issue are particularly relevant to children's and adult bathrooms, and other isolated spaces where a balance of security and privacy is important.

A fourth issue deals with suspicion of parental child abuse or neglect. As discussed above, educators and other human service providers are mandated reporters of suspicions of child abuse. Therefore, policies regarding indicators of abuse and procedures for reporting should be clear.

These policies are important to the surrogate parent for several reasons beyond the legal mandate. First, injuries, marks, or conditions that lead to suspicion are likely to be of undetermined origin at the time they are discovered. Though it is not the duty of the educator or most other human service providers to investigate their cause, the possibility exists that parties accused may attempt to redirect blame at a later time. The accused may do this by claiming that a child was harmed at school or in some other community facility.

For this reason, school and human service personnel should observe every child at the beginning of every day for injuries or conditions that might be construed as signs of abuse. If such injuries are present, even in cases where the teacher or other adult in charge does not suspect abuse, the child should be sent to the facility's medical office to at least document that the child arrived at the facility with a preexisting condition. If the school nurse or physician suspects abuse, then a report should be filed at that point.

All of the policies discussed above address issues that are loaded with potential for adversarial struggles between educators and children or their parents. These struggles may pertain to disciplinary actions, accusations about the actions of one's colleagues, supervision and protection of a child, or accidents and injury to a child. In general, policy regarding these issues and their various manifestations should be designed to assure the best possible support, protection, and supervision for children. However, such policies also must seek to minimize potential for conflict between staff and other adults involved with children, and provide a strong legal position for staff who are falsely accused of impropriety.

SOUND JUDGMENT AND SELF-PROTECTION FOR THE SURROGATE PARENT

While sound, well-implemented policies offer some protection, they are no substitute for the exercise of sound judgment on the part of the individual educator or service provider. This is particularly true for those who find themselves in the position of surrogate parent.

Some guidelines about the exercise of good judgment follow. These guidelines are intended to add rationality to what may seem to be a purely intuitive process. Though artistry is an important part of good education and human service, one must always be prepared to explain, in words and logic, the reasoning behind actions that others call into question.

The first guideline is to create and prepare participants, from the start, to understand and follow rules, routines, and procedures. Educators and other persons in charge must communicate clearly about the limits and boundaries of productive and acceptable behavior, and their own responsibilities to monitor such behavior. When necessary they should explain, demonstrate, and provide opportunities to rehearse any special procedures or routines that are important to participation in activities. As persons in authority, they should not wait until problems arise to solve them in a reactive manner.

In this way, potential for dangerous, activating emotions, such as anxiety or anger is reduced. Additionally, when adults in charge exercise control in clearly defined circumstances, there will be few surprises and a minimum of shaken confidence. Understandably, a strong protest awaits the punishment or restraint of a child or adolescent for violating a rule about which he was unaware. Moreover, to reject that protest by saying "Well, now you know!" may damage trust and generate powerful resentment.

A second guideline is to maintain appropriate social distance. As discussed at length in Chapter 7, adults in authority must establish and maintain healthy limits and boundaries of intimacy. Violating these limits and boundaries creates troubling illusions for children, along with feelings of having been cheated when the illusions dissolve. Such violations also create circumstances that can arouse the suspicion of children and adult observers about inappropriate behavior. This heightens one's vulnerability to accusation.

Unnecessary physical contact, off-color jesting, and seductive or flirtatious behavior can all lead to a bad end. Thus, the surrogate parent must seek and find ways to be close, and to express affection, caring, and concern that serve the child but also protect self.

A third guideline is to keep interpersonal aspects of work with a child within the confines of the activities at hand. If the surrogate parent is an art teacher, relations with children should be primarily focused on artistic endeavors. If the surrogate parent is an athletic coach, then relations with players should be primarily limited to sports participation. The same is true for band directors rehearsing for concerts, drama teachers preparing for the school play, clergy conducting Bible study, and recreation leaders taking hiking expeditions.

If young artists, chess players, scientists, athletes, or others, from time to time, ask for advice or seek to discuss issues in their lives, it is certainly appropriate to be helpful. However, to become overly involved in social activities that are peripheral to the primary activity may, again, create unwarranted expectations and fantasy, and a window of vulnerability to disappointment and accusation.

When tempted by such extra-curricular possibilities, the adult must look inward to discover what personal needs would be satisfied if business is mixed with pleasure. In all likelihood, responsible adults will conclude that their own needs are best met through participation in enjoyable activity and satisfying relationships with their own peer group.

OTHER SAFEGUARDS

The policies and guidelines discussed above are all aimed at the goal of developing and strengthening trust between service providers, children, and their parents. Because of this, the goal and its supporting policies and guidelines are consistent with the role of surrogate parent.

In addition, this goal and the recommendations above also serve purposes of protection for those who would fill this role. The first of these purposes is to minimize ambiguity and maximize clarity about the motives and intentions behind the behavior of educators and other service provides. In this way, the possibility of suspicion can be minimized. Furthermore, strained interpretation, innuendo, and distortion leading to gossip, dubious presumptions, and malicious accusation will have no credibility should a problem arise.

The second of these purposes is to reduce the likelihood of conflict which causes service providers, children, and their parents to become hostile adversaries. The anger and antagonism that are often generated under such circumstances can at times drive reasonable people to act out in dangerously unreasonable ways. The policies and guidelines above work to defuse confrontations before they lead to violence or accusation.

Unfortunately, the effects of good policies and sound judgment can be undermined by personal habits and tastes. In some schools and service settings, educators and service providers must conform to fairly strict rules regarding dress and grooming. Other service settings may impose few, if any, such demands. Also, some educators and other service providers may work with populations that are very sensitive to personal habits and tastes while others may serve populations who are oblivious to them.

In this instance, the important concerns are a service provider's personal habits, dress, and grooming. If any of the above shake confidence or create other problems for children, a time to pause and reconsider is at hand. Not only is trust at issue, but the adult's importance as a role model is jeopardized. These are very sensitive matters to those providing surrogate family opportunities to children.

Examples of such problems include the attractive female high school teacher wearing tight-fitting and revealing clothing to work, or the handsome muscular male gym teacher displaying his physique in similar fashion; or, on the other hand, the bohemian art instructor who shows up at a recreation center in paint-spattered and torn denim overalls and a sweatshirt. Similar examples can be conjured up for other human service settings, as well.

Though the clothing in the examples above may in no way be reflective of incompetence or irresponsibility on the part of its wearers, it conjures up impressions and fantasies about them as people. Sadly, for some children, especially very young ones, the boundary that separates impression and fantasy from reality is weak at times. For this reason, personal behavior that may be too easily interpreted as seductive, distracted, or slovenly and careless should be avoided by educators and other service providers when they are on the job. This is doubly true for the surrogate parent.

This recommendation states that, for their own security, service providers present themselves as being intently focused on providing the service for which they were hired. They should do so in all the ways possible. They should avoid flaunting their good looks or making political and social statements in their presentation of self, unless those actions are important to the programs in which they are engaged. They need to display the important message that they have no distracting or questionable motives or intentions. Appropriate grooming and attire for an individual's role transmits this message and contributes to confidence and trust in an individual's professionalism.

The same is true for the work space where service is provided. This applies to a classroom, a rehearsal hall, an office, a gymnasium, or an art studio. Its cleanliness, orderliness, comfort, the appropriateness of its decor, and the adequacy and condition of its supplies and equipment communicate important messages. These messages translate quite readily into impressions about the trustworthiness of the service provider. The recommendation in this case is that educators and other service providers constantly monitor and maintain their work space for appearance, safety, healthfulness, and function.

These safeguards are consistent with the policy recommendations and the guidelines discussed above. Certain principles drive them all. Safety and security in educational and other community centers of activity are enhanced by the creation of clear impressions about the conditions of provided service. Educators and other practitioners communicate these conditions in their verbal statements and their actions. Statements and actions should be consistent with one another, open and visible for all to see, and express an abiding commitment to the best interests of those being served.

Thus, the alarming dangers of physical, social, and legal violence described much earlier in this chapter need not intimidate those committed to helping children in need. However, the current environment is not one to enter carelessly or with a cavalier attitude. The social problem of abused children, and the problems caused by them and their violent families pose some risks to those who would help. The current atmosphere of hysteria surrounding the protection of such children amplifies these risks. The environment is to be entered with caution and care.

Fortunately, the suggestions presented above for reducing these dangers are simple and practical. They are by no means exhaustive either. What is important here, is that the risks inherent to good work as a surrogate parent can be minimized, if not eliminated, without drastic expenditures of time and energy. The establishment of policies, procedures, and practices that protect the interests of children and assure one's own security is an important key. The use of sound judgment in interpersonal transactions between ourselves and the children we serve is another. Finally, vigilance, interest, and thoughtfulness about the impressions we create about ourselves among those we help is yet another key to safety and success.

REFERENCES

American Humane Association. (1989). *National Analysis of Official Child Abuse and Neglect.* Washington, DC.

Aronson, S. S. (1991). *Health and Safety in Child Care.* New York: Harper Collins Publishers, pp. 182-193.

Berrick, J. D. and Barth, R. P. (1991). "The Role of the School Social Worker in Child Abuse Prevention." *Social Work in Education,* Vol. 13, pp. 195-202.

Camp, B. and Bash, M. A. (1980). "Developing Self-Control Through Training in Problem Solving: The Think Aloud Program." In D. Rathjen and J. Foreyt (eds.), *Social Competence: Interventions for Children and Adults.* New York: Pergamon Press, 1980, pp. 24-53.

Carnegie Foundation for the Advancement of Teaching. (1988). *The Conditions of Teaching: A State by State Analysis.* Princeton, New Jersey.

Ceci, S. J. and Bruck, M. (1993a). "Suggestibility of the Child Witness: A Historical Review and Synthesis." *Psychological Bulletin,* Vol. 113, No. 3, pp. 403-439.

Ceci, S. J. and Bruck, M. (1993b). "Child Witnesses: Translating Research into Policy." *Social Policy Report of the Society for Research in Child Development,* Vol. 7, No. 3, Fall.

Cox, R. D. and Gunn, W. B. (1980). "Interpersonal Skills in the Schools: Assessment and Curriculum Development." In D. Rathjen and J. Foreyt (eds.), *Social Competence: Interventions for Children and Adults.* New York: Pergamon Press, pp. 113-132.

Crouch, J. L. (1994). "Does Abuse as a Child Result in Irreparable Harm in Adulthood? No." In E. Gambrill and T. Stein (eds.), *Controversial Issues in Child Welfare.* Boston: Allyn and Bacon, pp. 29-33.

Daro, D. and Mitchel, L. (1990). *Current Trends in Child Abuse Reporting and Fatalities: The Results of the 1989 Annual 50 States Survey.* Washington, DC: National Commission for the Prevention of Child Abuse.

Finkelhor, D. (1979). *Sexually Victimized Children.* New York: Free Press.

Gardner, R. (1993). "Modern Witch Hunt–Child Abuse Charges." *The Wall Street Journal,* February 22, p. A10.

Gil, D. (1979). *Child Abuse and Violence.* New York: AMS Press.

Gordon, T. (1970). *Parent Effectiveness Training.* New York: Wyden.

Hegar, R. L. (1994). "Are Legal Definitions of Child Abuse Too Broad? Yes." In E. Gambrill and T. Stein (eds.), *Controversial Issues in Child Welfare.* Boston: Allyn and Bacon, pp. 211-215.

Hendricks-Mathews, M. K. (1991). "A Survey of Violence Education: A Survey of the STFM Violence Education Task Force." *Family Medicine,* Vol. 23, pp. 194-197.

Kaufman, J. and Zigler, E. (1987). "Do Abused Children Become Abusive Parents?" *American Journal of Orthopsychiatry,* Vol. 57, pp. 186-192.

National Center on Child Abuse and Neglect. (1992). *Child Abuse and Neglect: A Shared Community Concern.* Washington, DC.

Paige, R. M. and Paige, T. S. (1993). *Fostering Emotional Well-Being in the Classroom.* Boston: Jones and Bartlett, pp. 205-233.

Price, J. H. "The Family and Child Abuse."(1986). In R. Patton (ed.), *The American Family: Life and Health.* Oakland, California: Third Party Publishing Company, pp. 285-293.

Rabinowitz, D. "Deception: In the Movies, on the News." *The Wall Street Journal,* February 22, 1993, p. A8.

Rathjen, D. P. (1980). "An Overview of Social Competence." In D. Rathjen and J. Foreyt (eds.), *Social Competence: Interventions for Children and Adults.* New York: Pergamon Press, pp. 1-23.

Rivara, B. and Widom, K. (1992). "Childhood Victimization and Violent Offending." *Violence and Victims,* Vol. 5, pp. 19-35.

Robin, A. (1980). "Parent-Adolescent Conflict: A Skill-Training Approach." In D. Rathjen and J. Foreyt (eds.), *Social Competence: Interventions for Children and Adults.* New York: Pergamon Press, pp. 147-211.

Rotheram, M. J. (1980). "Social Skills Training Programs in Elementary and High School Classrooms." In D. Rathjen and J. Foreyt (eds.), *Social Competence: Interventions for Children and Adults*. New York: Pergamon Press, pp. 69-112.

Schrumpf, F., Crawford, D., and Usadel, H. C. (1991). *Peer Mediation: Conflict Resolution in Schools*. Champaign, Illinois: Research Press Company.

Schrumpf, F., Freiburg, S., and Skadden, D. (1993). *Life Lessons for Young Adolescents*. Champaign, Illinois: Research Press Company, pp. 111-148.

Spivack, G., Platt, J. J., and Shure, M. B. (1976). *The Problem Solving Approach to Adjustment*. San Francisco: Jossey Bass, 1976.

Sullivan, R. (1994)."Are Legal Definitions of Child Abuse Too Broad? No." In E. Gambrill and T. Stein (eds.), *Controversial Issues in Child Welfare*. Boston: Allyn and Bacon, pp. 216-221.

Toner, R. (1994). "The Doctor is Rarely In." *The New York Times*, Sec. 4, February 6, p. 1.

Weinbach, R. W. (1994). "Does Abuse as a Child Result in Irreparable Harm as an Adult? No." In E. Gambrill and T. Stein (eds.), *Controversial Issues in Child Welfare*. Boston: Allyn and Bacon, pp. 42-46.

Wodarsky, J. S. and Hedrick, M. (1987). "Violent Children: A Practice Paradigm." *Social Work in Education*, Fall, pp. 28-42.

Zuravin, S. J. (1994). "Does Abuse as a Child Result in Irreparable Harm in Adulthood? No." In E. Gambrill and T. Stein (eds.), *Controversial Issues in Child Welfare*. Boston: Allyn and Bacon, pp. 36-41.

Chapter 10

Ethical Issues for the Surrogate Parent

Introducing the topic of ethics in the final chapter of a book about fostering trust may seem odd. Since ethics are so important to trust, one would expect the topic to be presented first rather than last.

Nevertheless, the prior chapters of this book describe how an educator or other human service provider may establish trust with distrustful young people, and do not mention "ethics." Though Chapter 9 addresses current sensitivities about unethical behavior, the emphasis there is on minimizing some of the burdens and dangers that are inherent in being a surrogate parent.

These preceding chapters describe how to help young people repair, maintain, and strengthen themselves after their capacities for trust have been damaged. The discussion about theories, strategies, and tactics does not speak in moral or ethical terms, but one can readily identify many ethical and moral implications. Certainly one can probe the ethics and morality of the hostile, irresponsible, or incompetent adults and peers whose behavior wrought such damage in the first place.

Unfortunately for those who alreay have been victimized, an examination after the fact may be too late and mean too little. The very young victims of unhappy circumstances have no grasp of the idea that those, who caused them to suffer, behaved immorally or unethically. Instead, they learn of pain and disappointment, the world as a dangerous place, and self-blame.

This does not mean that the ethical concerns of surrogate parents are to be relegated to the trash heap of intellectual afterthought. Nor is the fact that ethics is the final topic of this book intended to promote such an idea. Rather, the intention here is to argue that ethical considerations specific to the surrogate family do not achieve primary importance until after an individual becomes a surrogate parent. Only then does the unusual power of the position become a concern.

In part, this occurs because the surrogate parent is only indirectly involved with the negative history of children in need. Also, most human service professions have codes of ethics to define morally acceptable behavior in standard practice. These codes of ethics are a part of the background of contexts in which educators and other practitioners normally provide service.

However, when young people attribute surrogate parent status to an adult, ethics jump to the foreground. Because the surrogate family can be so helpful, yet so disarming for such children, the surrogate parent must go beyond intuition, expedient practicality, and personal values when confronting ethical issues. This is necessary because the ethical choices and decisions of the surrogate parent must ultimately become part of a positive new legacy for vulnerable children in need.

Further, parental surrogates have heightened access to the private life of, and profound influence over, individuals who form such a special attachment with them. Ethics are irrelevant in the absence of power (Weinstein and Lagudis, 1980), but once a surrogate parent acquires special powers, they must be exercised with great care. Therefore, stringent ethical discipline is an absolute necessity.

As implied above, this writing was organized to stress the belief that the surrogate parent's power is derived from success at filling the role rather than any automatic predetermined status. There is no official position of "surrogate parent" and one does not enter the human service environment with a badge or insignia telling those being served that they must adopt the practitioner as a parental substitute. The educator or other human service provider earns that status when individual young people trust the individual enough to grant it.

Thus, the power of the surrogate parent's position comes last, not first. And, when shaken trust jeopardizes one's position as a surrogate parent, one loses one's power first, not last. Therefore, this, the final chapter, describes important and, at times, sensitive ethical issues about maintaining one's status in this fragile position after it has been achieved.

THE DELICATE MORAL POSITION
OF THE SURROGATE PARENT

The position of surrogate parent is fragile because of the very special powers and responsibilities that are inherent to it, and the ease with which those powers may disappear. As mentioned above, these powers emerge from an enhanced potential to influence individual and peer group beliefs, values, attitudes, and behavior. The surrogate parent is also in an advantaged position to interpret custom and tradition. Similarly, the surrogate parent acquires unusual access to the private world of young people, individually and in groups. These powers are the product of trust.

The surrogate parent must not underestimate the magnitude and importance of these powers. In medical settings, patients cite trust as the most important factor in accepting recommended treatment and consider this trust largely a product of interpersonal relationship (Penman et al., 1984). In fact, the influence can be so profound that even placebos have curative powers when enthusiastically offered by a well-liked and trusted physician (Goleman, 1993). In this vein, there appears to be great potential for the advice and recommendations of well-liked, trusted, and enthusiastic practitioners to be accepted and followed in other human service settings.

Therefore, exercising such power benevolently and managing the responsibility to do so are foundational to trust. In many ways, helping children in need of surrogate family experience is similar to catching a very large fish with a very light fishing line and a flimsy fishing pole. A few poorly timed mistakes, and both child and fish are lost. If one is not careful, one may find oneself in hot water, as well. But, when these prizes are carefully reeled in, the fisherman and the surrogate parent can have profound influence over the destiny of each.

This chapter on ethics addresses issues about the positive and negative potential of such profound influence. To retain this power of influence, an individual must not be corrupted by it. The surrogate parent must operate from the important moral high ground.

ETHICS AND THE ROLE OF SURROGATE PARENT

Generally, when one considers ethics, one thinks of them in connection with organized professions. In fact, the readers of this book most likely will be members of a human service profession that has a code of ethics to guide practice. Though a code of ethics is important to each profession, there is no such thing as a professional surrogate parent. Because the role of surrogate parent emphasizes issues of trust as a powerful ancillary focus, surrogate parenting might best be considered a propitious extension of one or another form of professional service.

The mentally, socially, and emotionally healthy surrogate parent may possess the right instincts and inclinations to be trustworthy. Still, informed moral and ethical consciousness, and an understanding of ethical principles that underlie trust are indispensable to surrogate parents as professional persons. This is partly so because the surrogate parent must make decisions about many actions which raise ethical or moral issues with no clear-cut resolutions (Northouse and Northouse, 1992, p. 255; Greenberg and Gold, 1992, p. 6).

Additionally, the most emotionally robust individual has personal blind spots and vulnerability to ill-considered knee-jerk response. Because we are all human in this way, others may rightfully demand explanations of decisions with which they are forced to live. Consciousness and intellectual awareness can successfully guide the exercise of power in complicated situations where instinct and personal inclination cannot. Intelligent understanding also provides language and reasoning to communicate to other people the rationality behind important decisions and actions.

Because trust is so fragile, surrogate parents must answer a challenge whenever they are asked to account for their actions. If children share power in the surrogate family, the surrogate parent is invariably responsible for the outcomes and consequences of his actions, whether intended or unintended, and foreseeable or unforeseeable (Callahan, 1976). This is particularly relevant when the surrogate parent's actions violate the wishes and values of children affected by those actions.

ETHICAL PRINCIPLES AND SYSTEMS

The complexity of the environment in which education and other human services are offered has great potential to raise bewildering moral issues. On one hand, the practitioner must maintain an abiding awareness of the needs and best interests of those served. On another, institutional policies and resources guide and limit practitioners' options in the work setting. And on yet another, the current epidemic of violence and abuse in many communities requires that self-protection be an important priority. Hence, the surrogate parent, from time to time, ends up on the horns of one or another of a dizzying array of confounding ethical dilemmas.

Ethics, as a branch of philosophy, represents an aspect of human intellectual development that attempts to add rationality to value-laden cultural and emotional concerns about moral issues. The social and legal concerns discussed in the introduction to this section, and again in Chapter 9, and potential issues and problems created by new technologies, have caused ethics to become a serious concern and a rapidly developing field. For instance, biomedical ethics is a prominent focus of current attention.

In very basic terms, ethics, morals, and morality address the problem of determining the rightness, or goodness, of various choices and actions. When we say that certain actions are unethical or immoral we have decided that they are incorrect, wrong, or bad.

Such decisions do not merely represent idealistic dreaming or metaphysical contemplation. They are of critical importance to the strength and vitality of human relationships. Not only do ethics and morals serve as internal controls on the behavior of persons with status and power, they also provide the foundation of trust between people as peers. Thus, ethics and morals codify and explain many social norms and expectations. They provide logic and words to define the nature of exchanges, protections, and cooperations that make social existence possible.

Because morality is so important to the integrity of the community, society has developed ethical principles and systems for defining what is moral and what is not. The principles serve as rules or definitions of moral and immoral actions (Greenberg and Gold, 1992). Society not only attempts to explain and persuade in regard to morality, it exacts social penalties for immoral behavior. Punishment, shame, and guilt are powerful negative reinforcers.

Because society can remove special rights and privileges it initially grants to the professions, professional communities must be responsive to ethical issues. With this in mind, health care and other professional communities have developed ethical codes that provide principles to guide practice. A principle common to many professional codes of ethics defines as immoral any behavior that causes harm, fails to prevent harm, or does not remove harmful potential. By the same reasoning, refraining from harming others, preventing harm, and removing potential harms is moral. For this reason, abuse, neglect, betrayal, exploitation, and abandonment not only are immoral, but they destroy trust, and jeopardize professional standing (Ceci and Bruck, 1993).

Similarly, many professional codes oblige members to actively contribute to the well-being of others in addition to demanding that they perpetrate no harm. Immoral behavior includes instability, inconsistency, rigidity, unrealistic perspectives, and response to crisis that deny others the benefits of service or raise potential for harm. In contrast, benevolence may be identified as moral behavior, while it also strengthens trust and professional standing.

Autonomy and justice are still other ethical principles that guide democratic society (Greenberg and Gold, 1992). These principles define seduction, corruption, and coercion as immoral because they wrest personal control from individuals. Further, they may deny individuals a fair share of their own entitlements. Such immoral actions prey upon one's vulnerabilities to deception, temptation, and superior strength. Informed personal choice, persuasive argument, equity, and fairness are moral counterpoints to behavior that tyrannizes.

Though the above principles appear to be simple and clear cut, their application is not. In some instances, applicable ethical principles are in conflict with one another. In others, mitigating circumstances must be considered in deciding what is moral and what is not. In still others, the benefits and protections of the individual must be balanced against the proportionate good of others. Clearly, ethics and morality cannot be served by simple recipes that one can follow in a mechanical fashion. Values, perceptions, beliefs, attitudes, and ideology can all intrude upon ethical decisions.

To cope with this complex problem, two ethical systems appear to have emerged for deciding about moral issues. Each addresses one side of the polar opposite needs described in Chapter 4. As a result, each has certain advantages and weaknesses relative to the other in guiding the application of ethical principles.

These human needs indicate that ethical principles must be stable and time-tested on the one hand, and that they be open to flexible interpretation on the other. Thus, "rule ethics" is a system that acknowledges the need for stability, and "situation ethics" is a system that acknowledges the need for flexibility. However, when either system becomes entrenched and monolithic in any social context, serious problems of trust arise.

Though rule ethics offers confidence inspiring stability, the system's rigidity and absolutism separate it from the practical problems it must address. Choices are defined in black or white with no shades of grey in between. Various actions are considered to be intrinsically evil or good, and inherently right or wrong regardless of circumstance. As a result, moral judgments are responsive to doctrine rather than reality. This leads to great difficulty in coping with complex issues in dynamic and changing social environments.

In contrast, situation ethics permits one to weigh the conditions and circumstances under which ethical issues arise and ethical principles need be applied. This system has real advantages in coping with a rapidly changing world. Yet, ethical principles may get lost in the shuffle as actions deemed immoral at one time may be judged to be moral at another. As a result, the system is very vulnerable to subversion and expediency by those who subscribe to it.

As one can readily see, we have no foolproof ethical principles or systems for applying them. As a result, some moral decision making may feel more like an emotionally charged wrestling match than calm, intellectual deliberation. Therefore, the surrogate parent must ultimately make many moral choices guided by ethical principle and wisdom, yet truly representing leaps into an abyss. For better or worse, one must be prepared to live with and accept responsibility for the consequences of each decision and action.

SUGGESTIONS FOR COPING
FOR THE SURROGATE PARENT

Fortunately, the surrogate parent can exercise a number of helpful personal prerogatives for coping with ethical issues. As stated earlier, the major ethical concerns of surrogate parenthood, above and beyond the ethics of a profession, involve the use of personal influence and access to information about children's private lives. An individual can create and implement personal policies and exercise personal judgments that may ease some of the burden of these responsibilities.

First, as a general policy, surrogate parents should work within the confines of the activities that bring them together with children in need. Teachers, band directors, athletic coaches, and others should not, in any way, solicit children as "therapy patients." However, if children ask for help by revealing unsolicited personal information about matters unrelated to activity, that is another matter. When this happens, surrogate parents must balance the limits of their abilities and commitments against the needs of the child. Inappropriate overinvolvement is one danger and abandonment is its opposite pole.

In such cases, the surrogate parent must be prepared to respond in any of three limited but constructive ways. If the child presents a real and immediate crisis, the surrogate parent must provide reasonable and appropriate "first aid" until those charged with managing the problems that underlie the crisis can be summoned. If the child presents a problem that poses no immediate danger but does require protective or remediative intervention, then the surrogate parent must be prepared to make a referral to an appropriate resource. In either case, to provide the child with timely assistance, the surrogate needs to know about available resources and who can be requested to help. Neglect is the important ethical concern in such situations.

If the child presents a problem that poses no foreseeable danger but is nevertheless a source of discomfort, the surrogate parent should respond in as supportive a fashion as possible in the context of activity. In providing support, one should avoid soliciting additional information beyond what the child's own initiative volunteers. The surrogate parent should not ask probing questions, and should avoid offering advice.

A sympathetic and caring ear is often all that is needed and possible. However, in some cases a child may reveal information the surrogate parent must report to a person in authority. The report may be mandated by law as in the case of child abuse, or by institutional policy as is possible in cases such as delinquency, crime, alcohol and drug abuse, or a teenage pregnancy.

In some instances, the situation may be complicated if a child asks and expects information to be held in strict confidence. The adult may feel that the fact of his possession of privileged information will remain a secret, too. Such circumstances force the surrogate parent to choose between concern about betraying the child and personal jeopardy that comes from breaking rules. This is a difficult moral dilemma, especially if one is confronted by a child who can turn to few, if any, other trustworthy adults.

As a part of general personal policy, such dilemmas should be addressed in advance. Surrogate parents must inform children of their obligations and commitments regarding privileged information before it is disclosed. In this way, adults may conform to the contractual obligations of their positions, and avoid acts of betrayal.

In all instances, the best interests of the child should be served. So, in unforeseeable or anomalous cases, careful decisions must be made about what to report and what not to report. In these kinds of situations, the surrogate parent will be greatly aided by clear ethical principles that are amenable to enlightened interpretation.

Giving advice to children creates another set of difficulties. Advice is often necessary and appropriate in the context of activities, but offering advice has inherent risks when it concerns issues extrinsic to the activity. Appropriate behavior includes a baseball coach advising a child about how to hit a curveball, a band director giving advice to a young trumpet player about selections for a recital, or a teacher recommending some books to take out of the library.

On the other hand, advice about sex, drugs, problems with parents, family difficulties, internecine struggles with boyfriends or girlfriends, and other very personal topics has inherent risk. Therefore, the surrogate parent must exercise great care when a child raises personal issues about such topics. This is especially true when a child struggling with a personal problem approaches the surrogate parent with questions such as "What should I do?" or the statement "I don't know what to do."

Such approaches are very seductive and have considerable potential to entrap a well-meaning person who wishes to be helpful. Advice about "what to do" is risky because the individual providing the advice may be held responsible for the consequences of following it. If a child sought and followed advice for a problem which is not solved or is worsened, there is considerable potential for the child to blame the advisor. The child not only avoids responsibility for personal actions, but can also vent frustration at a convenient target. The child's subsequent disappointment and anger may seriously damage trust in the surrogate parent.

Another risk of such advice is that some children really know what they want to do but feel a need for "adult permission" to do it. Advice can easily be interpreted as permission by these children. Significantly in many personal areas of a child's life, the surrogate parent is in no position to grant such permission.

Usually, children may seek advice about concerns related to personal values, goals, and methods of coping in connection with challenges and problems of everyday living. In some instances, children may need special assistance because of unusual or unanticipated difficulties. However, many of children's challenges and problems stem from developmental issues of growing up. Children's struggles revolve around the themes of self-care, coping with social difficulties, and having fun.

Though these themes are of greatest importance in the broader context of childrens' existence, they are also alive and well in the specific activities of which the surrogate parent is a part. The strategies and tactics of self-care, social interdependence, and finding enjoyment in ongoing but circumscribed activity can be extrapolated to life outside. Because schools and other community resources offer a great diversity of activity, children can emerge from them with many recipes or models for coping. The broader usefulness or transferability of these models should be taught in a conscious and purposeful manner while children are engaged in activity.

Therefore, for problems that are external to activity, the surrogate parent should not give advice about or attempt to solve problems "for" a child. The "lessons" of the activity should be used whenever possible to help a young person find viable options for external problems.

In instances when this is not possible, if there is time and energy, confidentiality is not a concern, and a problem has relevance to other participants, the underlying issues may be examined and explored with the surrogate parent in dialogue with the peer group. Thus, while participants wait for the paint to dry on their woodworking project, their pottery to bake in a kiln, as they walk together on a nature hike, or travel to the destination of a field trip, there are many opportunities to chat and shmooze.

In summation, the children should be helped to solve their own problems in a way that uses and contributes to the surrogate family. The surrogate parent needs to resolve the important ethical dilemma of how to avoid compromising a young person's autonomy or privacy on the one hand, or neglecting, betraying or abandoning the child on the other. The surrogate parent will struggle with the dilemma in connection with many problems and their variations and permutations. Because one cannot do justice to even a partial list of these problems in a single brief chapter, the intention here is to alert the reader to their existence and suggest some general guidelines for effectively coping with them.

IN CLOSING

A central theme of this book is that we do not make our way through life alone. When we feel as though we are too alone, there is probably something wrong. To be utterly alone is neither natural nor healthy, especially when one faces difficult tasks and responsibilities. Times when we struggle with moral issues and ethical dilemmas can certainly test our metal.

For this reason, educators and other human service providers who, from time to time, accept the role of surrogate parent must establish a helpful network of supportive, protective, and supervisory relationships. Collegial peers with whom one works, the customs and traditions of one's field as defined by the organized professional community, and supervisory staff may all contribute to solving important problems and issues.

Joining with others to address ethical concerns can be helpful in many ways. It can serve an educational or informational function in helping practitioners to understand the issues and tasks of ethical decision making. It can also contribute to the process of creating policy to guide such decisions. And finally, those with whom we join become a resource to ourselves and each other in coping with difficult individual problems.

Thus, the very resources that the surrogate parent draws upon in helping children from disrupted families has analogues for the adult professional. Most important, this network should be established before crisis occurs.

REFERENCES

Callahan, D. (1976). "Ethical Responsibility in Science in the Face of Uncertain Consequences." *Annals of the New York Academy of Sciences*, No. 265, pp. 1-12.

Ceci, S. and Bruck, M. (1993). "Child Witnesses: Translating Research into Policy." *Social Policy Report of the Society for Research in Child Development*, Vol. 7, No. 3, Fall, pp. 23-25.

Goleman, D. (1993). "Placebo Effect is Shown to be Twice as Powerful as Expected." *The New York Times*, August 17, p. c3.

Greenberg, J. and Gold, R. (1992). *The Health Education Ethics Book*. Dubuque, Iowa: Wm. C. Brown Publishers.

Northouse, P .G. and Northouse, L. L. (1992). *Health Communications: Strategies for Health Professionals*. 2nd ed. Norwalk, Connecticut: Appleton and Lange, pp. 249-272.

Penman, D. R., Holland, J. C., Bahna, G. F., Morrow, G., Schmale, A. H., Derogatis, L. R., Carnrike, Jr., C. L., and Cherry, R. (1984). "Informed Consent for Investigational Chemotherapy: Patients' and Physician's Perceptions." *Journal of Clinical Oncology*, Vol. 2, No. 7, pp. 849-855.

Weinstein, S. and Lagudis, M. (1980). "Health Ethics." In G. B. Dintiman and J. S. Greenberg (eds.), *Health Through Discovery*. 1st ed. Reading, Massachusetts: Addison-Wesley Publishing Company, pp. 505-518.

Index